Paul A. Sommers, PhD

Alignment
A Provider's Guide to Managing the Practice of Health Care

The Haworth Press, Inc.

Alignment
A Provider's Guide
to Managing the Practice
of Health Care

HAWORTH Marketing Resources
Innovations in Practice & Professional Services
William J. Winston, Senior Editor

New, Recent, and Forthcoming Titles:

Alignment
A Provider's Guide to Managing the Practice of Health Care

Paul A. Sommers, PhD

The Haworth Press
New York • London • Oxford

The Haworth Press, Inc., 10 Alice Street, Binghamton, NY 13904-1580

Cover design by Jennifer M. Gaska.

Library of Congress Cataloging-in-Publication Data

Sommers, Paul A.
    Alignment : a provider's guide to managing the practice of health care / Paul A. Sommers.
        p.   cm.
    Includes bibliographical references and index.
    ISBN 0-7890-0635-9 (alk. paper).
    1. Medicine—Practice. 2. Health services administration. I. Title.
R728.S57   1999
362.1′068—dc21   98-39594
                                                                                        CIP

CONTENTS

ABOUT THE AUTHOR

Paul A. Sommers, PhD, is Vice President of Data Services for Ingenix/ United HealthCare, Inc. in Minneapolis, Minnesota. He is also Adjunct Professor of Health Policy and Management in the Carlson School of Management at the University of Minnesota, Minneapolis, and Preceptor for MBA students in Medical Group Management at the University of St. Thomas Graduate School, also in Minneapolis. Over the past twenty-two years, Dr. Sommers has served with various medical groups and integrated health systems such as the Marshfield Clinic in Marshfield, Wisconsin; the Gundersen Clinic in LaCrosse, Wisconsin; the Ramsey Clinic in St. Paul, Minnesota; and Allina Health System/Medica Health Plans in Minneapolis. In addition, he is the author of more than eighty journal articles, textbook chapters, and publications related to healthcare, including *Medical Group Management in Turbulent Times: How Physician Leadership Can Optimize Health Plan, Hospital, and Medical Group Performance* (The Haworth Press, Inc., 1998) and the upcoming book *Consumer Satisfaction in Medical Practice.*

Preface

What makes some information in health care practice more important than other information? Why do certain practices that depend on information succeed while others fail?

Luck and random chance play a role. If the practice is in the right place at the right time with the right product or service, success is possible—at least temporarily. However, the more successful the practice, the greater the possibility of increased competition, thus the need to optimize key factors to produce excellence and sustain success. One way to achieve success is to establish a decision support system that continually aligns its focus and resources toward the most important aspects, while minimizing error in the decision-making process.

For the purpose of this text, alignment is defined as the shortest distance from initiation to successful completion of any desired activity. Achieving alignment, and thus excellence, in health care practice begins with "focused" (top priorities ONLY) work efforts to complete goals/objectives (organization-wide, departmental, and individual) that are directly supported by resources (FTEs, capital, and operational dollars).

Health care providers (physicians, all other practitioner types, and health care management) compose the audience. Proven methods, strategies, and outcomes derived from successful practices form the unique basis of each chapter. *Alignment* was written specifically to help providers define information and use it to distinguish themselves from the competition, while improving patient outcomes, daily operations, and satisfaction with services as practice effectiveness and efficiency increases.

Paul A. Sommers, PhD

Introduction

Health care providers must be more proactive and customer focused than ever before. Rapid changes are affecting all areas of health care, including hospitals, health plans, physicians profit and nonprofit health organizations, academic health centers, and more. There is not just one faction controlling the reform and reorganization of health care. Instead, various combinations of health care systems, providers, and benefactors are forging new and sometimes quite unique alliances to create change that will positively affect the results of health care practice.

The approach presented in *Alignment* is single-minded—that being to arm providers with information that will help them produce value-based quality care. Portions of this book also appear in *Medical Group Management in Turbulent Times: How Physician Leadership Can Optimize Health Plan, Hospital, and Medical Group Performance* (1998), also by the author, and published by The Haworth Press. The incorporated material includes fundamental elements of medical practice that reinforce the importance of particular aspects of quality care, such as physician leadership, strategic planning, consumer satisfaction, and the shift in medical practice from intervention toward prevention and wellness education. Answers to the following questions and related issues are addressed in this text:

- What must providers do to prepare for turbulent times?
- What must be done to integrate clinical and economic responsibility with the delivery of health care?
- Where does the alignment process begin?
- How does a health care provider align and sustain "focus" through measurement and continuous improvement to achieve excellence in desired outcomes?

Key issues underlying the preparations to be made by health care providers to become and remain proactive through alignment are addressed. Straightforward recommendations are presented along with time-tested methods and techniques applied in successful practice that can be put to immediate use in any health care provider's practice operations. From the aspect of applications, *Alignment* is most unique in that all examples used have come directly from successful practice operations.

Each chapter has been established with proactive considerations setting the tone for each unit to be addressed by the text. A summary of highlighted questions follows each chapter to focus the reader's attention to the most important information, which becomes of most value when the reader applies it directly to health care practice.

Chapter 1

Changes in Health Care Practice: Prevention and Management of Disease

PROACTIVE CONSIDERATIONS

- Physicians must lead by example, and other health care providers will follow. However, physicians must be armed with information that will help them produce value-based quality care predicated on the integration of clinical and economic responsibilities.
- The provider's role must enhance its focus to include prevention along with intervention, leading to effective patient care, education, and self-help. The ability to convey the elements required for a patient's lifestyle enhancement will become an important tool for the contemporary provider's "black bag." This must be done at a time when reimbursement is shrinking and health care expenses are increasing due to consumer demand and rising costs of technology. All sectors of the health care industry are experiencing significant financial strain, with providers being the focus of attention. New approaches to accomplish more quality outcomes at less cost are requirements.[1]
- A seamless system for excellent care and service that is consumer focused and programmed toward the development of healthy lifestyles are targeted goals. Consumers are more involved in their health choices and decisions than ever before. "Choice" has become a resounding requirement from the entire consumer-purchasing community.
- "Build it and they will come" is not going to be the hallmark for leading health care systems in the twenty-first century. Instead, the best practices will be designed to meet patients' needs. Clearly communicate, orally and in writing, exactly what your patients need to know to correct their current problem(s) while enhancing their health status to prevent the occurrence of future problems. Participation in the process of curriculum development with your local public and private schools is a good place to begin. Provide schools with consultation and infor-

1

mation on health education, prevention, and lifestyle enhancement for kindergarten through twelfth grade curricula.

- Among the most respected community leaders, health care providers can have significant and lasting impact as healers, educators, and counselors. Active community participation as a health care provider will serve to enhance the quality and lifestyles of individuals throughout the communities supporting the practice.

- Consumer satisfaction, disease-free lives, and enhanced lifestyles are desired outcomes. Leading health care systems are developing consumer-based programs that provide personal care and services that accompany financial incentives to reward the consumers' thirst for information, value, and quality outcomes, which results in more preventive care and less acute emergency room care.

- Providing individual care plans to patients, with ongoing enhancements as needed, supported by educational materials and self-improvement training programs, will rapidly distinguish your practice from the competition. Today's practices continue to struggle with the task of balancing revenue and expenses with less reimbursement overall. Practitioners must make better use of patient information to enhance patient outcomes while balancing the budget.

- Sustaining a focus on health improvement rather than curing illness and healing injuries requires educational programs designed to develop new leadership skills among current practitioners. The switch in focus from intervention to prevention will yield long-term return-on-investment results that are positive for patients and practitioners alike:
  a. Healthy lifestyles will reduce the need to focus on expensive corrective actions, while promoting wellness and self-care.
  b. Medical and worker compensation expenses will be reduced, thereby decreasing the burden of illness currently carried by business, industry, and the tax-paying public.

- Outcomes form guideposts for patient diagnosis, evaluation, and treatment. The measurement of performance and results is the process used to determine the status of outcomes. In the past, some physicians took issue with the application and interpretation of performance measurement information because it was used by payers and other purchasers to control physicians and other providers. If your performance scores are interpreted to be low, the payment for services rendered would be discounted, withheld, or otherwise diminished. *Alignment* shows physicians how to build decision support systems that integrate clinical and economic responsibilities into each individual and group practice to produce predefined patient and practice outcomes.

PROVIDER'S SELF-ANALYSIS, TARGETS, AND BENCHMARKS

The need for timely and accurate information has reached its highest level. Practice and physician performance information is a critical success factor for all medical groups. The Medical Group Management Association (MGMA) produces annual survey reports that provide comparison tools for virtually all aspects of practice.

- Watch your competitors. What are they up to?
- If you want to know what health plans in your area or around the state are doing, call the insurance commissioner to find out who is applying for licenses.
- Physician income stayed flat for a second straight year, according to the MGMA in 1998. Both primary care physicians and specialists are affected, as illustrated in the Physician Compensation and Production Survey (1998 report based on 1997 data).[2]
- Understand your expenses in comparison to both incoming revenue and benchmark expenses from similar practices. Net revenue growth must be balanced by adequate FTE and related resources to avoid quality problems and/or staff burnout.

PROVIDER GROUP SELF-NEEDS ASSESSMENT

Available comparison tools from the MGMA include the following annual printed survey reports furnished to all MGMA individual members from responding medical groups:

- Cost Survey
- Physician Compensation and Production Survey
- Management Compensation Survey

Respondent Benchmark Reports assist practices through a direct comparison of specifically defined measures in a customized report. The benchmark is the median value among similar practices. The Interactive Physician Compensation and Production Survey includes software tools that are provided with analytic and graphic assessment functions for application to medical practice data. Spreadsheet and report-writing capabilities are part of the package. Key indicators can be compared to target group performance, through various data tables for selected states, and by geographic regions. The Cost Survey Best Practices Report is a direct comparison of practice performance to data from Cost Survey respondents chosen for "best performance," based on overall financial stability and cost per procedure.

An internal checklist that has proven useful as a provider/organization "self-needs assessment" follows. Determine how your organization compares to the competition in the following areas:

1. Budget forecasts:
   * What are current year needs and desired percent revenue versus expense?
   * What are future budget expectations for the next three years?
   * What changes could impact the budget (e.g., Medicaid payment reductions, increase in surtax on managed care products, etc.)?
2. What are the top clinical, service, and/or community priorities in the provider group's strategic plan? How do they compare to the competitors'?
3. What have the auditors recommended in their management letter accompanying the last three auditor's reports? The management letter should offer business enhancement advice to sustain practice viability.
4. Define the provider group's managed care capabilities:
   * Document the use of practice guidelines and/or best-of-practice standards.
   * What are per member per month (PMPM) expense rates for each managed care product?
5. Information systems:
   * What are current system dimensions, connectivity, and overall capacities?
   * What are statistical analysis, interpretation, and reporting capabilities (e.g., do you know what the most important information is to your practice and how to use it)?
6. Medical records:
   * Are they integrated with hospitals where patients are admitted?
   * What is the degree of computerized/electronic automated records?
   * Has the record system been reviewed for completeness/accessibility?

7. Customer satisfaction scores/comments: Is satisfaction information defined by individual practitioner and by delivery site (e.g., as measured by consumers, patients, employer/purchaser, state/government, other)?
   - How current are the results?
   - Is information trended?
   - List action plans that have been implemented to improve less than excellent care and/or services.
8. Are provider information reports available by individual practitioner and by specialty (e.g., pharmacy, lab, diagnostics, inpatient and outpatient practice profiles, etc.)?
   - List current provider utilization and cost for each service provided by the practice (by specialty and in total for the group). Are outcomes included?
9. List inpatient utilization measures for individual practitioners and for the whole group (total number admissions, hospital days, average length of stay, PMPM, etc.).
10. Calculate ratio of nonprovider FTEs to provider FTEs. How do they compare to similar practices in your area, in the state, and nationally?
11. List outpatient utilization measures for individual practitioners and the whole group (number of patients per day/annually, PMPM).
12. List lab/X-ray/pharmacy utilization (by provider, specialty, clinic, PMPM, etc.).
13. Define how outcomes are measured.
14. What comparative benchmarks are used by the group?
15. List charges, revenue, and expenses for each provider in the group (include health plan billed claims information). How do they compare to those annually published by the American Medical Association and the Medical Group Management Association?
    - How are billed claims for each health plan served included in the overall analysis?
16. Does a strategic plan exist? If yes, what are the "key indicators" of success for each strategic priority?

Following an analysis of the provider group's needs assessment results, the findings are reviewed with the provider group's staff and management. Variances from priority targets are identified, and plans are developed to eliminate these variances. Typically, monthly monitoring reports are developed to chart progress and provide documentation to continually enhance care and service toward each target. The information is summarized and reported to the provider group on a quarterly basis and used for annual systemwide strategic plan development and budgeting.

Benchmarks, targets, and other points of comparison are important to know and use. If not used, it is quite possible that the provider(s) will wonder why patients have left and contracts are being lost. Peer group comparisons at the local and national levels are used to highlight similarities and differences. Such information is regularly reviewed by most employer and government purchasing groups to select the best health providers. If provider scores show poor utilization of resources, higher costs, or unsatisfactory outcomes, the organization is in jeopardy of losing business. Proactive management of this information to guide care and service levels toward excellent outcomes will help to correct problems before they occur.

The following is an example of what purchasers and payers want to know about medical service provider performance before they decide to contract for services:

1. Type of patients of health plan members served
   - Age and gender
2. Utilization results
   - Inpatient results
      a. Acute admits per/1000
         - By admit type
         - Cost by diagnostic category (including maternity)
      b. Acute days ALOS
      c. Nonacute admits per/1000
      d. Nonacute inpatient days per/1000
      e. Nonacute ALOS
      f. Total inpatient admits per/1000
      g. Total inpatient days per/1000
      h. Total inpatient ALOS
   - Outpatient results
      a. Emergency department visits per/1000 members
   - Physician office visits
      a. Top ten diagnoses for visits by frequency and cost
      b. Visits per/1000
      c. Top ten costs by provider specialty
   - Pharmacy
      a. Top ten claims cost by therapeutic class
      b. Top ten prescriptions by cost
      c. Prescriptions per/1000 members
   - Distribution of health care costs
      a. Top five diagnostic categories
      b. Costs by outpatient, inpatient, physician, and pharmacy

Health plans typically furnish their health plan Employer Data and Information Set (HEDIS) results to prospective purchasers and clients as "quality indicators." HEDIS is a program of the National Committee for Quality Assurance (NCQA). The program was designed to permit employers to comprehend what value their health care dollars buy and to give purchasers the information necessary to hold health plans and other health care organizations accountable for excellent clinical care and service results. HEDIS measures health plans in the areas of quality, access, utilization, satisfaction, and finance to allow purchasers to compare plans across many key areas.

The eight clinical HEDIS measures are:*

- Advising Smokers to Quit
- Beta Blocker Treatment (after a heart attack)
- Breast Cancer Screening
- Cervical Cancer Screening
- Cesarean Section Rates
- Childhood Immunizations
- Diabetic Eye Exams
- Prenatal Care in the First Trimester

The physician is an essential key to benchmark development, utilization review, and continuous improvement. It is the physician practice that serves as the comparative standard against which all utilization, financial, and quality analyses are based. It is mandatory that each provider be given the tools and necessary information to offer the best care to each patient. If this is done, the following can be expected:

- The physician is armed with the most accurate and timely information possible that facilitates value-based quality care to each patient. The results of excellent patient care improve the bottom line of the physician's medical practice.
- The patient receives excellent results at an appropriate price. The patient therefore returns to the same provider and tells others about the experience.
- Excellent care provided on a patient-by-patient basis enhances bottom line of entire practice, improving chances for long-term retention of patient and attracting new patients by word-of-mouth referrals from satisfied customers.

---

*Reprinted with permission from the National Committee for Quality Assurance; *The State of Managed Care Quality* (1997); Copyright ©1997 by NCQA.

- Hospital bottom line is enhanced as physician practice is responsible for inpatient care. This increases long-term patient retention and attracts new patients in need of hospital care through referrals from satisfied customers.
- The health plan meets financial, utilization, and quality targets because of providers' excellent care to each member/patient. Bottom line is enhanced and chances of gaining new referrals from satisfied members/customers are increased.

How does one provider, or a group of providers, compare to others in the same specialties? Include as broad a set of benchmark characteristics as possible to provide the most comprehensive profile. An example of elements to consider follows:[1]

1. Financial indicators
   - PMPM expenses for pharmacy, lab, radiology, episodes of care, inpatient, outpatient, mental health/CD, same-day surgery and others as needed (for an example record of PMPM indicators, see Figure 1.1)
   - Operating income (monthly and year to date)
   - Days' cash-on-hand
   - Days of net revenue available in accounts receivable
2. Indicators of volume serviced
   - Adult and pediatric inpatient days (monthly and year to date)
   - Adult and pediatric admissions (monthly and year to date)
   - Visits to the emergency room (monthly and year to date)
   - Cases served in the operating room (monthly and year to date)
   - Visits to outpatient clinics (monthly and year to date)
   - Same-day surgery cases (monthly and year to date)
3. Human resources indicators
   - Total FTEs employed
   - Ratio of physician to nonphysician staff
   - Rates of turnover among providers
   - Rates of turnover among nonproviders
   - Number of staff physicians, by specialty, by year
   - Percentage of staff employed who are minorities
4. Indicators of service and quality
   - HEDIS scores
   - Complaints from inpatients
   - Complaints from outpatients
   - Complaints from users of the emergency room
   - Mortality rates
   - Loss and gain of patients from year to year

- Disenrollment rate among health plan members by product
- Consumer satisfaction ratings and comments
- Underutilization or nonuse by health plan members by insurance product

Managed care will continue to expand and, in many cases, will be driven by employer groups and other segments of private industry. The Buyers Health Care Action Group (BHCAG) in Minneapolis/St. Paul, Minnesota, the John Deere Company in Iowa, and others serve as examples. These purchasing groups have set their own expectations and invited health care providers to participate, if they agree to abide by the purchasing groups' delivery, utilization, service, quality, and financial standards. Health care premiums and employer-sponsored health insurance costs are trending down as an effect of the private industry influence.

Purchasers are receiving small increases in health care costs as medical expenses continue to rise. Health insurance premiums for managed care buyers have experienced slight increases, with expenses markedly surpassing premium increases from 2 to 4 percent. The losses have caused significant restructuring and layoffs among many health plans. It is expected that providers for Medicare and Medicaid will receive less reimbursement now and in the future. The U.S. government's Office of Managed Care, Health Care Financing Administration (HCFA) sees the growth in Medicare managed care as an important trend. Although only a health maintenance organization (HMO) option is available today, several hybrid options are being considered for future establishment in every major market. HEDIS measures and other comparative shopping findings will be distributed to Medicare constituents in 1999. This information will be published for all to see in the form of a comparative information chart, according to HCFA Director, Policy and Improvement, Jean LeMasurier. Health care markets across the United States are experiencing the effects. Table 1.1 shows the decrease in hospital bed days per 1,000.[3] Table 1.2 illustrates an expanded perspective that further complicates the provider's problems.[4] Along with a ratcheting down of bed days from a median of 275 in 1994 to 253 days in 1995, the related medical expense loss ratio increased from $80.68 PMPM in 1994 to $82.93 PMPM in 1995.

OPTIMIZING THE PROVIDER'S ROLE

The need for physician leadership to return the focus of health care back to the individual patient has never been as evident as it is today. The emphasis on achieving top results through best practices at least cost, on a

FIGURE 1.1. Per Member Per Month (PMPM) Expense Indicators for Insurance Products

SERVICES	PMPM Insurance Product #1	PMPM Insurance Product #2	PMPM Insurance Product #3
Lab			
Outpatient			
Physician			
Total			
Radiology			
Outpatient			
Physician			
Total			
Diagnostic Testing			
Pharmacy			
Emergency Room			
Outpatient Surgery (facility only)			
Physical Therapy			
Inpatient Facility (excluding alcohol/drug/abuse/psych)			
Total Physician			

Source: Sommers, P. A. Internal study. Allina Health System, Minneapolis, MN, 1997-1998.

TABLE 1.1. Decrease in Hospital Bed Days

Market	Days/1,000 Population, 1995	Days/1,000 Population in 100% Managed Care Market	
Boston	1,014	366	
Chicago	692	354	
Los Angeles-Long Beach	474	337	
Minneapolis-St. Paul	548	348	37% ↓
San Diego	460	352	
Seattle	469	363	
St. Louis	752	365	

patient-by-patient basis, pales in comparison to daily media events that pit one element of the delivery system against another, without regard for the individual patient. The time is right to reestablish physician leadership to integrate both clinical and economic responsibilities in a patient-centered health care system.

Why? Because only physicians can admit patients to hospitals, write orders, and prescribe medications and special equipment. The physician is a most valuable resource in every health care environment. When given a "choice," patients will most often follow their doctor's advice. This defined leadership must be leveraged in partnership with health plans and hospitals.

Groups who understand these facts and integrate the providers into active, problem-solving teams within their organization optimize mutual success. Provider participation and leadership in a planned manner (e.g., strategic and operational leadership roles including positions on the board, as department heads, as committee chairs, etc.) should be encouraged and actively supported. Clinical and economic responsibilities can be joined if physicians are active participants in the highest levels of organizational governance.

For more than a decade, Paul Ellwood, MD, and Leland Kaiser, PhD, (considered two of the very best visionaries in health care) have called

TABLE 1.2. Further Complications for Providers—Medical Loss Ratio

	1995	1994	1993
Total Members, Current Year	34,488	37,991	39,303
Enrollee Change Ratio	1.13	1.09	1.09
Inpatient Days per 1,000			
All Enrollees	253	275	263
Nonphysician Encounters per			
Member per Month	0.02	0.02	0.02
Physician Encounters per			
Member per Month	0.18	0.19	0.18
Nonphysician to Physician			
Encounters (Ratio)	0.08	0.11	0.09
Current Ratio	1.18	1.18	1.15
Days in Accounts Receivable	8.71	7.89	7.47
Days in Claims Payable	62.12	62.11	62.02
Unpaid Claims per Member			
per Month	12.71	10.65	10.74
Debt Service Coverage Ratio	24.69	39.13	44.23
Total Expenses As Percent			
of Revenue	98.77	96.37	96.54
Inpatient Expense As a Percent			
of Total Medical Expense	0.27	0.28	0.28
Outside Referral Expense As			
a Percent of Total Expense	0.07	0.07	0.09
Total Medicaid and Hospital			
Expense	42,779,638	36,045,653	40,462,757
Percent Total Medical			
Expense	84.49	85.07	86.56
Medical Expense Loss Ratio	82.93	80.68	81.98
Percent Total Administrative			
Expense	15.51	14.92	13.44
Administrative Expense As			
Percent of Revenue	14.79	13.82	12.63
Premiums	45,731,798	48,329,569	48,704,012
Net Income Margin	0.01	0.03	0.03
Total Profit Margin	0.96	2.64	2.88
Total Net Worth	5,793,957	4,609,364	4,527,588
Return on Assets	0.02	0.07	0.09

attention to the need for change. They predicate the need for change upon the presence of a cultural revolution—a revolution in technology, politics, and economics—and there is no stopping it. Growth of managed care and managed competition has made the American medical economy the sixth or seventh largest economy in the world. That is, the United States spends more on medical care than China spends on everything.[5]

The process of integrating clinical and economic responsibilities into the physician culture may not be an easy task. Many physicians believe in a separation between what is best for the patient, what the care costs, and how the process is managed. At this point, physician-administrator teams can be an asset. By working as "partners," the physician can set the clinical care goals and actively encourage, support, and reinforce administrative efforts to accomplish the same patient-focused outcomes.

THE NEW MEDICAL ECONOMICS

Up until now, the game has been all about trading off doctor's visits for days in the hospital (based upon the way expenditures for medical services were shaped: 68 percent for hospitals and 32 percent for physicians). The payment system has been reversed: 45 percent for hospitals, 55 percent for physicians, with smaller overall total expenditures. Remaining dollars are used to (1) attract patients (members) by giving more benefits in exchange for choice, (2) provide incentives to providers to hospitalize less, emphasizing outpatient care, and (3) bring financial profit to the organization(s) managing the process.

Currently there is an oversupply of hospital beds, but more aggressive hospitals find margins positive despite rates of occupancy being at their lowest levels. To promote these positive margins, they use cost containment, reengineering of operating systems, and/or planned integrations among groups of providers and hospitals to consolidate duplicate services. In addition, visits to providers are declining, along with related income. Systems for reimbursement are being changed to offer incentives for use of less expensive outpatient-based primary care services and to eliminate, where possible, referrals to specialty services. Providers must unite and seek out mutually rewarding opportunities with hospitals and health plans.

To achieve value-oriented care, physicians will have to shift away from fee-for-service thinking, originally instituted by the federal government as a means to attract physicians to serve the special and expensive health care needs of Medicare and Medicaid patients. The goal should be to attract all of the fee-for-service business that is possible, while changing the methods of practice toward managed care by instituting the use of benchmarks, RVUs, PMPMs, consumer satisfaction systems, and HEDIS measures. Other methods of leveraging revenue include the following:

1. Adding same day/ambulatory surgery capabilities (including "stand alone" ambulatory surgery centers)
2. Enhanced laboratory services
   - Link diagnosis and outcomes to lab results
   - Prices should be competitive to commercial competitors
   - Added value gained if physician interpretation can accompany report
3. Enhanced diagnostic services
   - Link diagnosis and outcomes to diagnostic results
   - Competitive prices
   - Physician interpretation of each report adds value
4. Physician ownership (where laws permit)
   - HMOs
   - Direct contracting
   - MRIs, CT scans, and other diagnostic services
   - Physical, occupational, speech, and other forms of therapy services
5. Keeping patients out of the hospital
   - Home care
   - Urgent care services
   - Extended office hours
   - Rotate open appointment times among provider schedules to work in "walk in" patients

MENTAL ATTITUDE, MIND-SET, AND CONSCIOUSNESS

To quote from Ellwood and Kaiser:

The Universe is full of garbage and gold. Watch your bucket, because you collect just what you are looking for! What's out there is a set of building blocks. There is no determinism in those blocks. They are just blocks—blocks to be used optimistically or to be viewed pessimistically.[5] (p. 17)

Your future is between the ears of the people who make up your group. How long does it take you to change your future? Answer: As long as it takes to change your mind. How long does it take to change the future of a medical group? Answer: As long as it takes to change its collective mind.

How do we change what's out there? Answer: The two most critical strategies for a medical group are the production of better ideas and long-term acquisition of capital.

- Your group's ultimate limitation is the imagination available among its providers.
- Capital is the single most important issue. In a capitalistic society, the one with the most capital "wins." One can buy into a market. One can also artificially lower prices.

Ways to position yourself—promotion of wellness, prevention, sensible policies regarding tobacco, alcohol, stress—all those are coming along very quickly, as we move toward improvements in lifestyles. The money in this business is in better lifestyles, not in medical care. The super-meds may buy up the medical schools—You have to educate the people in your own system: in residencies, internships, fellowships—the whole thing! This also means research: acquire the best minds to invent the devices, the implants, and the transplants (for example, an artificial heart), and commit maybe $2 million dollars to it, and when the kinks are ironed out, it may earn you $20 million annually! The medical group of the future will be "amoeboid" ("constantly changing shape"). The winning medical group will be able to make any decisions of any order of magnitude in less than ninety days. This will require the rapid acquisition and effective use of information (alignment) and of contemporary informational systems and networks.

CHANGING ROLES, ISSUES OF REIMBURSEMENT, AND CAPITATION

If you are right but slow, you are dead.[5]

In his book *Strong Medicine*, George Halvorson, head of HealthPartners, advocates the influencing of physicians' practices by realigning payments to encourage the direction toward which the payer would like to see the health care practice move.[6] To use his example, from the perspective of a health plan, when a baby is delivered, the medical providers involved should be paid for having promoted healthy mothers and healthy babies. The system providing their payment should not encourage any particular medical procedure over another, unless that encouragement is based on clear standards for quality of care.

He further notes that fee-for-service payments do not reward quality. In many communities, physicians ignore the issue of hospital costs, since their income is based on their own fee schedules, not on the efficiency of the total care to which they contributed. This makes sense when the hospital's costs are not related to the doctors' own costs of doing business. In such a case, no financial incentive exists for the provider to use hospital care conservatively and efficiently. Once providers become aware of the impact of their decisions upon total costs, and once they are in positions where they can keep any excess capitational payments as a reward for efficiency, but would have to pay for any excess care out of their own clinic's bank account, they will quickly become more efficient. Such a situation would be likely with the integration of clinical and economic responsibilities.

Halvorson contends that physicians' pay is not the financial problem; rather, the problem is physician-created expenses. Physicians make 80 percent to 90 percent of all decisions in health care, so their styles of practice drive the system. Their direct personal compensation, after overhead and expenses, probably accounts for only about 12 percent to 15 percent of the total bill for health care in America. That is clearly not the lion's share of costs. Their incomes are increasing more rapidly than inflation by a significant margin, but even that increase is not a truly significant problem for consumers and payers. The overwhelming problem is that the decisions they make create other substantial costs within the system. Physicians' decisions made in favor of more extensive care significantly increase the overall cost of care for each patient. Halvorson believes that no reform of the system will succeed unless it takes into consideration the leveraging impact of physicians' decisions. Doctors will become more efficient once they are aware of the impact of their decisions and have learned to balance clinical and economic demands.

Rewarding efficiency is the clearly heralded solution presented in the book *Strong Medicine*. Halvorson indicates that the best way to reward efficiency and not volume is to prepay teams of physicians a fixed amount of money per patient to meet all of the medical needs of each patient. That general approach is referred to as "prepayment," and such payments are generally called "capitation" because they are paid "per capita" or per person rather than "per service." Prepayment now has decades of experience behind it—and it works, as evidenced by the growing number of successful health plans that base their operations on this method. The science of capitation has also progressed significantly since those early days. Modern capitation approaches put the doctors at less financial risk and instead focus risk on issues over which the doctor has more direct control. Many physicians experienced in managing capitation have optimized the method to their financial advantage. From the perspective of a health plan, the challenge is how better to align payments with goals so that doctors can focus on efficiency, quality, and most important, on prevention and the development of healthier lifestyles.[6]

Although "efficiency" has been improving, it is important to balance the health of the patients in the equation to produce a win-win outcome. An example of capitated care going too far in the efficiency direction is when the Minnesota legislature decided to extend the amount of time health plans covered hospital stays for the mothers of healthy newborns. Insurers had stated that the health plan would only cover one day of a mother's stay in the hospital after giving birth (unless there were complications). Less than satisfactory experiences were documented by health plan members. The state legislature acted to extend insurance coverage for mothers' hospital stays to two days for a normal delivery. Just because a system or plan is efficient does not mean it is quality patient care. A balance is needed, which means testing options through continuous quality enhancements and being willing to change when less than appropriate outcomes are evident.

HEALTHY OUTCOMES—ONE PATIENT AT A TIME

The fact remains that health systems, providers, and their patients are far better off working together to achieve healthy lifestyles—one patient at a time. It will be most efficient, from every aspect, for health care organizations to focus on preventive educational and self-care programs rather than on intervention activities. On behalf of each patient, providers must be knowledgeable about available resources and services from participating health plans, hospitals, and the community.

The following examples show how two health care systems, Allina and HealthPartners, based in Minneapolis and St. Paul, addressed improvements in health among their members and communities. The goal of each organization is to be the best system for delivering and financing health care. Both are integrated systems that include multiple health plans to meet any defined need; both own or contract with hospitals in every area where patients and members live, and both include over 11,000 physicians who participate in both systems. The organizations both have missions *focused on improving the health of their members and the community*. To achieve this defined goal, specific initiatives toward prevention and healthy outcomes have been implemented by both groups.

Allina has a number of formal initiatives for both health plan members and Allina employees that focus on determining one's current health status (health risk appraisal and past medical history, etc.) and what to do about it. Monthly publications, television public service spots, sponsorship of local and regional events that have health or the enhancement of one's quality of life as the theme—all are part of the organization's efforts toward healthy living. Each member receives a handbook that serves as a resource directory and self-help educational guide that addresses solutions to common health problems. Suggestions are provided that allow members to choose self-help care options before they visit the provider and/or emergency room.[7] Gordon Sprenger, Allina CEO, stresses prevention and the need to team up with communities to address violence, problems of our youth, unemployment, and housing with the same vigor used to attack illness. Allina established a free clinic for poor kids at an elementary school near one of its hospitals, the first of its kind in the United States. Allina providers have begun working with local police to counsel former gang members and remove their identifying tattoos. Company executives are lobbying state legislators for antitobacco and gun control initiatives. As Sprenger sees it, aggressive community health is the only way to stay in business.[8]

HealthPartners has similar programs and services for its members and employees.[9] It created employer interest for prevention and health-focused activities in 1994 when it was selected by the Business Health Care Action Group (BHCAG), a large Twin Cities employer-based purchasing group, to insure employee health plan members from many Minneapolis/St. Paul companies. Although many other providers, including Allina, are part of the BHCAG network, HealthPartners' emphasis on prevention and wellness attracted employer group interest with aspirations of significant health care improvements.

HealthPartners' example of preventive approach to healthy living is educationally based and aimed at patient members. To reach patient members effectively, however, and to achieve measurably "improved" health status, the providers (i.e., physicians, hospitals, health plans, supporting staff of each provider, and any other participating providers) *must* function as teachers. It becomes necessary to teach the benefactors how to optimize the effectiveness of their services on behalf of patient members. The transfer of information from each expert source to the patient member is a main objective. In this example, the organization provided consumer education through a center on health promotions staffed with health educators, nurses, and dietitians to help members develop and maintain healthier lifestyles. By providing comprehensive educational resources and presenting consumer education programs and services, individuals were assisted in making choices that promote optimal health. A brief listing of subjects addressed follows: [9]

- Stress and Relaxation • Heart Health • Smoking Cessation
- Fitness • Weight Management • Healthy Eating

Developing new skills for personal growth and enrichment:

- Parenting • Self-Esteem for Adults and Children • Assertiveness
- Couples' Communication Workshop • Understanding Shame
- Women's Midlife Power Surge • Anger Management
- Coping with Loss

Taking an active role in managing your health conditions:

- Toward Better Blood Pressure • Fibromyalgia • Infertility
- Pulmonary Rehabilitation Program • Diabetes • Cholesterol

Give your child the best possible start in life by preparing for a healthy pregnancy, birth, and baby:

- Planning a Healthy Pregnancy • Expecting the Best: Early Pregnancy Orientation • Breast-Feeding Your Baby • New Baby, New Family Care Class • Childbirth Preparation Classes

Subjects of written materials available to health plan members:

- Routine Physicals Get a New Twist—preventive screening, lifestyle counseling are replacing the old annual physical. Created by physicians, the guidelines specify the best way consistently and effectively to prevent a given condition in your health.

Applied Focus on the Consumer

The preventive services focus calls for more than just disease testing. It also emphasizes disease prevention. Most preventable illnesses occur because of people's behavior. New guidelines will move the focus away from routine medical testing to discussion about how you can prevent illness down the road.[9]

Individual characteristics are used by the patient's physician to examine lifestyle risk factors—dietary habits, weight, physical activity, tobacco use, and other behaviors that one can control to reduce risk of heart disease, diabetes, hypertension, and other life-threatening illnesses. In the past, a visit to the doctor included a few minutes of talk and a lot of time on the exam table. With the new guideline, you probably will spend less time on the exam table and a lot more time talking about family medical history and discussing preventive issues. Those conversations may occur with your physician, or they make take place with a registered nurse, a nurse practitioner, a certified nurse midwife, or a health educator. For example, depending on your age and situation, you may find yourself talking with your provider about such diverse preventive topics as your use of seat belts, the importance of smoke detectors, safer sex, and stress and coping skills. You will receive educational materials and support to make changes that can help ensure your continued good health. Based on your conversation and your level of risk, your doctor may decide that you do not need a certain test or, conversely, that you should have additional tests.

Self-Determination

This component of the guideline gives you a central role in maintaining your health. You become a key player in your own well-being by making responsible lifestyle choices and staying current with preventive care screenings.

Lifestyle changes such as eating well, getting exercise, wearing seat belts, getting appropriate screenings can save more lives than the annual physical.[14] The most important piece of prevention for men 50 or younger is lifestyle changes. Pap tests and mammograms are essential services for women over 50.[14]

The benefits of having this preventive services guideline include better patient outcomes, a best of practice standard that reduces treatment variations among providers, reduced health care costs, and the opportunity to improve health care continuously. For example, by understanding what causes heart attacks, you can take steps to significantly reduce your chances of ever having one. The key is to understand the process so that you can make the right decisions, right now—today—about your heart. The information can help you avoid being among the 20 percent of Americans who suffer from some form of heart disease or one of the 920,000 people who die from it each year. In many cases, heart disease can be prevented. If the disease has already developed, you can manage it and, in some cases, actually reverse it.[14]

The message is clear: prevention and "lifestyle" go hand in hand and are based on education.

Allina has established its patient care focus[15] within the context of an "excellent health care experience whenever, wherever, and in whatever manner they have need of Allina products and services," according to K. James Ehlen, MD, President.[16] Under the direction of John H. Kleinman, MD, System Vice President at the time, clinical care priorities have been set.[15,17] Each priority is addressed through a model that encompasses the best-of-practice clinical goals, guidelines, and tools developed by clinical action groups composed of more than 650 physicians, other health care professionals, and medical policy experts. Use of this model will reduce the costs incurred by the delivery of poor quality care; enhance the care experience; ensure the appropriateness, effectiveness, and efficiency of care; integrate clinical and operational services; and improve community health.

The model is initially applied to six clinical priority conditions including: breast cancer, colon cancer, diabetes mellitus, cardiac disease, pediatric asthma, and pregnancy care. For example, in the case of diabetes mellitus, therapeutic efforts will focus on the elimination or severity reduction of its more complex complications: blindness, severely debilitating neuropathy, early death from preventable cardiac disease or renal failure, and severe birth defects in children of diabetic mothers. Adherence to clinical action group recommendations will, in the long run, substantially reduce the economic cost of diabetic care and improve patient outcomes.[13]

CHALLENGES OF THE TWENTY-FIRST CENTURY

The health care industry continues to react to significant changes and expectations coming from many directions. Consumers, purchasers, and payers want excellent care, service, and results at competitive prices. Certain basic requirements must be addressed by providers to prepare for these expectations while proactively developing a patient-focused delivery system based upon preventive medicine and healthy lifestyles. The following are some prerequisites:

- Return the physician to the center of health care. This transition can be accomplished most successfully when the physician integrates clinical care and economic responsibilities into his or her practice.[1,18]
- Arm providers with accurate and timely patient care, utilization, quality, cost, and outcomes information at the time patient care plans are developed. Healthy lifestyles are not random events. Information technology can help to assemble and interpret the most important information and related attributes. An integrated, patient-centered health care delivery system can provide the information when it is needed and continue to manage desired outcomes.[19]
- Incorporate the quality performance indicators developed by NCQA/HEDIS through the measurement of care and service results provided to more than 37 million health plan members throughout the United States.[20] This information base offers an unprecedented opportunity to examine and compare performance across the managed

care industry and to produce national, regional, and state averages, as well as benchmarks, on specific measures of care and service. This report takes advantage of those capabilities to provide answers to the following questions:

a. What can HEDIS tell us about the managed care industry's ability to deliver high-quality health care and service?

b. How much do HMOs and other managed care plans vary in their delivery of quality care within and between local areas? What do these variations signify? What is their impact on the health of the American public? (See Table 1.3 for estimated impacts.)

c. How do HMOs and other managed care organizations compare to fee-for-service insurers across vital clinical and service dimensions?

d. How satisfied are HMO enrollees with the care and service they receive?

• Think like consumers, purchasers, and payers. Managed care trends have shaped the way purchasers and payers deal with health care providers. Government purchaser models, for example, Medicare and Medicaid, will be emulated by others. Private businesses and employer groups have slowed the rise in health insurance premiums by establishing and tightly managing what, where, when, and how much they are willing to pay for specifically defined health care services.[21] If you want to be part of a health care delivery system that serves one or more of these payers, you (your group) will have to play by their rules.

Managed care trends that can be expected during the twenty-first century include the following:

• Continuation of managed care company mergers
• Physician-based provider network growth and direct contracting with employer groups and other purchasers
• A shift in focus toward partnerships among physicians, hospitals, health plans, and patients balanced with the integration of care and financing
• Healthy outcomes achieved through preventive medicine and wellness education on a patient-by-patient basis

Wellness, personal fitness, and self-help; prevention versus intervention; disease management; and outcome measurement/management are basic considerations for the leading integrated health care systems. Individual patient responsibility will be required more than ever before. Part of

TABLE 1.3. 1997 NCQA Quality Compass National Averages

The Eight Clinical HEDIS Measures and Member Satisfaction	National Average	Benchmark	Impact if All Health Plans Performed As Well As the Best Plans
Advising Smokers to Quit This measure estimates the percentage of adult smokers or recent quitters age eighteen and older who received advice to quit smoking from a health professional in the plan in 1996.	61%	70%	If industrywide performance were brought up to the ninetieth percentile benchmark of 70 percent, an additional 4.2 million enrollees who smoke would be advised about the benefits of quitting, and nearly 26,000 people would likely quit smoking each year, resulting in approximately $22 million saved in health care costs over the next seven years.
Beta-Blocker Treatment After a Heart Attack The rate of beta-blocker treatments is the percentage of plan members at least thirty-five years of age (and for whom beta-blocker therapy would not cause problems and is not contraindicated) who were discharged from the hospital after a heart attack with a prescription for one of these agents.	61.9%	85%	If industrywide performance were brought up to the ninetieth percentile benchmark of 85 percent, 1,600 cardiac deaths would be avoided among 57 million HMO enrollees each year. The number of future heart attacks avoided would be even higher. The total cost of medical care and lost productivity due to heart disease is $60 billion annually.
Breast Cancer Screening The breast cancer screening rate is the percentage of women in the health plan between the ages of fifty-two and sixty-nine who have had at least one mammogram during the prior two years.	70.4%	80%	If industrywide performance were brought up to the ninetieth percentile benchmark of 80 percent, an additional 1,200 breast cancer cases could have been detected, and 1,800 years of life could be saved (among 57 million HMO enrollees) each year. Regular mammography screening can reduce mortality from breast cancer by as much as 23 percent. Early detection and treatment of breast cancer would help save almost $4 billion in treatment and lost productivity costs associated with this illness.
Cervical Cancer Screening The cervical cancer screening rate is the percentage of women in the health plan age fifteen to thirty-four who had at least one Papanicolaou (Pap) smear during the past three years.	70.4%	83%	If all health plans nationwide were brought up to the ninetieth percentile benchmark (83 percent) of managed care plans, almost 500 deaths could be averted each year.

TABLE 1.3 *(continued)*

The Eight Clinical HEDIS Measures and Member Satisfaction	National Average	Benchmark	Impact if All Health Plans Performed As Well As the Best Plans
Cesarean Section The Cesarean section rate is the percentage of women in a health plan who had a live birth in 1996 through Cesarean section rather than vaginal delivery.	20.6%	13.5%	The estimated risk of a woman dying after a C-section is four times higher than the risk of death following a vaginal delivery. C-sections are also typically followed by longer hospital stays and longer recovery times. Currently, 80 percent of all health plans report C-section rates between 14.8 and 38.4 percent.
Childhood Immunizations The childhood immunization rate is the percentage of children in the health plan who received appropriate immunizations by their second birthday. The completed series of vaccines includes four DTP/DtaP (diptheria-tetanus-pertussis), three polio (OPV/IPV), one MMR (measles-mumps-rubella), one Hib (H influenza type b), and two HepB (Hepatitis B). Note that this measure is more inclusive than the measure reported by the Centers for Disease Control (CDC), which does not include the HepB and Hib vaccines.	65.3%	85%	If all health plans were brought up to the ninetieth percentile benchmark (85 percent), unnecessary morbidity and mortality among children would be prevented, thus saving lives, life years, and associated costs. The Children's Defense Fund estimates that providing immunizations yields a 10:1 economic return on investment in terms of reduced medical expenditures.
Eye Exams for Patients with Diabetes The eye exams for diabetics rate is the percentage of plan members with diabetes age thirty-one years and older who received an eye exam in 1996. Because some diabetics can safely be screened less frequently than annually, one would not necessarily expect a screening rate of 100 percent in each plan.	38.4%	57%	It is estimated that more than 2,500 cases of blindness would be prevented each year if the industry benchmark of 57 percent was attained.

The Eight Clinical HEDIS Measures and Member Satisfaction	National Average	Benchmark	Impact if All Health Plans Performed As Well As the Best Plans
Prenatal Care in the First Trimester The prenatal care in first trimester rate is the percentage of pregnant women in the plan who began prenatal care during the first thirteen weeks of pregnancy. Prenatal care consists of patient education, evaluation of the pregnant woman for physical or historic factors requiring special care, careful assessment of gestational age, and determination of the success with which the mother and fetus(es) are tolerating the pregnancy.	84.5%	94%	Reductions in a woman's likelihood of delivering a low-birth-weight infant and other maternal and infant health problems could be achieved if the industry moved toward the ninetieth percentile benchmark of 94 percent. Very low-birth-weight infants accounted for 1.2 percent of all births, but 64.2 percent of all neonatal deaths. Prenatal care is cost-effective and becomes even more so when provided as an integral part of primary care services during routine health promotion.
Member Satisfaction These measures assess members' overall level of satisfaction with the health plan, as well as the level of satisfaction in specific areas, including choice of physician, referrals to a specialist, waiting time, and available information on members' rights.	56.2%	N/A	56.2 percent of members indicated they were "completely" or "very" satisfied with their current health plan. (Note: previously, overall satisfaction ratings reported by NCQA included members indicating that they were "somewhat" satisfied. NCQA changed the way it reports this data to make it more useful for distinguishing between plans.)

Observations from this initial report:
1. Only a beginning point. Annual trending that begins with 1998 report will help.
2. Significant opportunity toward prevention and healthy lifestyle development.
3. Potential cost savings, reduced morbidity and mortality, and increased satisfaction.

Source: Information reprinted with permission from the National Committee for Quality Assurance; *The State of Managed Care Quality* (1997); Copyright ©1997 by NCQA.

25

the requirement will involve learning more about one's personal health risk characteristics. Personal health care information can be obtained through the completion of a health risk assessment profile. Once an individual health risk profile has been completed, the patient's personal physician can work in partnership with the patient to address each risk factor for correction. A lifestyle improvement plan can be jointly developed between patient, physician, and the health care team. Such a profile is compiled keeping the following information in mind:

1. Characteristics of the health risk appraisal:[22]
   - Influenced by the choices made by each individual
   - Shows how lifestyle choices affect the ability to avoid the common cause of death for each participant (by age and sex)
   - Not a substitute for a check-up or physical exam
   - Not designed for individuals with cancer, heart disease, kidney disease, or other significant illnesses
   - All information kept confidential
2. General categories of assessment:
   - Physical dimensions, blood pressure, and cholesterol level
   - Health-related behaviors, for example, smoking, use of medications, alcohol, driving record and habits, food selections, amount of physical activity, amount of sleep, participation in health improvement programs
3. Quality-of-life indicators, for example, general satisfaction with life, job satisfaction, social habits, general physical health perspective, any factors of personal loss (job loss, divorce, etc.), work missed due to illness
4. Medical history and self-care, for example, family members with medical problems, any personal problems with back pain, high blood pressure, and gender-related concerns:
   - Women—last mammogram, family history of breast cancer, hysterectomy, Pap test, menstrual history, children, breast exams, last physical exam
   - Men—last prostrate exam, last testicle exam for lumps
5. Personal information, for example, marital status, race/origin, education level achieved, type of occupation, type of employment

Following the completion and review of health risk appraisal results, a report of major findings and recommendations for preventive care is developed. A written personal report is provided to the patient and typically shows an overall total health profile score and what health improvements could be made to improve that score. Good habits are outlined, as well as specific actions to be taken to improve the risk profile.

Example of Health Risk Appraisal Results

Sex: Female   Weight 200 lbs.   Blood Pressure: 120/75
Age: 26   Height: 5' 7"

Good Habits	What to Do to Improve Risk Profile
• Regular Pap tests • Safe blood pressure (120/75) • Good seat belt use • Low alcohol risk • No tobacco use • Dietary fat within guidelines	• Reduce driving speed to legal limit • Exercise three or more times weekly • Reduce weight (acceptable range: (132-148 lbs.)

Recommended Preventive Services for Women Under Forty:

- Cholesterol (every five years)
- Blood pressure (every two years)
- Dental care (every six to twelve months)
- Breast self-exam (monthly)
- Breast exam and Pap smear test (every one to two years)
- Rubella vaccine (once)
- Tetanus-diphtheria booster shot (every ten years)

SUMMARY

After consideration of the information and issues presented, answers to the following questions about your practice will give you an idea of where its current focus is and the direction needed to achieve customer-focused care, service, and healthy lifestyle development.

- Has care been delivered as a customer service to each patient in a smooth and effective manner? Are all needs being met without duplication, on a low-cost, high-quality basis? Have patients become healthier under your health care guidance (e.g., as a group, are patients living longer, more disease-free lives)? List the prevention activities practiced. Are they working? What outcomes are measured to determine success?

- How do outcomes compare to benchmarks?
- Are operating costs as low as they could be? How do they compare to peer group costs?
- Do consumer satisfaction ratings show excellent care and service? Which aspects are most important to consumers? Are consumers directly connected to the delivery system (e.g., patient-centered care versus a care system in which patients must try to fit in)?[23]
- Are providers receiving ongoing continuing medical and/or other preventive care education to stay a little in advance of the times? What new skills have been added within the last year? Do providers regularly contribute health care information for public and private school curriculum development and instruction on an annual basis? What percent of staff members routinely provide consultation to schools, nursing homes, and other community groups?
- Are consumer satisfaction scores adequate compared to peer groups? Is satisfaction increasing in known problem areas? Is the percentage of disease-free membership/patients increasing? Where have the most significant gains been made? Is the number of patients leaving the system or disenrolling from the health plans comparable to your competition? Why are consumers leaving the practice?
- What refinements have been made to enhance the clinical care, daily operations, and consumer satisfaction with services? What areas need further refinement?

Chapter 2
Using Information

PROACTIVE CONSIDERATIONS

- How well is the practice positioned to achieve its clinical, service, and financial targets? Whether the practice succeeds or fails should not come as a surprise. Success can be optimized through alignment.
- The objective of alignment is to connect practice priorities → goals → required management support → resources. Three essential steps are needed:
  1. Selecting targets on which to base success.
  2. Developing measurable actions to guide the implementation of activities related to targeted outcomes.
  3. Defining information that links alignment goals, intervention activities, and outcomes.
- Leveraging alignment to impact target goals is the basis of proactive management. The concept requires analysis of current results compared to forecasted desired outcomes. Midcourse corrections are made to change activities responsible for poor performance bringing practice results back on line to meet or exceed each forecasted outcome.
- Resources are allocated toward practice priorities.

The business of health care is replete with enough information to make effective decisions toward achievement of desired financial, operations, and patient care outcomes. The problem is to decide what the most important information is for each desired outcome and how to use it. For example, the most important business information establishes the key indicators that should be used by the CEO, administrative staff, board of directors, and other health care leaders to monitor the business. Key indicators should be reviewed at each board of directors meeting; executive management systems must be built to optimize indicator performance; at year end, auditors validate key indicator business results; and, annual reports should reflect indicator performance in association with company vision, mission, and goals accomplished.[1] All decision makers must know what the key indicators of their business success are, the meaning and value of relationships between and among indicators, and what continuous improvement action is needed to optimize desired outcomes by aligning resources and operational focus on priorities.[2] The following material covers the concept and application of principles associated with alignment and defining the most important information.

DEFINING ALIGNMENT

Alignment can be on an individual provider or provider group level and is calculated or defined by drawing a direct path from current or actual performance to desired targets. A plan is required to show activities that connect the essential priority steps. The task is to identify each required step and provide the necessary manpower and financial support to achieve the desired results.

Example: Reduce the length of time it takes to process a health care bill and resolve the account following the delivery of service to a patient. [2]

Goal: Reduce actual number of days to achieve target number.

Objective: Based upon the size of the provider group's accounts receivable, one day's worth of billings could range from $50,000 to $1 million or more. In Figure 2.1, the clinic takes forty-eight days when it should take thirty-nine. Nine days must be eliminated to achieve alignment, thus creating increased cash flow and additional interest income.

Figure 2.2 illustrates the steps required to process a bill through the hospital component of an integrated system from which twenty-five days need to be eliminated.

The objective of alignment shown in each figure is to achieve the target number of days to complete each step in the billing process. Alignment is achieved when forecasted target and actual days are the same. The major components of the billing process are listed from beginning to end in sequential order, using a procedure called process mapping. Specific actions or steps compromise each component and serve as the focal points for in-depth review and analysis. The intent and purpose is to eliminate unwarranted actions, redundancies, or other nonproductive, time-consuming activity.

Components of Billing Cycle

CLINIC	HOSPITAL
Encounter	Average Length of Stay (ALOS)
Coding/Charge Ticket	Bill Hold
Claims Generation	Coding/Charge Ticket
Payer Turnaround	Claims Generation
Errors/Resubmits	Payer Turnaround
	Errors/Resubmits

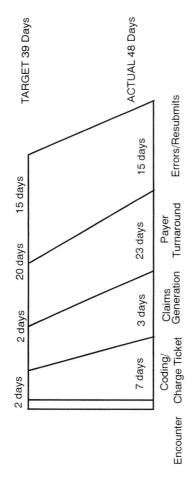

FIGURE 2.1. Clinic Days to Process a Bill

Source: Sommers, P. A. and Torgerson T. Internal study. Allina Health System, Minneapolis, MN, 1997-1998.

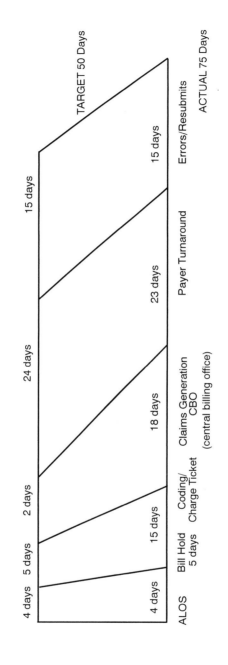

FIGURE 2.2. Hospital Days to Process a Bill

Source: Sommers, P. A. and Torgerson T. Internal study. Allina Health System, Minneapolis, MN, 1997-1998.

A detailed review of process mapping applied to both clinic and hospital billing cycle components is addressed in Chapter 6, "Special Applications."

What Is the Most Important Information?

To determine whether the provider, hospital, health plan, and/or combined efforts to achieve mutual outcomes have been successful, targets composed of information found in each organization's outcomes database(s) must be evaluated. For example, although many health care organizations with mutual interests have addressed the consolidation of efforts, as evidenced by the growing number of formally integrated organizations, few of the emerging hybrids have quantifiably documented the results to determine if the reasons for consolidating have been successfully achieved.[3,4] If the intent to produce a desired outcome is not clearly defined and agreed upon by all parties at the outset, determining if the resultant outcomes are appropriate becomes a difficult matter. Once the desired targets have been defined, it is a routine task to measure achievement toward desired outcomes.

Database Development

Knowledge of the relationships between and among the key indicators composing the provider's practice, and its hospital and health plans performance, is essential. The development of reliable and valid information sources representing each business unit is a requirement. For example, the data illustrated in Tables 2.1 and 2.2 represent one medical practice. The information is similar to what would be presented at routine physician group board of director's meetings and becomes part of the knowledge base upon which practice business decisions are based. Information of importance to the organization's viability should be reported, monitored, and managed at the highest level. Strategic plans are established to guide the practice toward defined success targets represented in the database.

Equally important to the physician group information is the hospital database associated with physician practices. It is important to evaluate provider, hospital, and health plan results to determine the most important information associated with clinic, hospital, health plan, or combined organization success targets.

Hospital financial and combined physician-hospital volume/activity factors are shown in Table 2.3, which is similar to the type of information presented at routine hospital board meetings.

TABLE 2.1. All Physicians Clinic Actual and Budgeted Administrative Expenditures—1987-1995 (Dollars in Thousands)

ADMINISTRATIVE COSTS	Actual 1987	Actual 1988	Actual 1989	Actual 1990	Actual 1991	Actual 1992	Budget 1992	Actual 1993	Budget 1993	Actual 1994	Budget 1994	Actual 1995
Executive Office	891	771	842	685	531	535	538	502	519	552	550	619
Legal	N/A	N/A	N/A	N/A	N/A	86	101	164	173	119	171	113
Marketing and PR	624	287	353	50	50	71	71	114	114	117	117	94
Operations	78	104	73	76	0	0	0	0	0	0	0	0
Medical Director's Office	N/A	N/A	(30)	51	43	43	40	37	41	68	54	58
Risk Management	70	70	58	80	82	103	112	103	116	106	132	105
Human Resources	156	219	284	305	352	304	346	338	362	336	371	382
Professional Services	N/A	N/A	N/A	N/A	N/A	82	99	142	140	149	162	169
Managed Care/Quality Control	N/A	15	24	31	64	73	72	78	78	90	90	74
Accounting			347	398	429	495	489	509	509	504	504	702
Financial Services			0	0	(94)	69	69	35	121	52	(56)	251
Credit and Collections			993	1,042	983	1,127	1,108	1,273	1,226	1,290	1,291	1,230
Management Information Services			704	703	730	767	807	886	934	970	970	1068
Investment Income Fee Management			240	208	40	0	0	0	0	0	0	0
Central Registration			40	40	0	0	0	0	0	0	0	0
TOTAL BUSINESS OFFICE	1,964	2,179	2,264	2,391	2,088	2,458	2,473	2,703	2,790	2,816	2,709	2,896
Business Services Reps	N/A	N/A	N/A	N/A	N/A	N/A	N/A	186	150	246	269	437
Surgical Coding Department	N/A	N/A	N/A	N/A	0	8	0	(14)	0	11	22	27
Zoned Registration	N/A	N/A	N/A	N/A	N/A	N/A	N/A	56	56	95	95	0
Ramsey Health Care	N/A	N/A	N/A	N/A	69	157	153	337	198	233	218	218
Parent Company	N/A	N/A	N/A	N/A	69	157	153	337	198	233	218	218
Ambulatory Care	N/A	N/A	N/A	N/A	N/A	N/A	N/A	99	101	103	104	114
General Fund and Other	248	(105)	(482)	346	173	128	166	204	173	202	221	197
TOTAL ADMINISTRATIVE OVERHEAD	4,031	3,540	3,386	4,060	3,452	4,048	4,171	5,049	5,011	5,243	5,291	5,503
Medical Department Net Revenue	33,503	35,073	36,666	41,693	45,622	49,546	50,686	53,798	53,969	57,594	57,133	60,019
Medical Department Direct Expense	25,382	28,000	31,466	34,922	39,446	42,558	44,326	46,426	46,843	50,064	49,351	52,104
Medical Department Net Income Available to Cover Corporate and Indirect Expenses	8,121	7,073	5,200	6,771	6,176	6,988	6,360	7,372	7,126	7,530	7,782	7,915
Administrative/Overhead as a percentage of Medical Department Net Revenue	12.03%	10.09%	9.23%	9.74%	7.57%	8.17%	8.23%	9.39%	9.28%	9.10%	9.26%	9.17%

Source: Sommers, P. A. Internal Study, Ramsey Clinic/St. Paul-Ramsey Medical Center, St. Paul, MN, 1995.

34

TABLE 2.2. All Physicians Clinic Actual and Budgeted Corporate Expenditures—1987-1995 (Dollars in Thousands)

CORPORATE COSTS	Actual 1987	Actual 1988	Actual 1989	Actual 1990	Actual 1991	Actual 1992	Budget 1992	Actual 1993	Budget 1993	Actual 1994	Budget 1994	Actual 1995
Branch Administration	229	322	282	205	193	184	193	315	261	169	146	277
Branch Clinics	795	944	1,003	1,116	574	650	351	930	304	743	671	733
Ambulatory Care	N/A	118	95	88	51	107	89	N/A	N/A	N/A	N/A	N/A
Campus Clinic	185	451	346	516	409	479	523	353	532	387	501	454
Neonatology	N/A	N/A	159	157	200	212	188	322	204	277	285	317
Neurosurgery	N/A	N/A	N/A	262	158	151	61	103	83	79	40	13
Walk-in Clinic	N/A	N/A	N/A	N/A	N/A	27	0	116	100	128	46	163
Specialties	109	27	10	19		10	0	0	0	0	0	0
Emergency Medical Services	N/A	107	132	30	115	259	258	262	262	271	271	244
Contribution to Foundation	291	168	0	307	67	0	0	0	0	150	150	150
Venture Funds	332	22	137	132	2	173	267	204	329	(14)	108	99
Workers Compensation Program	N/A	N/A	N/A	N/A	N/A	N/A	N/A	0	0	46	70	55
Incentive Plan	500	0	0	0	0	0	0	0	0	0	0	0
Insurance Contingency	600	1,031	927	(913)	(674)	(54)	0	(114)	0	(18)	0	0
Corporate Profit (Loss)	787	193	(1,260)	2,994	2,781	1,144	410	255	483	587	500	602
Other Corporate Costs	273	18	0	4	(108)	(108)	66	154	59	63	68	0
Total Corporate Costs	4,101	3,401	1,831	4,917	3,876	3,223	2,406	2,900	2,617	2,868	2,856	3,106
Total Corporate and Administrative	8,132	6,941	5,217	8,977	7,328	7,271	6,577	7,949	7,628	8,111	8,146	8,609
Net Clinic Revenues	39,105	43,234	44,356	49,779	53,220	55,863	57,595	60,883	60,843	64,140	64,865	67,792
Clinic Expenses	38,318	43,041	45,616	46,785	50,439	54,719	57,185	60,628	60,360	64,553	64,365	67,109
Corporate Profit (Loss)	787	193	1,260	2,994	2,781	1,144	410	255	483	587	500	602
Physician Salaries	17,115	18,918	22,040	23,322	26,093	27,831	27,848	31,284	30,035	34,883	32,625	35,129
Physician Salaries As a Percentage of Operating Expenses	44.67%	43.95%	48.32%	49.85%	51.73%	50.86%	48.70%	51.60%	49.76%	54.04%	50.69%	52.20%
Affiliation $ As a Percentage of Net Revenue	12.68%	13.22%	14.36%	13.85%	14.06%	14.17%	13.84%	13.47%	13.48%	13.88%	13.69%	14.68%
Affiliation $ As a Percentage of Medical Center Total Expenses	4.88%	5.54%	5.58%	5.28%	5.87%	5.23%	5.28%	5.05%	5.03%	4.99%	5.20%	5.21%

Source: Sommers, P. A. Internal study. Ramsey Clinic/St. Paul-Ramsey Medical Center, St. Paul, MN, 1995.

TABLE 2.3. Hospital Financial and Physician/Hospital Volume/Activity—Historical Financial Data —1985-1994 (Dollars in Thousands)

	1985	1986	1987	1988	1989	1990	1991	1992	1993	1994
Licensed Beds	427	427	427	427	427	427	427	427	427	427
Beds in Service	292	292	292	292	292	292	292	292	292	292
Average Daily Census	231.30	219.30	228.60	220.80	226.80	234.20	244.10	257.10	260.10	268.70
Percent Occupancy	79.20	75.00	78.40	75.30	77.20	79.40	83.60	82.40	83.10	85.80
Patient Days*	84,441	80,038	83,437	80,830	82,776	85,491	89,088	94,118	94,924	98,078
Admission*	13,607	13,276	13,725	13,211	12,495	13,001	13,921	15,401	16,005	17,164
Average Length of Stay*	6.21	6.03	6.08	6.10	6.60	6.60	6.40	6.10	5.90	5.70
Observation Status Patients	N/A	N/A	N/A	305	1,778	1,827	1,275	405	511	1,055
Outpatient Clinic Visits**	219,471	230,971	241,270	242,477	253,836	269,324	268,345	265,635	278,859	283,671
Emergency Room Visits**	53,830	54,067	55,795	57,421	54,779	57,090	55,745	59,437	56,626	56,584
Deliveries	1,257	1,217	1,118	1,086	1,171	1,396	1,658	1,649	1,601	1,674
Operating Room Cases	N/A	N/A	7,029	6,515	6,015	6,297	6,396	6,124	6,093	7,115
Radiology Procedures	N/A	N/A	106,900	105,126	110,189	113,028	111,542	113,252	113,456	
Lab Procedures	N/A	N/A	586,686	611,492	692,340	718,283	718,751	723,382	724,267	757,551
Full-Time Equivalents	N/A	N/A	2,017.80	1,949.30	1,956.20	2,051.20	2,149.80	2,151.30	2,180.70	2,281.90
Inpatient Referrals										
Net Patient Revenue	98,022	84,695	96,697	99,816	110,240	124,811	133,868	146,507	157,279	173,864
Other Operating Revenue	7,238	8,792	9,631	6,136	6,618	9,749	10,045	11,803	13,444	13,479
Operating Expenses	88,913	92,919	104,630	102,633	113,366	131,536	140,088	154,121	165,806	181,631
Income from Operations	16,347	568	1,698	3,319	3,492	3,024	3,825	4,189	4,917	5,901
Prior Year Adjustments	0	0	0	3,598	(504)	(3,323)	(881)	0	(19,869)	0
Nonoperating Revenue	1,048	867	685	577	985	597	361	363	(2,346)	(42)
Excess of Revenue Over Expenses	17,395	1,435	2,383	7,484	3,973	298	3,305	4,552	(17,298)	(5,859)
Operating Fund Cash	6,639	3,068	6,247	8,480	5,187	509	3,660	9,769	17,433	20,552
Depreciation Fund Cash	9,056	8,858	7,318	9,060	9,894	9,774	9,010	9,428	9,764	9,893
Patient Accounts Receivable	13,423	12,555	14,706	18,152	20,477	24,953	26,832	25,406	27,667	31,858
Net Land, Buildings, & Equipment	34,391	37,573	38,263	39,516	43,206	48,744	50,306	52,581	55,189	70,951
Additions to Land, Buildings, & Equipment	7,560	8,061	5,924	6,431	8,863	11,100	7,385	8,732	9,696	24,050
Total Assets	73,665	76,926	80,704	90,950	97,993	104,605	113,236	199,883	167,257	178,997
Fund Balance	47,542	49,958	53,474	61,992	67,056	68,501	73,037	78,661	62,364	67,686

Source: Sommers, P. A. Internal study. Ramsey Clinic/St. Paul-Ramsey Medical Center, St. Paul, MN. 1995.

* Statistics from 1985 to 1991 have been adjusted to remove data related to neonatal and convalescent nurseries.
** Walk-in Clinic visits in all years are included in outpatient clinic visits.

SELECTING TARGETS FOR BUSINESS SUCCESS

Is the business doing what was originally intended? A process used for determining which factors are most important toward achieving the plan's mission and vision is essential. Questions about quantitative outcomes and the ability of results to stand the rigor of scientific inquiry and the test of time must be addressed. Because multiple factors may have a bearing on preferred outcomes, an evaluation process capable of analyzing such situations is necessary.[5] Revolutions begin long before they are officially declared, stated Eccles, on the subject of performance measurement. He also noted that, for several years, senior executives in a broad range of industries have been rethinking how to measure the performance of their businesses. At the heart of this revolution lies a radical decision to shift from treating financial figures as the foundation for performance measurement to treating them as one among a broader set of measures.[6]

Several years ago, a balanced scorecard approach was developed by Kaplan and Norton to help organizations link their financial budgets with their strategic goals.[7] The balanced scorecard supplemented traditional financial measures with criteria that measured performance from three additional perspectives—those of customers, internal business processes, and learning and growth. It therefore enables organizations to track financial results while simultaneously monitoring progress in building the capabilities and acquiring the intangible assets needed for future growth.

Peter Drucker underscores the need for organizational redesign based upon a new set of tools and concepts. Drucker notes that we have both overestimated and underestimated our tools: we failed to realize that they would drastically change the tasks to be tackled:

> Concepts and tools are mutually interdependent and interactive. One changes the other. That is now happening to the concept we call a business and to the tools we call information. The new tools enable us—indeed, may force us—to see our businesses differently.[8] (p. 36)

Although the balanced scorecard approach expands the primary driver of business success beyond considering just financial to include the additional perspectives of customers, internal business processes, and learning and growth, it remains somewhat constrained. The mutual interdependence and interactivity between and among the factors accounting for business success discussed by Drucker need to be considered. Such consideration requires the freedom of all potential success drivers of a business to align themselves with the other related drivers, regardless of their origin (i.e., from providers, hospitals and/or health plans). For example, if a health care organization believed that it would be mutually advantageous to consolidate or integrate services or operations with others to create greater leverage while reducing overhead costs, it would be imperative to evaluate success differently than if each organization would conduct its business alone. If a provider group and a hospital integrated, three business efforts could be evaluated to determine success:

- Impact on provider group
- Impact on hospital
- Impact on combined physician-hospital entity

The targets of success for each organization may be different depending upon the desired integration expectations. Specific goals and objectives would be described in a jointly developed strategic plan. If a decision is determined to be positive to the physician group, negative to the hospital, but overall positive to the combined physician-hospital entity, action would be taken with full knowledge of each potential interaction. Provisions would be made to minimize the negative effects while optimizing positive results. Although individual organization situations may change, the goal would be to enhance the overall results for integrating business efforts in the first place.[9,10,11,12]

A multidimensional approach capable of producing quantifiable results is well suited for use in the evaluation and management of outcomes for the integrated organization. Since a successful organization is based upon an appropriate mix of excellent care and service elements to meet defined patient/purchaser needs for health care in the market to which services are provided, it is necessary to determine both the influence of market conditions upon care provided in the provision of services and the influence upon each participating business entity.[13,14]

Longitudinal analyses using a multidimensional model, simple regression, were applied to the physician and hospital data shown in Tables 2.1, 2.2, and 2.3. Using combined physician and hospital net revenue as a success target, the analysis was used to determine which indicators among all the listed possibilities are most important in predicting combined net revenue growth. Once determined, the top indicators would receive focused attention, with resources (human, capital, and financial) directed to optimize each indicator's positive contributions to further increase combined net revenue.

Linear regression analyses were applied to data collected from 1987 to 1994 to examine predictive relationships between the factors accounting for the positive combined physician-hospital net revenue results. Several key indicators were identified in rank order and are as follows: (1) year, (2) clinic visits, (3) physician salary growth as a measure of total operating expense, and (4) referrals. Tables 2.4 and 2.5 display the results associated with the analyses. R^2 defines the percent of variance found in the prediction of combined medical center and clinic revenues attributed to each of the indicators selected for analysis, and p-level indicates the degree to which error is responsible for the results.[15]

An increasing number of outpatient clinic visits, physician salary growth as an increasing percentage of the clinic's total operating expense budget, and increasing referrals of admitted patients from area physicians are statistically significant ($p < .02$) predictors of the positive combined net revenue trend. These indicators receive focused attention at the time the strategic plan is developed. The elements underlying each key indicator are traced back through the databases to their points of origin in the physicians' and hospital practices. Specific goals and objectives are developed to monitor and, when needed, enhance the performance of each element. Budgets are developed to reflect the necessary financial incentives and support required activities to achieve the desired outcomes.

The Medical Group Management Association (MGMA) provides comparative benchmarks that can be used to determine appropriate operational standards. Annual surveys to MGMA members throughout the United States gather confidential data on charges, revenue, expenses, earnings, and staffing in medical practices. Comparative payment rate standards are determined by establishing frequencies of use for each procedure. Relative value units (RVUs) are payment measures used as baselines for calculating capitated rates. The RVU was developed by the government as a basis for physician payment for services. Cost, productivity, RVUs, and other benchmark reports are updated annually and shared with MGMA members.[16,17] The information provides guideposts from which judgements can be made about the appropriateness of implementation of innovative changes.

IMPLEMENTING ACTION
TO ACHIEVE DESIRED OUTCOMES

Action Plan #1: Increasing Combined Physician Group and Hospital Net Revenue Growth

Results from Tables 2.4 and 2.5 were integrated into an annually revised "joint" physician-hospital strategic plan, budgets, and current year goals and objectives for each organization. The analysis showed that specific implications focused on five main indicators, of which two pertain to the hospital, one to the clinic, and two to the "combined" physician and hospital efforts. Activities implemented are described in Table 2.6.

TABLE 2.4. Combined Net Revenue Predictors (Rank Ordered from 1 to 5)

1991 Predictors	p-level	R²	1992 Predictors	p-level	R²	1993 Predictors	p-level	R²	1994 Predictors	p-level	R²
1. Year	.01	94%	1. Year	.01	96%	1. Year	.01	98%	1. Year	.01	98%
2. Outpatient Visit	.01	92%	2. Inpatient Days	.01	88%	2. Inpatient Days	.01	92%	2. Inpatient Days	.01	95%
3. Phys. Compensation As % of Expense Budget	.02	92%	3. Outpatient Visits	.01	86%	3. Outpatient Visits	.01	86%	3. Outpatient Visits	.01	86%
4. Inpatient Days	.02	81%	4. Inpatient Referrals	.01	85%	4. Phys. Compensation As % of Expense Budget	.01	79%	4. Phys. Compensation As % of Expense Budget	.01	85%
5. Inpatient Referrals	.02	79%	5. Phys. Compensation As a % of Expense Budget	.01	83%	5. Inpatient Referrals	.01	79%	5. Inpatient Referrals	.01	76%

Source: Sommers, P. A. Managing Medical Service Outcomes by Predicting and Achieving Success: An Inferential Approach. *American Medical Group Association*, 42(3): 24, 26-28, 30: May/June 1995.

Year as a key predictor demonstrates that the relationship between combined medical center and clinic net revenue has grown stronger and becomes more predictable over the course of the study. An increasing number of outpatient clinic visits, inpatient hospital days, physician compensation growth as an increasing percent of the clinic's total operating expense budget, and increasing referrals of admitted patients from area physicians were found to be most predictive of combined net revenue. Although rank order of the key predictors has changed slightly, the same factors have consistently remained the top predictors since 1991.

R² coefficients were derived from simple pairwise regression analysis with combined net revenue.

TABLE 2.5. Prediction of Combined Medical Center and Clinical Revenues—
1987-1991

Variable	B Slope	t	p	R^2
(9) Year	13,621.0	10.56	.002	97%
(10) Patient Days	6.074	2.43	.093	66%
(1) Referrals	20.911	4.64	.091	88%
(2) Admissions	1.820	0.09	.935	2%
(3) Clinic Visits	1.467	5.97	.009	92%
(4) Physician Salary Growth As a Measure of Total Operating Expense	6,884.8	5.07	.015	90%
(11) Administrative Overhead As Percentage of Medical Department Net Revenue	-11,586	-2.84	-.066	73%

CORRELATIONS

	Combined Revenue	Year	Patient days	Referral	Admits	Total Visits	Physicians' Salary As a % of Expense Budget	Administrative Overhead
Year	.987		.815	.937	.015	.960	.946	-.853
Patient Days			.730	.925	-0.17	.942	.921	-.913
Referrals				.670	.538	.718	.831	-.556
Admits					-.245	.919	.941	-.811
Total Visits						-.080	.049	.059
Admin. Overhead							.846	-.729

Source: Sommers, P. A. Longitudinal Analysis of a Physician-Hospital Collaboration That Works: The Ramsey Model. *Group Practice Journal,* 43(3): 14, 16-18, 20, 22-23, 26, 55, 1994. Reprinted with permission.

Hospital Indicators

Continued positive outcomes require increased admission, with adequate reimbursement, of appropriate patients who stay for optimum periods of time. This outcome relates to two main indicators: inpatient referrals and inpatient hospital days.

Inpatient referrals (actions taken). Strong emphasis was applied to enhancing the existing primary care physician referral relations program; refining and expanding the branch clinic primary care network; sponsoring continuing medical education courses that appealed to referring physicians;

TABLE 2.6. Predicting Combined Net Revenue—1991-1994

Results	Factor	Implications
Five key factors accounted for the prediction of combined net revenue in 1991-1992-1993. Although the factors rotated their order slightly over the years, the *same* five remained the top predictors.	*Year:* The longer the partnership lasted, the more combined net revenue growth.	*Needed Action:* Continue integrated physician-hospital partnership.
	Patient Days: Inpatient hospital days.	*Needed Action:* 1. Encourage referral of increased fee-for-service business through excellent care, low costs, and high consumer satisfaction. 2. Operations improvement. Reduce costs/improve operations. 3. Anticipating increased capitation shift care delivery from "in" to "outpatient," i.e., same-day surgery, home care, promotion of healthier lifestyles, etc.
	Referred Inpatients: Patients referred for inpatient hospital care by area primary care physicians.	*Needed Action:* 1. Make rapid and accurate communication back to referral source through referral communication network, "a way of doing business." 2. Target marketing dollars on specialty service utilization versus primary care. 3. Opened new burn center and new ER. 4. Expand CME offerings about critical care skill enhancements to primary care physicians. 5. Market research findings about referral center capabilities to underscore state-of-the-art, leading-edge medical care services.
	Outpatient/Ambulatory Care: Patients seen by physicians in an outpatient/ambulatory care setting.	*Needed Action:* 1. Expand referral communication network to respond to outpatients referred for specialty service needs. 2. Operations improvement (improve customer services while decreasing costs). 3. Prepare space and facilities to serve patients in a seamless, customer-oriented manner.
	Physician Compensation: Total compensation with incentive dollars included.	*Needed Action:* 1. Increase incentive opportunities for physicians in the direction you would like to see their practices move. 2. Reduce administrative and non-revenue producing overhead. Begin zero-based budgeting.

software enhancements to refine services of the inpatient referral communication system; and construction of a new burn center to further expand specialty service capabilities for burn and trauma patients.

The following program changes were implemented in 1993-1994: (1) an outpatient primary care physician referral communications program was added to the existing inpatient system; (2) a broader network of affiliation contracts was developed with primary care providers for purposes of becoming their critical care/specialty service hospital; and (3) a communications plan was implemented to inform primary care providers about the significance and related capabilities associated with the recognition received from the American College of Surgeons that the new emergency medical facility and program was identified as a Level 1 Trauma Center.

Inpatient hospital days (actions taken). A window of opportunity for fee-for-service (FFS) patients was present in the western Wisconsin catchment area. Many of these patients were not covered by capitated insurance programs, which made them very attractive to regional hospitals who provided specialty and tertiary care services. Marketing programs targeted each of the FFS communities with campaigns focused on ensuring its constituents the best specialty care at the lowest prices with the highest consumer satisfaction. Most important, the communities were told that the patients would be returned to the community and their local physicians once the specialty serviced had been delivered.

Within the hospital, operations were redesigned to better serve each patient while reducing duplication and, thus, overhead expenses. Drilling deeper into the databases using multiple linear regression analysis revealed that 93 percent of the variance associated with inpatient days and FTEs is accounted for by knowledge of three variables:

	R^2
1. Inpatient revenue by day	49%
2. Patient days	38%
3. Operations' expense of nurses	6%
	93%

Patient days and full-time equivalent (FTE) employees were identified as the "targets" and analyzed from an inpatient-revenue-by-day perspective. Knowledge of inpatient revenue by day is the best predictor of inpatient days per FTE and accounted for 49 percent of the variance. This indicates that as revenue per day go up, inpatient days per FTE go down. This finding raises a question concerning the increasing severity of illness among patients needing hospitalization, since the number of tests and procedures are greater, thus increasing revenue on a daily basis. This is occurring simultaneously with increased admissions, which creates fewer inpatient days per FTE.

Knowledge of patient days individually accounted for an additional 38 percent of the variance, which indicates that as patient days increase, inpatient days per FTE also increase (the more patient days, the busier the hospital, thus more inpatient days per FTE). An additional 6 percent of the variance is attributable to knowledge of nurses' operating expenses. As operating expenses for nurses go up, inpatient days per FTE go down.

In preparation for an anticipated increase in capitated patients and strong price wars with the competition, the hospital shifted its delivery system toward outpatient services (i.e., same-day surgery, home health care, etc.) Costs were reduced simultaneously with aggressive pricing aimed at attracting more patients in need of specialty care.

Physician factors. The recruitment and retention of physicians was a major issue. The physician turnover rate was two to three times greater than benchmark comparisons with similar practices. *Physician compensation as a percent of the clinic's expense budget was a key factor.* Overall, physician compensation was less than other similar groups, which made it difficult to recruit and retain providers.

Physician compensation (actions taken). Strong emphasis was placed on the development of competitive compensation packages. Medical department-based productivity-driven incentive programs were established to extend further compensation opportunity to interested physicians. The physician turnover rate declined as compensation increased.

Hospital and physician factors combined. Continued combined success will require ongoing trust and joint efforts. The factors of time and outpatient/ambulatory care clinic visits have been addressed jointly.

Time. Time relates to long-term growth and success through joint planning, programs, and budgeting efforts. The longer the physician and hospital groups worked together in an integrated environment, the more combined net revenue increased.

For purposes of examining this relationship without the influence of time, multiple linear regression analysis was conducted of the same variables, excluding time as a predictor while adjusting for seasonal trends and inflation. Two variables account for 93 percent of the variance:

	R^2
1. Clinic FTEs	87%
2. Hospital admissions	6%
	93%

The implication is that fewer clinic FTEs (nonphysician) should be caring for more patients. An increase in the outpatient base will increase the probability of more patients requiring admission for hospitalization. By using more provider extenders (for both physicians and nurses) and fewer FTEs overall, it was possible to provide more care to sicker patients at less overhead expense, thus increasing overall combined clinic and medical center net revenue.

Outpatient/ambulatory care clinic visits (seasonally adjusted). Multiple linear regression analysis was applied to review the relationship between outpatient visits and FTEs. Of the variance associated with outpatient visits per FTE, 91 percent is accounted for by knowledge of three variables:

	R^2
1. ER visits	37%
2. Outpatient clinic visits	23%
3. Operating expenses of nurses	31%
	91%

The more outpatient visits there are, the more visits per FTE. Simultaneously, the more nursing expenses, the fewer outpatient visits per FTE. Staffing was a main cost driver addressed through an operation improvement process within the organization. The desired result was a smaller yet more efficient staff.

Actions taken: The hospital enhanced the outpatient clinic facilities and physician offices and expanded the emergency medical center to include a customer-friendly, nonemergency walk-in clinic that did not require prior appointments. The walk-in clinic charged lower outpatient rates than the emergency room and was open twenty-four hours a day, seven days a week. Ongoing assessment of required FTEs to produce desired results was included in the initiation of a zero-based program-budgeting process cycle that reduced the number of nurses. Because of the medical department-based productivity incentive plans, fewer physicians cared for more patients.

Action Plan #2: Decreasing Physician Staff Turnover

The physician group turnover rate had been averaging 13.5 percent per year from 1981 to 1991. When the integrated organization was established in 1987, an understanding was reached between the hospital and clinic that the hospital would use its resources to build essential facilities and to purchase the necessary equipment for physician use (e.g., MRIs, CTs, lasers, etc.). The clinic agreed to focus its resources toward competitive physician compensation, with the belief that the recruitment and retention of quality physicians would contribute as a significant success factor for the integrated organization. In fact, the integrated physician-hospital model was predicated upon physician leadership followed by an organization-wide commitment to institute the programs and services called for by the physicians. The success targets were instituted in the jointly developed annual strategic plan.

Efforts to enhance the physician workforce led to a decrease in the turnover average from 13.5 percent to 6.1 percent at the end of 1994, as shown in Figure 2.3. An inferential analysis of the factors accounting for the improvement in retention of physician staff documented three main predictors including (1) administrative overhead reduction as a percent of medical department net revenue, (2) net clinic revenue, and, (3) physician salary growth as a measure of overall clinic operating budget. Figure 2.4 illustrates the trend of administrative overhead as a percent of medical department net revenue, and Figure 2.5 shows the increasing trend of physician compensation as a percent of the clinic's total operating expense.

Physician staff turnover was decreased. Activities related to those factors responsible for physician staff retention are illustrated in Table 2.7.

Physician compensation as a percent of the physician group's expense budget has had a significant impact on combined physician group and hospital net revenue growth. Over the course of the study, the physician group and hospital implemented overhead reduction programs and developed department-based, productivity-driven physician incentive plans to enhance its salary-based compensation opportunities. Contrary to the tendency to reduce physician compensation because of shrinking reimbursement from some payers, the clinic added productivity-based incentives to encourage enhanced physician effectiveness on an organization-wide basis.

While physician compensation consistently increased, turnover decreased to an all-time low. In addition, the physician group financially experienced its most successful years (1991, 1992, 1993, and 1994).

Setting the Stage for Health Plan and Care Delivery System Interventions

Application of NCQA's clinical HEDIS indicators and baseline measures published in 1997 will help health plans and delivery systems understand how they compare to others. Second, the information will show what measures may need further analysis and, possibly, additional resources. The

FIGURE 2.3. Decreasing Physician Turnover

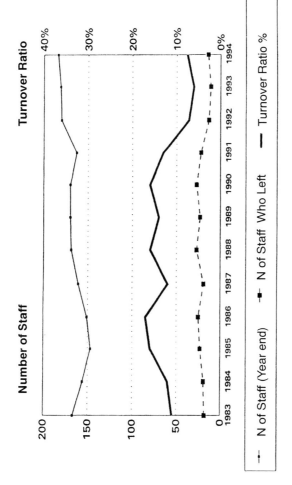

Source: Sommers, P., Luxenberg, M., and Sommers, E. CQI Longitudinally Applied to Integrated Service Outcomes. *Medical Group Management Journal*, 42(2): 50-54, 56-58; March/April, 1995. Reprinted with permission.

FIGURE 2.4 Reduction of Administrative Overhead As a Percentage of Net Revenues

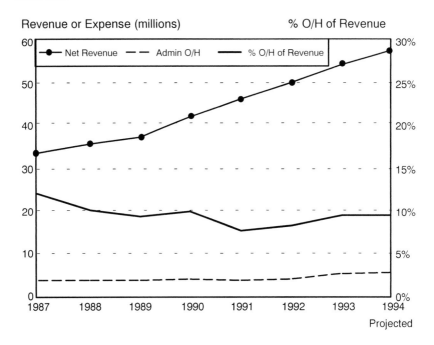

Revenue or Expense (millions)   % O/H of Revenue

Source: Sommers, P., Luxenberg, M., and Sommers, E. CQI Longitudinally Applied to Integrated Service Outcomes. *Medical Group Management Journal,* 42(2): 50-54, 56-58; March/April, 1995. Reprinted with permission.

following list shows the measures that represent health plan and delivery system performance in 1996, as reported in NCQA's *Quality Compass* (1997). More than 300 health plans participated.[18]

SUMMARY

- Has the use of information in health care practice been aligned to serve the top priorities? Does a direct path connect priority goals, objectives, and management support to resources?
- Does more than one alignment pattern exist to describe practice operations? How many nonpriority services/activities are being supported by the budget? Eliminate ASAP!

FIGURE 2.5. Physician Compensation As a Percentage of Clinic's Total Operating Budget

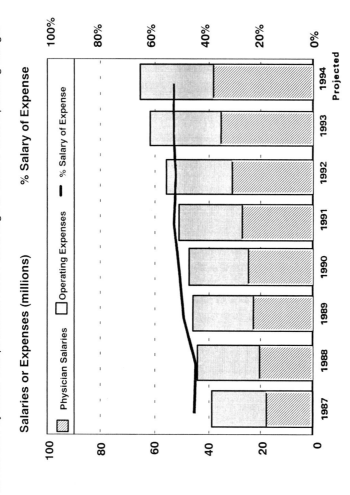

Source: Sommers, P., Luxenberg, M., and Sommers, E. CQI Longitudinally Applied to Integrated Service Outcomes. *Medical Group Management Journal*, 42(2): 50-54, 56-58; March/April, 1995. Reprinted with permission.

TABLE 2.7. Activities Related to Physician Staff Retention

1991-1994		
RESULTS	**FACTOR**	**IMPLICATIONS**
Three key factors accounted for the prediction of decreasing physician turnover and are presented in rank order.	*Factor 1:* Administrative overhead reduction as a percent of medical department net revenue.	*Needed Action:* 1. Reduce expenses supporting nonrevenue-producing services. Use zero-based budgeting process. 2. Ask departments to consider LPNs or RNs and PAs instead of additional physicians. Cross-train support staff wherever possible. 3. Consolidate duplicate services.
	Factor 2: Net clinic revenue.	*Needed Action:* Complete each recommendation outlined in Table 2.6.
	Factor 3: Physician salary growth as a measure of the clinic's operating expense budget.	*Needed Action:* 1. Implement department-based, productivity-driven incentive plans. 2. Supplement department incentives with clinicwide incentive opportunities. 3. Instead of hiring "new" physicians, ask existing staff to see one new patient per day and/or add more capitated members to their practice.

Source: Sommers, P. A. Internal study. Ramsey Clinic/St. Paul-Ramsey Medical Center, St. Paul, MN, 1995.

- Has each success target been clearly defined? Each must be measurable and the outcomes oriented to be proactively managed. What benchmarks are important to use as comparative measures?
- Focused action plans must be in place to achieve each desired outcome. More than one action plan may be needed to achieve various aspects of each target. All staff members of the organization must have their functions directly aligned with priorities—if staff are not fully committed and responsible for achieving one or more aspects of the action plans, their services should not be needed.
- The key to proactive management is leveraging current activities and results toward forecasted outcomes. A predefined time line should be used to monitor progress. Midcourse corrections must be implemented to enhance activities associated with poor performance. It is important to identify and make adjustments to each responsible activity as soon as it appears "off track," instead of waiting for traditionally acceptable reporting periods, (i.e., annual, semiannual, or quarterly). Continuous improvement must become the way to do business.

Chapter 3

Top-Down ↓ Bottom-Up ↑ Planning

PROACTIVE CONSIDERATIONS

- What is the organization's defined vision and mission? The twenty-first century will bring an increased interest from consumers of health care. Considerations for addressing the needs of each consumer are warranted since excellent care and service will go hand in hand with successful health care practices.
- Health care practices grounded on core values supported by personal conviction and commitment will have an advantage in weathering the storms of price wars, unethical competition, and consumer concerns about quality and return on investment. When costs cannot be reduced due to the needs of advanced, cutting-edge medical care and lifesaving technology, the practice that ties strong core values to the delivery of patient-focused care will prevail.
- How much do you know about the competition? The more you know, and the ability to effectively use that information, can place the practice in a strong market position. This process begins with a marketplace analysis that compares each practice strength, weakness, opportunity, and threat to each competitor.
- Strategies are needed to position the provider organization for purposes of exploiting the competition's weaknesses while capitalizing on its own internal strengths.
- Defined goals, objectives, and action-based plans are standard operating procedure for each individual within the provider organization. Common organizational priorities must exist between and among all FTEs. Defined in writing, with performance reviewed on a regular basis, the resultant outcomes can be matched with priority fulfillment. In each case, the outcomes achieved at the individual level are used as a basis for determining salary and/or incentive opportunities.
- Outcome analysis and results management decisions are facilitated through application of the principle of continuous improvement. Once

set, plans must be flexible toward change. Although the top priorities may remain the same, each plan's activities must be of a dynamic nature to take advantage of opportunities as they arise.

Planning is a process used to guide the provider's practice from where it is today to where it should be in the next one, five, ten, and fifteen years. To provide a complete picture of the organization's future direction, given the competitive nature of health care, "strategic thinking" (positioning the medical practice to take advantage of competing health systems) becomes a principle in the development of plans. The plan is based on direction from the governing body but requires active participation from each member of the organization. Other valued groups (formal or informal partners) at risk of gain or loss should also be considered for joint participation, (e.g., other providers, hospitals where the group's physicians admit patients, etc.). The value of joint planning with those who have mutual interests includes:

1. additional resources to focus on specific activities;
2. potential cost savings through consolidation of duplicate activities and systems; and
3. overall greater leverage associated with more points of influence focused on key success targets.

The strategic planning process identifies the mission, which is a view of the future, and defines goals as targets to be achieved to move the practice toward actualizing the mission. Strategies are maneuvers selected to guide planned activities toward achievement of desired outcomes. Since plans will be affected by market conditions and the environment in general, they will need to be flexible to take advantage of opportunities. Regardless of the size of an organization, some basic concepts must be considered if the plan is to develop.

Vision, mission, and core values of the organization are set by the CEO/president and board of directors. The plan states desired outcomes and commitment to achieving the mission and vision. A dynamic plan is not rewritten every year, but is reviewed regularly and only changed when appropriate. The plan consists of targets, called goals, which are broad actions that define how mission and vision will be achieved. Objectives are included for each goal, and specific measurable programs and services reflect the focus of each objective. Throughout the entire organization, each business, administrative, patient care, and service unit has specific goals and objectives aimed at the same companywide priority targets.[1] Figure 3.1 shows a structure of planned activity.

FIGURE 3.1. Model for Mission-Based Planning Formed Around Desired Key Targets

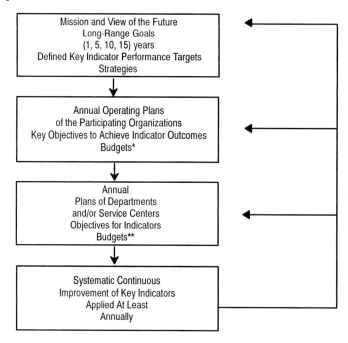

Source: Sommers, P. A. International study. Allina Health System, Minneapolis, MN, 1997-1998.

* Incentive dollars available for achieving organization-wide goals/objectives.
** Incentive dollars available for achieving individual merit and department-wide goals/objectives.

ORGANIZATION-WIDE PARTICIPATION

Bottom-up elements are reflected as implementation of programs and services occurs toward achievement of departmental (direct customer/member/patient interaction) targets. If what is happening at the direct customer/member/patient level is not congruent with the mission and vision of the organizational goals, outcomes achievement will be random. To ensure top-down/bottom-up congruence, continuous improvement (CI) is applied to monitor systemwide performance against key indicator goals and objectives. At least an annual comprehensive evaluation of progress is required, while quarterly and monthly updates serve as markers of intermediate outcomes. The ability to predict and define the path to desired outcomes is a significant strategic advantage. As the CI process shows new or changing patterns among key factors, it is important to "drill down" to the information source(s) and make the necessary adjustments at that level and time of identification.

The concept of a dynamic or "rolling" plan facilitates the CI principle. Simply put, the basic plan, predicated on the mission and vision of the health care system that represents the main business units, moves from year to year without a great deal of variation. The successful business establishes its reputation by being excellent in specific areas that allow for the concentrated focus of resources. Over time and through repeated focus and superior performance, the main business units and their specific product lines acquire a reputation for excellence. A dynamic plan invites changes organized for inclusion into the main product lines, and if warranted, past activities are dropped when their factors no longer significantly contribute toward the attainment of priority goals.

Success Essentials

Planning for success requires the understanding and application of proven business principles that have been applied to successful medical practices and health services.[2] The basic steps of strategic plan development, as described in Figure 3.1, are outlined in the following material for a metropolitan multispecialty physician group and regional tertiary care hospital. Subsequent examples in this chapter apply the planning process to (1) a metropolitan-based multispecialty physician group and regional tertiary care hospital; (2) a community-based primary care physician group and hospital setting; and (3) an HMO managed care environment.

CASE EXAMPLE: STRATEGIC PLAN DEVELOPMENT FOR METROPOLITAN-BASED MULTISPECIALTY PHYSICIAN GROUP AND REGIONAL TERTIARY CARE HOSPITAL

Mission and Vision

A mission statement summarizes what we are expected to do over the long-term future; the vision statement outlines our hopes and dreams for the future medial practice. For example, the medical practice will:

- continue to be the innovator in critical care services through leadership in research and education;

- develop efficient and convenient outpatient services through dedication to the needs and preferences of patients;
- remain true to its tradition of community service through commitment to conservative financial management;
- become the obvious choice for health care in the metro area through rigorously high standards of excellent patient care and service; and
- continue to develop joint ventures with providers and other health systems that share its mission.

Core Values

Core values outline the medical group's expectations for each individual within the organization. Six individual commitments are key to achieving its mission and vision of the future:

1. *A commitment to integrity.* The physicians are composed of a multitude of individuals, all of whom will act ethically, with personal honesty, conviction, and mutual respect. Many come from professional disciplines, each having a code of conduct. Although the group's success depends on effective working relationships among all individuals, it is equally important that individuals rigorously adhere to their own ethical and professional standards.
2. *A commitment to merits.* Decisions must be based on facts and substance, not form and procedure. Concordance with the group's mission, vision, goals, and strategies will take precedence over the desires and opportunities of individuals.
3. *A commitment to openness.* Each member must plan and act with the greatest possible openness and participation. Individuals are encouraged to speak their minds and adopt a positive questioning attitude, both of their own thinking and that of colleagues.
4. *A commitment to equal opportunity.* A commitment to equal opportunity for all, regardless of race, color, creed, religion, national origin, sex, sexual or affection orientation, marital status, status with regard to public assistance, membership or activity in a local commission, disability, age, political affiliation, or place of residence.
5. *A commitment to using resources responsibly.* The conservative and economical use of human, financial, and other resources is required for long-term success.
6. *A commitment to learning.* Learning is the basis by which we move from where we are today toward the successful achievement of excellent care and service. Continuous improvement is the process

of integrating learning with long-term practice success, evidenced by healthy lifestyle enhancements of the patients served.

Summary of Strategic Plan

The strategic plan states a commitment and expresses the conviction to achieve the physicians' mission and vision of the future. The plan is not rewritten every year, but is reviewed regularly and changed when appropriate. The strategic plan consists of:

- *Goals* are broad actions that define how we will achieve our mission and fulfill our vision. The physicians' group has seven goals:

  1. Provide unified medical leadership and strategic direction
  2. Provide excellent care and service
  3. Improve internal corporate culture and external image
  4. Increase the patient base by improving services, facilities, and technology
  5. Strengthen the financial position and improve net income
  6. Recruit qualified staff to support this vision and mission
  7. Enhance continuing medical education activities, to be seen as excellent in primary care medicine and critical care practice

- *Strengths, weaknesses, opportunities, and threats (SWOTs)* are issues we face that must be managed (i.e., either exploited or overcome). The provider's self-analysis, targets, and benchmark scores should be included in SWOTs.
- *Strategies* are the approaches the physicians take to address issues. Strategies provide direction for services and/or departments. For example, "Here is a specific opportunity; here is how we will use it." For purposes of emphasizing current-year groupwide importance, the strategies within this plan are listed in prioritized order. Subsequent years' emphases may or may not remain the same based upon CI analysis.
- *Objectives and programs* are specific ways to deal with SWOTs and implement strategies. Generally, they are quantifiable in terms of dates, actions, etc., and are incorporated into capital and operating budgets. Objectives should fit stated strategies; otherwise, why expend the resources? These objectives, which are seen as key indicators of specific service strengths, were extracted from more detailed lists.

Key Position Strategies

An example: The medical group has six overarching, or "positioning," strategies. They are selected from the plan and emphasized to indicate strategic intent, reputation, image, and points of difference from the competitors that the group wants to place in the minds of its customers:

◆ Succeed as part of an integrated system of care that seeks to improve health

❏ Combine academic physicians' group practice and teaching hospital

❏ Use continuing medical education to create superior health care capabilities

❏ Maintain ER and trauma care leadership role and dominant market share

❏ Continue to develop ER, main campus clinics, and branch clinics to provide an outpatient base for majority of hospitalizations and specialty referrals

❏ Strengthen service commitment to, and relationships with, referring MDs

> Key: ◆ New ❏ Ongoing

Goal #1: Provide Unified Medical Leadership and Strategic Direction in Concert with Hospital and Health Plan

SWOTs	Strategies	Objectives/Programs
S: Physician-hospital partnership. S: Reputation as a teaching facility has a positive effect (e.g., cutting edge, high-tech). S: Expanded vertical integration with health plans as integrated service network.	◇ Combine academically inclined physicians' group and teaching hospital. ◇ Use continuing medical education to create superior health care capabilities. ◇ Place physicians in lead role in marketing and planning. ◆ Adopt managed care as a way of doing business en route to successfully integrating physicians into the new parent organization.	Clearly define mission, vision, core values, goals, and strategies. Effectively communicate corporate message to nonphysician personnel and seek their commitment. Determine expected utilization target and activity patterns by physician and hospital inpatient and outpatient departments. Develop MIS capability to provide department with the necessary information on a timely basis (monthly), to understand their current performance in relation to expected performance. Develop departmental reimbursement systems that align incentives under capitated reimbursement.

Key:
◇ Ongoing
◆ New
Strategies are in priority order.

Goal #2: Provide Quality Care and Service

SWOTs	Strategies	Objectives/Programs

SWOTs

W: Long waits for appointments and long waiting times in clinics.

W: Communication with referring MDs inconsistent.

O: New, powerful customer groups have emerged (e.g., payers and purchasers of care, referring professionals, prehospital providers), with explicit expectations for information outcomes and service.

T: Payers and purchasers imposing stricter utilization controls.

T: Patients have many choices; therefore, technical excellence is not enough.

T: Government and purchasers rapidly moving to service contracts based on cost, outcomes.

T: Important payers will tend to use their own care systems.

W: Continuing medical education model may influence certain aspects of care.

Strategies

◇ Meet or exceed expectations of customers for service quality and value.

♦ Restructure referral services as an operations activity under business office/customer services and include outpatient referrals in addition to inpatients.

♦ Become an active participant in health care guideline utilization.

◇ Demonstrate top management commitment to Continuous Quality Improvement.

Objectives/Programs

Seek to design new clinic space to make it more patient friendly.

Seek to improve systematic, timely feedback to referral sources for outpatients and inpatients.

Develop outcomes measurement and reporting methods.

Develop internal capability to respond to multiple data needs of providers, patients, payers, and purchasers.

Establish and formalize practice guidelines.

Monitor patient surveys to improve responsiveness to patient demands.

Implement demonstration projects at department level, showing use of consumer satisfaction information to improve operation (e.g., pediatrics, surgery).

Key:
◇ Ongoing
♦ New
Strategies are in priority order.

Goal #2 *(continued)*

SWOTs	Strategies	Objectives/Programs
T: External demand for outcome measures. T: Cost reimbursement rates are declining. T: State legislation calls for control of high technology equipment. S: Physicians' commitment to continuous quality improvement (CQI).	◇ Standard patient care quality improvement model. ◇ Utilize care delivery models that maintain quality while taking into account reimbursement rates. ◆ Coordinate CQI planning and activities.	Maintain quality improvement model through continuing education, database analysis, and process enhancement. Develop plan to provide customized services that maintain quality of care. Develop plan to ensure access to necessary new technology and equipment. Incorporate appropriate CQI training and coordinate among all providers. Compare and contrast quarterly performance and focus, continuing education on eliminating the difference between expected and actual performance.

Key:
◇ Ongoing
◆ New
Strategies are in priority order.

Goal #3: Improve Internal Physician Group Culture and External Image

SWOTs	Strategies	Objectives/Programs
W: Many nonphysician employees do not understand the strategies and direction.	◇ Make understanding of strategic plans an important priority.	Communicate key strategies to the appropriate audiences.
W: Interdepartmental and external referral patient flows are relatively low in comparison to other settings.	◇ See internal and external MDs and residents as customers. ◇ Involve physicians early in decision making.	
O: MDs control patient hospital volume.		
S: The external public has a relatively strong understanding of the integrated physician group's role and identity.	◇ Retain present positioning as an excellent critical care provider.	Develop a communications plan to support an integrated organizational identity program and positioning and to enhance external image.
S: A member of an integrated physician-hospital health plan organization.	◆ Participate in helping to establish the value of an integrated organization to individual patients and each group of consumers.	Develop a communications plan to optimize physicians as members of the integrated group.

Key:
◇ Ongoing
◆ New
Strategies are in priority order.

Goal #4: Increase Patient Base by Improving Services, Facilities, and Technology

SWOTs	Strategies	Objectives/Programs
T: Aggressive competition critical care services are moving into marketplace.	◇ Maintain emergency and trauma care leadership role and dominant market share.	Achieve Level 1 Trauma and critical care service.
O: Inpatient services provide financial base but require even larger outpatient base.	◆ Integrate organization to become provider of choice for specialty referrals, trauma, critical care, and emergency/ urgent care services.	Design and implement new ambulatory care building, remodeled ER, and walk-in clinic.
		Develop plan to bid on competitor contracts with primary care physicians for their specialty care needs.
S: MD and EMS transport patterns show increased use of physicians and good understanding of service specialists.	◇ Strengthen service commitment to, and relationships with, referring MDs.	Monitor sources of referring revenue.
		Strengthen MD support of Physician Referral Network.
O: Substantial portion of existing business comes from referring MDs.		Transition the management of referral physician services from marketing into operations (e.g., business/customer services).
T: Current market share is increasing, but competitors directly compete with group.	◇ Seek competitive advantage over closest competitor.	Strengthen and emphasize cardiology and orthopedics.
	◇ Increase continuing medical education skills and latest outpatient techniques.	
T: A new competitive threat has moved into your primary catchment area.	◆ Reposition All Physicians Clinic within the network to counteract new primary care competitor.	Consider the integration of select services as valuable added options for community.
		Consider relation of All Physicians Clinic.

Key:
◇ Ongoing
◆ New
Strategies are in priority order.

Goal #4 *(continued)*

SWOTs	Strategies	Objectives/Programs
O: Government support is critical to facilities, numerous contracts, and reimbursement arrangements.	◇ Have superior ability to interface with county and state government. ◇ Strengthen OB to contain competitive threats from the new primary care competitors.	Strengthen OB and Urology coverage to enhance primary care. Coverage and value-added specialty urological services.
S: Pediatric service has expanded.	◇ Meet the pediatric care needs of the community through collaboration with other providers.	Strengthen our relationship with community service. Review psychiatry to increase services without expanding campus facilities.
T/O: Demand for psychiatry services has been steadily growing, with relatively weak competition, but managed care cost controls are strictly limiting benefits and eroding the inpatient market.	◇ Seek opportunities to extend mental health and chemical dependency services' "reach" off-campus.	Meet with select health plans interested in capitated mental health and chemical dependency programs. Develop community provider relationships to be attractive as a referral service resource.
S: Full-service, integrated, tertiary care provider with expertise in critical care.	◆ Optimize the integrated organization options (i.e., health plan options, prevention versus intervention leading toward healthier patients/members, use of practice guidelines).	Expand inpatient service capabilities with private and semiprivate rooms. Determine physician service needs by specialty and regulate FTEs accordingly. Provide technology needed to establish All Physicians Clinic as the specialty care center of choice.

Key:
◇ Ongoing
◆ New
Strategies are in priority order.

Goal #4 *(continued)*

SWOTs	Strategies	Objectives/Programs
S: MD-hospital partnership.	◇ Develop and market managed care arrangements to increase market share and diversify customer mix (as an integrated organization there is strength in producing and marketing various health plan options that are based on consumer need/preference).	Capture and track patient data on cost, utilization, and outcome with linkage of the inpatient, outpatient, and branch systems.
W: Lower preference for, and use of, Physicians' Clinic in suburban areas.		Provide incentives for cost-effective medical management. Expand network for distribution of services to competitor patients and employer purchases.
W: Physicians' Clinic has perceived lower proficiency/quality in some services (e.g., cardiovascular).	◆ Position All Physicians Clinic to retain current Medicare volume in a capitated/managed care environment.	Develop globally priced packages within selected specialties for direct contract sales.
O: Growing market interest in "wholesale" and "sole-source" purchasing of health care services.		Enhance the "preferred" health benefit product for employees, and develop it further for external sales.
O: State law requires small employer health plans.		Work with health plan to identify and/or establish managed care programs in which current All Physicians Clinic Medicare patients can be enrolled as members.
T: Increasingly more people are enrolled in managed care plans and this will include Medicare.		
T: Managed care contracts restrict choice of provider, use of specialists/services, length of stay, charges.		

Key:

◇ Ongoing

◆ New

Strategies are in priority order.

Goal #4 *(continued)*

SWOTs	Strategies	Objectives/Programs
O: State law calls for programs to support rural health care.	◇ Meet community needs of branch market areas with on-site specialty coverage.	Increase specialty coverage in gynecology, ENT, orthopedics, and cardiology.
O: Influx of younger professionals into branch market areas.	♦ Increase market share of specialty referrals from neighboring state.	Develop a marketing strategy for neighboring state.
O: Populations of neighboring state counties in service area are growing.	◇ Actively nurture relationships with communities of color and new Americans.	Meet key opinion leaders. Sensitivity training for staff. Participate in minority community events.
T: Increasing competition for primary and specialty services in neighboring state.		
O: Minority populations in main catchment area are growing and All Physicians Clinic has unique strength in helping these groups.		

Key
◇ Ongoing
♦ New
Strategies are in priority order.

Goal #5: Strengthen Financial Position and Improve Net Income

SWOTs	Strategies	Objectives/Programs
T: Health care reimbursement is increasingly uncertain and most likely will decrease.	◇ To ensure continued financial strength, increase efficiencies and control operating costs and capital spending.	Operation Improvement Program. Reengineer current physician group, hospital, and health plan operations to increase customer service, improve quality, and reduce costs.
S: New parent company can provide a steady flow of patients.	◇ Seek revenue enhancements from current business.	
	◇ Maintain a conservative financial position.	Seek mutual cost savings opportunities within the integrated organization.
O: State will have captiated service networks and an all-payer system, parallel to federal program. Regulations are not published and there is opportunity for input.	◇ Use physician and hospital(s) strength to maintain one another's financial position.

♦ Support integrated organization in health policy development at the county, state, and federal levels. | |

Key:
◇ Ongoing
♦ New
Strategies are in priority order.

Goal #6: Recruit Qualified Staff to Support Physicians' Group and Mission

SWOTs	Strategies	Objectives/Programs
T: Shortages in some classes of health care workers.	◇ Offer higher quality services through physicians and other staff members who receive compensation that meets or exceeds competitive levels.	With MD input, consider the cost-effectiveness and impact on quality of using more physician extenders.
	◇ Seek to enhance teamwork between physicians, nurses.	
W: Physicians' Clinic MDs are relatively un-recognized.	◇ Seek public recognition and prestige for MDs as key sources for increased patient volumes. Continuing medical education opportunities present visibility through networking interactions.	Continue MD recognition program for contributions in patient care, teaching, research, and community service.
W: MD turnover is somewhat higher than peer group average.	◇ Enhance perception of clinic within medical community to attract and retain quality staff.	

Key:
◇ Ongoing
◆ New
Strategies are in priority order.

Goal #7: Enhance Activities in Continuing Medical Education, Research, and Undergraduate/Graduate Education

SWOTs	Strategies	Objectives/Programs
W: Academic and continuing medical education role is not well-known by our public.	◇ Have superior environment for residents and students.	Identify/implement enhancements that would make All Physicians Clinic resident programs unique and desirable.
T: Potential decrease in residents in area University medical training programs.	◇ Strengthen affiliation with area medical schools through collaborative efforts for services not provided by All Physicians Clinic.	Develop an alumni relations program.
W: Research is costly and reduces MD patient care income.	◇ Stress external research grants.	Increase the number of residents trained through All Physicians Clinic family medicine program.
T: Increased pressure for cost containment may include reduction of public funding for medical research and education.	◇ Actively promote and participate in a process to revise funding system for medical education and research.	Reconstituting Alll Physicians Clinic medical education committee to address ways/means of transitioning managed care into the training curriculum.
S: Incorporating managed care into the Physicians' Clinic medical education program.	◆ Organization to become a demonstration center to teach managed care techniques and management principles to medical students.	Develop collaborative educational programs between integrated organization's providers (physician and hospital) and health plan. Seek outside funding for demonstration medical education program teaching medical students how to be effective managed care providers.

Key:
◇ Ongoing
◆ New
Strategies are in priority order.

Monitoring Progress Toward Strategic Plan Targets

Quarterly updates of progress toward the strategic plan priorities are received from each clinical and administrative department within the physicians' group, hospital, and health plan. A comprehensive, in-depth analysis is conducted annually.

Formation of the annual budget follows development of the strategic plan, with rank-ordered consideration of financial and FTE support given toward those programs, services, and activities identifed as priorities.

OUTCOMES MANAGEMENT
AND CONTINUOUS IMPROVEMENT

Typically, outcome targets are evaluated comprehensively on an annual basis. At this point, it is important to determine if, and to what extent, the specified objectives and targeted outcomes of the strategic plan have been reached. New business activity and any service unit with an increased allocation of financial and/or human resources are assessed to determine whether any differences exist in the outcomes produced.

Evidence is reviewed to determine whether the business components are performing as expected and what refinements are needed. It is important to screen the information being collected to detect defects in procedural design and in the process of implementing the service. In this way, an organization can monitor the procedures for collecting data and document the observable effects—at the end of the evaluation cycle and throughout the process—to identify potential problems and to correct the operation of systems for delivering the service, as needed. A dynamic, continuously self-improving business system is the desired outcome of a thriving health care organization.

The process used to make a decision that is based on the concept of continuous improvement is one which moves an idea through rapid application/implementation (usually trial and error) to produce an outcome: following measurement of outcome(s) results, learning occurs, which in turn leads to enhancements (changes), thus producing the next idea. Figure 3.2 shows the cycle of events.

To be useful, outcomes must be measurable and documented. If outcomes are not measured, nor any findings recorded, no true results exist. Future events should be compared to the record of each preceding event to understand and learn what, why, and how to enhance efforts toward achievement of optimal outcomes. Transforming ideas into measurable

FIGURE 3.2. Cycle of Decision Making

Idea

Rapid Application/ Outcome

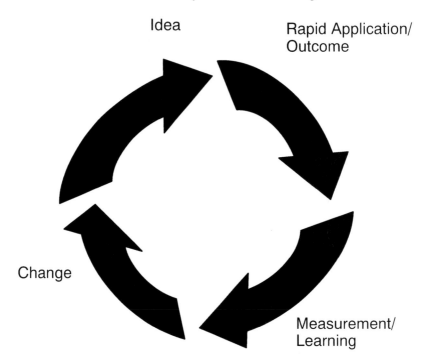

Change

Measurement/ Learning

goals, objectives, and plans, followed by actual "trials" in which reliable and valid findings are recorded, sets the stage for knowledge-based decision making.[3]

New Business Development Process

When a "new" business opportunity is identified, it is important to have a specific process to evaluate its potential. Such an opportunity could present itself at any time, which means it typically will not fit the budget cycle. However, if the opportunity has merit, it should be considered and, if deemed appropriate, implemented regardless of timing. Some organizations reserve a specific dollar amount or a percent of the budget for new business development. The process used to evaluate new business proposals should be consistent and widely known among the physician, hospital, and health plan leadership.

The new business development process should stimulate new growth opportunities based on the customers' (patients, referring professionals, payers and purchasers of care, prehospital providers, and medical trainees) needs and the organizational strategic plans. The process should stimulate ideas that will support the direction in which the business is intended to go.

A new business proposal will require review and approval through this developmental process when:

1. either the physicians, hospital, or health plan(s) is directly affected by the proposal;
2. the proposal is intended to produce new revenue or protect current revenue;
3. the proposal will require approval of the board(s) of directors, from either a policy or financial standpoint, prior to implementation; and
4. the proposal will require a capital expenditure of $25,000 to $50,000 or more.

The process works according to six steps.

Review Cycle Is Announced

New business ideas will be reviewed competitively on a quarterly basis or when a significant opportunity presents itself. Announcements of the start of a new review cycle will be made through internal publications in a timely manner. Certain projects may be reviewed on an expedited basis if timing is considered strategically important.

An Idea Is Proposed

The idea person completes the following background information about the opportunity to the greatest degree possible and submits it to the administrative head of the organization.

Criteria for initial evaluation of new business ideas. An administrative staff member should be assigned to help department heads and the idea person respond to the following:

A. Description
   1. Briefly describe who will benefit from the ideas and how it will work.
   2. Must we pioneer this idea? ____ yes ____ no
   3. What other successful models can we look at?

B. Mission
   1. Is this idea compatible with, and supportive of, defined organizational missions goals and strategic plans? ____yes ____no
   2. Briefly explain.
C. Competition
   1. What competition to this idea currently exists?
   2. How might the competition respond to our initiative?
D. Market Assessment
   1. Does the potential market demand for this idea exceed the capacity of existing providers? ____yes ____no
   2. If yes, on what information do you base your answer?
   3. How did end users' (patient, referring professional, business and industry, paramedical personnel) input play a role in developing this idea?
   4. What research has been done to support this idea?
E. Experience
   1. Does the organization currently have the experience and talent to develop and manage this idea successfully? ____yes ____no
   2. If no, how will these be provided?
F. Location and Space
   1. Do you currently have access to space in which to effectively implement this idea? ____yes ___no
   2. If yes, is this space easily accessible by users of the idea?
G. Staffing

   Primarily, how many and what types of people will be required to implement this idea?

Number of FTEs	New	Existing	Job Class
_____	_____		_____

H. Capital
   1. What is the preliminary estimate of the initial cost of equipment $____ and facilities $____ required to implement this idea?
I. Financial Results
   1. Is this idea believed likely to create revenue in excess of expenses? ____yes ____no
   2. If yes, on what information do you base your answer?
J. Timing
   1. How long will it take to develop the idea?
   2. Is the timing of introduction or development of the idea a critical factor to its success? ____yes ____no

K. Organizational Conflicts
1. Does this idea present any potential conflict with the interests of others (i.e., physicians, departments, clinic, or services)? ____yes ____no
2. If yes, describe potential conflicts.
L. Authorized Approval
Signature of authorizing individual: Date:

_____   _____

Ideas Are Screened with Initial Criteria

Responses to the initial evaluation criteria will be reviewed by administrative staff from the physicians' group, hospital(s), and health plan(s). The staff will then rank all ideas presented based on how well each addresses the criteria. Top-ranked ideas will receive authorization to become proposals. A time line will be set for review.

Proposal Is Developed

The criteria for approval of new business proposals follows:
A. Business Plan
1. The plan must address the first three years of operation.
2. The plan must satisfactorily respond to all of the criteria for initial evaluation.
3. The plan must state implementation timetables and responsibilities.
4. Promotional requirements must be outlined.
5. Evaluation criteria that will be used to measure project success must be explicitly stated.
6. A contingency plan must address what will be done with staff, space, equipment, cash, receivables, and liabilities if operations of the project do not meet expectations.
B. Financial Evaluation
1. A pro forma statement of revenues and expenses must be provided for the first three years of operation.
   a. Projects undertaken with an expectation of financial gain:
   • Physicians' group expenditures—the proposal must show a positive margin of net revenue over expenses, including the costs of promotion, by the second year of operation. The proposal must also recover any losses from the first year of operation by the end of the third year.
   • Hospital expenditures—the proposal must have a present positive net value of cash flows.

    b. Projects not undertaken for economic reasons must generate sufficient net revenue to at least meet the expenses of operation, including costs of promotion, by the third year of operation.

2. All assumptions regarding major business risks associated with the proposal—volume, market conditions, charges, payment sources, operational expenses, promotional costs, bad debts, discounts, and capital costs—must be explicitly stated and shown to be reasonable and consistent with industry norms.

3. Total capital requirements, recovery periods, and rates of return, etc., must be shown to be reasonable and in accordance with organizational requirements.

4. The allocation of operating and capital expenses among hospital, health plan, physicians, and foundation must be detailed.

5. The allocation of operating income among the hospital, clinic, foun-foundation, health plan, and medical departments must be detailed.

C. Other Considerations

1. Any regulatory, legal, or accreditation requirements must be anticipated and addressed.

2. Administrative responsibilities must be resolved (e.g., Who will manage the idea? Who will managers report to?)

3. The availability of development, foundation, or grant funds to supplement start-up operations must be considered.

The Proposal Is Approved

The physicians' group, hospital, and/or health plan or other strategic planning body, will recommend approval of proposals to the appropriate boards or other governing bodies based upon how well the approval criteria are satisfied.

Depending on the nature of the project, other hospital, clinic, or health plan or foundation committee reviews may be necessary. These will be scheduled before approval by the appropriate boards or other governing bodies.

The Operations of Approved Proposals Are Evaluated

Project operations and eligibility for additional funding after the first year will be evaluated annually by the strategic planning body. The evaluation will be based on how well the objectives of the business plan are being met and whether operations are on track with the pro forma estimates, as outlined in the approved proposals. Projects are expected to be self-supporting within one to three years of start-up, depending on the nature of the project.

Annual review updates should be submitted to the strategic planning body within sixty days of the anniversary date for each of the first three years of operation, unless otherwise directed by the committee. A notice of annual review and the required process will be sent to the authorizing individual. The anniversary data will be from the time the project received final approval.

New Business Development Annual Review

On at least an annual basis, progress toward goals, objectives, and financial targets should be reviewed. Many organizations require updates on the same quarterly reporting intervals as for strategic plan reporting. The following is an example of an annual review process:

Program Name:

Date Approved (anniversary date):

Date Operational:

A. Objective
 1. Has the primary goal or objective been achieved to date? Explain.
 2. Is this program still compatible with the hospital's, clinic's, health plan's, and foundation's defined missions, goals, and strategic plans? If no, explain.

B. Results

How do the actual volumes of service and financial results compare to the original pro forma projections? Please attach an updated pro forma showing projected and actual results.

C. Financial Viability
 1. Is the program now self-supporting? If no, explain how and when that will be accomplished.
 2. Will the program require additional operating or capital funds to continue? If yes, explain why additional funds will be necessary.

D. Changes

Does the program need to change from what was originally proposed? Explain.

E. Approvals

Signature of authorizing individual: Date:

_____   _____

CASE EXAMPLE: DEVELOPING
A COMMUNITY-BASED PRIMARY CARE GROUP
AND HOSPITAL STRATEGIC PLAN

The following example illustrates a community-based approach to be used by an integrated physician-hospital-health plan organization to build its primary care networks in a nonmetropolitan area.

Introduction

Primary care clinic development is crucial to long-term success for physicians, hospitals, and health plans. More and more care is being delivered by primary care providers to better meet consumer needs as close to their homes as possible. In addition, payers are reinforcing primary care development by paying specialists less. To be most effective, primary care service should be founded on the principle of local solutions to local problems. The focus of efforts is on ways and means to build networks from the individual communities up rather than being dependent on comprehensive service centers many miles away. Building effective networks requires (1) education of the participants and identification of benefits to provide the will, (2) a carefully defined networking process to provide the way, (3) sufficient financial and technical resources to provide the means, (4) adequate time to build trust among the participants, and (5) participant commitment and follow-through to ensure the attainment of mutual goals.

The organization can inspire needed changes by supporting the development of community-based planning processes to enhance local health systems. Accompanying this effort should be strategies to:

- enhance local leadership skills;
- educate and involve local citizens;
- support the integration of existing health resources between and among communities; and
- develop a vision of excellent care and services that clearly identifies the continuum of care citizens can expect, with primary care available as close to home as possible.

Community Health Care Development (Mission and Vision)

The mission of community health care is to support the growth and development of excellent primary care and service for all community residents within a ten-mile radius of the main physicians' group, hospital, and health plan center. The vision is to meet all constituent health care needs at the local level through partnerships and joint ventures with multispecialty physicians' groups, tertiary care hospitals, skilled nursing homes, home care agencies, and health plans focused on preventive care and lifestyle enhancement.

Core Values

Core values outline expectations for each individual within the community health care network:

- *A commitment to local leadership.* Efforts will focus on ways and means to build networks from the individual community up. Each constituent will be provided all necessary care and services as close to home as possible.
- *A commitment to the education and involvement of local citizens.* Effective networks will be built to ensure the education of the community-based constituents. Private and public schools and the local public health services will be the main network contacts to work with social services as medical group and hospital partners.
- *A commitment to self-examination and change, beginning from within each individual and leading to supporting the integration of existing health resources between and among communities.* Through education, community residents will be taught how to optimize and consolidate scarce human, fiscal, and capital resources to continuously enhance healthy lifestyle development.
- *A commitment to provide primary care as close to the patient's home as possible.* To succeed, we must be willing to learn. We must continuously search among care alternatives for ways and means to optimize the health and wellness of each citizen.

Strategic Plan Summary

The strategic plan states our commitment to achieving the mission and vision of the future. The plan is not rewritten every year, but is reviewed regularly and changed when appropriate. The strategic plan consists of:

- *Goals* are broad actions that define how we will achieve our mission and fulfill our vision. The following are the five community health care goals:
  1. Provide unified medical development and management services for internal and external consumers. Desired outcome: Provide leader-

ship to guide caregivers toward achievement of effective services delivered at the community level throughout the network.

2. Provide high-quality, low-cost program consultation to contracted primary, specialty, and hospital caregivers. Desired outcome: Save dollars, achieve consumer satisfaction, and enhance performance on a continuing basis.

3. Improve the management and effectiveness of administrative linkages between the organization-owned clinics and contracted caregivers. Desired outcome: Become the network support system of choice for primary care providers.

4. Enhance supportive and integrating care delivery processes. Desired outcome: Improve/extend caregiving capabilities.

5. Optimize the delivery and transformation of information communication capabilities with a consumer-oriented focus toward state-of-the-art performance. Desired outcome: Enhanced communica tions measured by internal and external consumer satisfaction that is refined on a continuing basis.

- *Strengths, weaknesses, opportunities, and threats (SWOTs)* are issues we face that must be managed (i.e., either exploited or overcome). Strategies are the approaches the organization takes to address issues.
- *Strategies provide direction for departments.* For example, "Here is a specific opportunity; here is how we will use it."
- *Objectives and programs* are specific ways to deal with SWOTs and implement with adequate strategies. Generally, they are quantifiable in terms of dates, actions, etc., and are identified in the capital and operating budgets. Objectives should fit the strategies; otherwise, why expend the resources?

Key Positioning Strategies

- Establish reputation and skill as the health care organization of choice among contracted physicians' groups. Save dollars while increasing effectiveness and achieving both internal and external consumer satisfaction.
- Strengthen service commitment (caregiver/provider and management) and improve relationships with contracted physicians' groups. Benchmark care outcomes, utilization targets, and service standards—develop/implement networkwide plan to measure and achieve outcomes through continuous quality improvement.
- Create state-of-the-art expertise and methods for practice guidelines development and practical approaches toward the development of healthi-

er populations (i.e., members and patients); expand/extend capability through electronic information exchange, including telemedicine and teleconferencing; and, enhance and extend medical and continuing education programs to both internal and external customers. Use medical and continuing education and research to create superior health care, administrative, management, and service capabilities.

- Enhance communication capabilities to meet caregiver/provider and management needs to deliver superior internal and external consumer service. Create/enhance comprehensive service networks to meet caregiver and management needs.

Goal #1: Provide Unified Medical Development and Management Services for Internal and External Organizational Consumers

SWOTs	Strategies	Objectives/Programs
S: Physician-hospital-health plan partnership.	◆ Combine networkwide resources toward collective priorities.	Clearly define mission, vision, core values, goals, and strategies.
S: Reputation as a community-oriented, full-service, vertically integrated health care organization.	◆ Focus services on internal and external consumer needs.	Reorient the delivery of services in the owned and contracted clinics and hospitals to enhance customer satisfaction and follow-up at all levels (e.g., offer needs assessment/consumer satisfaction evaluation to determine baseline).
S: Owned clinics will be marketed under one coordinated marketing plan.	◆ Use existing owned clinics and hospital to demonstrate integrated approach to meet health needs of constituents.	Promote the value of the family medical clinics and local community hospitals. Educate the community on the broad scope of primary caregiver capabilities from delivering babies to performing colposcopies to counseling adolescents (e.g., marketing plans of owned and contracted primary care groups must reflect unique attributes and produce the necessary outcomes to become network of choice).
S: Owned and contracted groups create an extensive medical service distribution system across the seven county metro area, eastern Minnesota and western Wisconsin. The network represents virtually unlimited health care service capabilities to a potential market of more than one million patients/members.	◆ Place physicians in lead role to market and deliver products.	Promote the "hometown clinic" you have grown up with on a personal basis. Encourage the physicians to participate in community events, the local schools, and athletic endeavors. The organization should offer resources as needed (e.g., a tailor-made health plan for the industrial park/Small Business Purchasing Alliance).

Goal #2: Provide High-Quality, Low-Cost Program Consultation to Contracted Primary, Specialty, and Hospital Caregivers

SWOTs	Strategies	Objectives/Programs
T: Hospitals may close, be purchased by another organization, or consolidate.	◆ Provide management and consulting services to help communities and hospitals through the transition to prepare them to meet community health care needs of the future.	Seek to be the organization most helpful to local communities in implementing educationally based wellness and healthy lifestyle programs. Offer resources to local physicians' groups and hospitals to facilitate health care planning (e.g., conduct community education needs assessments and offer follow-up plans to help communities meet defined
O: Competitors interested in western Wisconsin are not currently organized to systematically begin to take control of shaping the health care system of the future.	◆ Service local hospital and physician constituencies by helping them identify needs and "options" to meet current and future health care needs.	needs). Create the provider network needed to compete more effectively with other integrated systems. May require consolidation of duplicate services among caregivers (e.g., area physicians and hospitals for primary and secondary care; the hospitals of surrounding counties for home care; the physicians and hospitals of an adjacent county for emergency room service, etc.). Appoint a medical director to help marshall resources necessary to train local physicians and hospitals about managed care (e.g., connect clinics to organization electronically). Offer management information and claims processing systems. Interface with network practice guidelines.

Goal #2 *(continued)*

SWOTs	Strategies	Objectives/Programs
		Prepare and implement a strategic development plan for enrollment growth and for commercial risk contracting, medicare risk contracting, and other managed care opportunities (e.g., small employer purchasing alliances).
		Oversee utilization management and quality assurance functions, including clinical outcome documentation and other support services that can help local physicians and hospitals.
		Coordinate and manage specialists' panels across the network.
		Help to administer/allocate risk pools pursuant to risk-sharing arrangements between hospitals and physicians. Become a licensed HMO in Wisconsin. May need to develop PPOs and other companion managed care products to market through the network (e.g., industrial park model).
W: Currently no marketing plan has been developed to focus efforts on western Wisconsin.	◆ Market the network to employers and consumers.	Begin to strategically develop organizational connections throughout St. Croix, Polk, Pierce, and Dunn counties initially.

Goal #3: Improve Management and Effectiveness of Administrative Linkages Between Owned and Contract Caregivers

SWOTs	Strategies	Objectives/Programs
S: The comprehensive physician-hospital-health plan network.	◆ Become the network support system of choice for primary care providers.	Provide consultation on practice management and practice enhancement.
		Assist in physician development, recruitment, and retention for network growth.
		Provide CME Category 1 credit for physicians and appropriate continuing education for other staff.
		Provide administrative services on a "menu" basis to participating physicians and hospitals as requested. Manage selected practices (solo and/or group) as requested.
		Seek new/expand existing relationships in collaboration with local communities (e.g., Random Lake, etc.).

Goal #4: Enhance Supportive and Integrating Care Delivery Processes

SWOTs	Strategies	Objectives/Programs
O: No organized management service organization is effectively serving physicians and hospitals in western Wisconsin.	♦ Develop an organized management/services approach toward helping primary and specialty caregivers and hospitals optimize their service in the communities of western Wisconsin.	Provide administrative assistance to physicians and hospitals. Conduct hospital/ practice needs assessment to determine the best way to help each group (physician and hospital).

Present proposal to each pro-vider/hospital group on the following basis: flexible structure; no minimum physician or hospital requirement; can serve multiple physicians' groups and hospitals as well as solo practitioners; equal opportunity can be offered to both physicians and hospitals.

Provide selective administrative services to physicians; medical group retains control over practice, including "ownership" of patients and medical records (can build as much independence into each community as they desire).

From hospital's perspective—no pressure to buy goodwill from physicians.

Minimum regulatory requirements.

Initially begin by approaching all area primary care groups to discuss ways and means of promoting community understanding of health care and needs and fostering leadership toward healthier lifestyles.

Goal #5: Optimize the Delivery and Transformation of Information Communication Capabilities with a Consumer-Oriented Focus Toward State-of–the-Art Performance

SWOTs	Strategies	Objectives/Programs
W: Long waits for appointments and long waiting times in clinic.	♦ Meet or exceed expectations of customers (members, patients, other payers, purchasers, and other referral sources).	Develop outcomes measurement and reporting methods to monitor key consumer satisfaction performance.
T: Payers and purchasers imposing stricter utilization controls.	♦ Encourage active participation in the developing practice guidelines network.	Promote practice guidelines among owned and contracted groups. Provide electronically managed outcome and utilization reporting systems.
W: Expensive and time-consuming methods of providing specialty services to distant primary caregivers.	♦ Use telemedicine capability to reach out and provide specialty care throughout western Wisconsin initially, and subsequently throughout the organizational network.	Establish connectivity between the organization's specialty service center and distant primary care groups. Connect physically via electronics, cable, TV, and/or other undefined forms to promote ready access and immediate feedback of information about clinical care, outcomes, information updating, satisfaction, patient/member choices, ongoing education, and promotion of healthy lifestyles.
T: Important payers will tend to use their own care systems and support services.	♦ Network services must become exemplary from a cost, quality, effectiveness, and consumer satisfaction perspective.	Become the network of choice based upon ability to deliver most effective service at lowest cost to totally satisfied consumers. Network effectiveness to be demonstrated by meeting defined needs one customer at a time.

Goal #5 *(continued)*

SWOTs	Strategies	Objectives/Programs
T/O: There will be several competing major players in western Wisconsin.	◆ Use existing owned and contracted network to "seal out" competitor movement on market share of defined product lines.	Sponsor and help develop and implement joint strategic plans in collaboration with physicians and hospitals of western Wisconsin.

Goal Summary:
Program/Budget/Activity Responsibilities

Program Activity	Projected Budget Needed	Assigned Responsibilities
Goal #1:		
•Offer consultative assistance to the owned and contracted clinics for needs assessment/consumer satisfaction evaluation, and follow-up services.	$ In-kind-support	Managing Director Physician Liaison
•Offer consultative services to help owned and contracted services develop effective marketing plans to promote local market share growth in each community.	$25,000	Managing Director Marketing Department
•Complete design and actuarial work related to industrial park/ Small Business Purchasing Alliance PPO model.	$	Insurance Account Rep.
•Develop a permanent presence in western Wisconsin by establishing an agency office. Initial steps in 1996.	$15,000	Managing Director VP Network Services
Goal #2:		
•Conduct community education needs assessment and work with each community to develop a plan to meet defined needs.	$10,000	Managing Director Marketing Department
•Approach communities with offer to help coordinate consolidation of duplicate services between hospital and physicians for purposes of eliminating duplication and excess expenses, while demonstrating how working together provides mutual benefit.		Managing Director
•Establish connectivity between organization and owned/contracted clinics (e.g., electronic communications and/or telemedicine).	$ In-kind-support	Director, Network Mgmt. VP, MIS
•Assign account representatives to oversee utilization review, quality assurance, and clinical outcomes documentation.	$ In-kind-services	VP, Network Mgmt.

Goal Summary *(continued)*

Program Activity	Projected Budget Needed	Assigned Responsibilities
Goal #2 *(continued)*		
•Secure an HMO license to sell products in western Wisconsin.	To be determined by insurance dept.	
•Implement coordinated emergency medical service program between physicians and hospitals in the county.	$ In-kind-service	Managing Partner
•Complete home care business plan for the three hospitals of the county.	$25,000	Managing Partner Director, Home Care
Goal #3:		
•Offer consultative services to owned and contracted primary care clinics to increase management efficiency.	$ In-kind-services	VP, Network Mgmt. Managing Director
•Complete feasibility plans concerning Random Lake and Indo Scandian.	$25,000	Medical Director Regional Services Adm., Regional Services
Goal #4:		
•Provide consultation on practice management and educational development in communities as basis for management services organization. Interface CME/EMS training, education, and consultation services.	$25,000	Managing Director Physician Liaison
•Approach hospitals and physicians throughout the regional counties with proposal to help examine ways and means of enhancing community understanding of health care needs, while fostering leadership toward healthier lifestyles.	$ In-kind-services	VP, Network Mgmt.
Goal #5:		
•Develop a systems approach to monitor outcomes/reporting measures.	$ In-kind-support	VP, MIS Director, Network Mgmt.
•Sign clinics up/help prepare for participation in practice guidelines collaboration.	$ In-kind-services	Medical Director Practice Guidelines

Goal Summary *(continued)*

Goal #5 *(continued)*

•Establish connectivity (See Goal #2, $ See Goal #2
which covers same activity).

•Offer to develop joint strategic plans $ In-kind-services   Managing Director
with interested physicians and hos-
pitals of western Wisconsin.

1996 Total $125,000

CASE EXAMPLE:
HEALTH PLANS' MANAGED CARE STRATEGIC PLAN

Health Plans wants to offer what the purchasing community desires. Typically, this means that members of a health plan are targeted to receive a lifetime of health care options—prevention and wellness services and the highest quality, technologically advanced services, including home care, hospice, and long-term care services, if so desired. Each plan tries to differentiate itself in the marketplace with a broad range of options. Comprehensive plans emphasize a focus on building healthier communities to supplement individual member health improvement. Satisfaction and customer loyalty are required for long-term health plan growth and market-share enhancement, and both are significantly influenced by various unique factors, including easy access to health care, choice of providers, excellent care and customer service, and innovative preventive care programs.[3]

Vision and Mission

Health Plans strives for recognition as a leader aimed at improving the health of the community served and, specifically, the health of plan members.

Sample Key Positioning Strategies Outlined As Three-Year Goals (Examples Only)

1. Create greater customer value through improved choice, service, information, and price as measured by excellent satisfaction with care and service.
2. Measurably improve the health of plan members.
3. Align operations and strategies with top clinical and service quality priorities. Only top priorities will receive funding.

4. Increase membership by 30 percent (cumulative over three years) while achieving retention targets established for each product.
5. By end of year three, achieve 2 percent net operating income from operations.

Sample One-Year Goals (Examples Only)

1. Internal working environment:
   • Implement strategy to improve workforce capability and job satisfaction. It has been consistently documented that staff and consumer satisfaction rises and falls together.
2. Provider effectiveness:
   • Increase provider knowledge of ways and means to better utilize practice information to improve the care of each member (patient) while positively affecting the bottom line of the clinic.
   • Integrate health plan information into decision support system for provider use and application. System will monitor and manage pharmacy, lab, radiology, consumer satisfaction, and episode-of-care information.
3. External value:
   • Implement clinical and service quality goals.
   • Improve information to stakeholders by implementing models to predict and prevent disease-specific conditions. Create network-wide communications programs to inform providers about patient, service and system enhancements, including telemedicine, radio, and television.
   • Complete evaluation and redesign of products that are not meeting defined customer needs. Involve rank-and-file providers in the initial stages of development process to achieve "buy-in."
4. Health improvement:
   • Implement health risk assessment profile for plan membership.
   • Develop strategies with employer groups to identify high-risk employees and implement plans to reduce risk. Long-term strategy is prevention and lifestyle enhancement.
5. Finance:
   • Achieve $ _____ million in net operating income.
   • Redevelop financial and administrative assumptions to accurately reflect organization needs and priorities, complete with specific plans to achieve targeted priorities.
6. Growth:
   • Achieve at least _5_ percent growth in health plan enrollment. (Determine feasibility of percent market share.)

_____% Medicare

_____% Medicaid

_____% PPO

_____% Commercial

- Achieve member retention rate of at least 94 percent.

Examples of Preventive, Clinical, and Service Quality Priorities As Noted Under External Value Goals

Preventive Care Goals and Measurement Targets (Examples Only)

- Mammography target is 82 percent. (Benchmarks: 60 percent HEDIS, Healthy People 2000.)
- Pediatric immunization target is 91 percent. (Benchmarks: 90 percent HEDIS, Healthy People 2000.)
- Adult immunization—the current adult rate is being assessed by a phone survey on a random sample of members (1) over sixty-five years of age and (2) high-risk adults twenty-one to sixty-four years of age.
- Pap test (cervical cancer) target is 87 percent. (Benchmarks: 85 percent HEDIS, Healthy People 2000.)
- Otitis media—the current measurement will be through HEDIS 3.0 and will measure the number of children six weeks to sixty months old with an uncomplicated diagnosis of otitis media who were not prescribed first line of antibiotics. (Benchmarks: Healthy People 2000 is to reduce days of restricted activity and school absenteeism among children four years old and younger to 105 days per 100 children.)
- Mental illness—continue monitoring follow-ups after hospitalization through HEDIS 3.0. (Benchmarks: Healthy People 2000 is to reduce prevalence to less than 10 percent of mental disorders among children/ adolescents and reduce same among adults to less than 10.7 percent.)

HEDIS measures should be specifically included in each health plan's annual strategic plan. The immediate advantage to the health plan relates to the broad base for comparisons of their plan scores. Through a new report, "The State of Managed Care Quality" (1997), NCQA is now providing a description of what was measured, why it is important, and how the managed care industry is doing—both nationally and by census regions (highest and lowest performers).[4] The averages provided represent the performance of those plans that voluntarily submitted data to *Quality Compass*. The following list shows which states are included in each region.

- East North Central—Ohio, Indiana, Illinois, Michigan, Wisconsin
- Middle Atlantic—New Jersey, New York, Pennsylvania
- Mountain—Arizona, Colorado, Idaho, Montana, New Mexico, Nevada, Utah, Wyoming
- New England—Connecticut, Maine, Massachusetts, New Hampshire, Rhode Island, Vermont
- Pacific—Alaska, California, Hawaii, Washington, Oregon
- South Atlantic—Delaware, District of Columbia, Florida, Georgia, Maryland, North Carolina, South Carolina, Virginia, West Virginia
- South Central—Alabama, Arkansas, Kentucky, Louisiana, Mississippi, Oklahoma, Tennessee, Texas
- West North Central—Minnesota, Iowa, Missouri, North Dakota, South Dakota, Nebraska, Kansas

NCQA discusses what improvement could mean to the health of Americans and describes some steps health plans can take to achieve that improvement. Early findings include the following:

1. HMOs and other managed care organizations vary greatly, both within regions and across regions, in terms of preventive care, treatment of acutely ill and chronically ill patients, and member satisfaction:
   - Heart attack patients in the South Central Region are treated with beta-blockers less than 20 percent of the time in some health plans, but more than 90 percent of patients receive beta-blocker treatment in the best-performing plans.
   - Plans in the New England region scored highest in seven out of nine measures; plans in the South Central region scored lowest in seven out of nine measures.
2. If we could bring all plans up to the level of performance achieved by the best plans, it would have significant consequences for the health of Americans:
   - If all plans were brought up to the benchmark level in screening for breast cancer, an additional 1,200 cases would be detected each year, and 1,800 years of life would be saved.
3. Managed care enrollees, in general, are satisfied with the care they receive through their health plans, but have complaints about the system's service.
   - More than 85 percent report that they did not have a problem receiving necessary care, but only 39 percent rated their plan as "very good" or "excellent."

NCQA will be producing this report annually. *Quality Compass* collects information from NCQA's accreditation program—in which more than 330 health plans, covering three-fourths of all HMO enrollees, now participate—and HEDIS, which is in use by more than 90 percent of health plans. *Quality Compass* contains data on more than fifty HEDIS measures for all participating plans. For the first report, *The State of Managed Care Quality* (1997), the eight clinical HEDIS measures, previously discussed in Chapter 1, have received special attention. The care provided to children, women, and the chronically ill are featured and are meant to serve as important probes into the industry's overall performance. Patient satisfaction information is available for the first time this year to shed some light on how HMO enrollees view the care and service they receive from their own health plans.

Clinical Quality Priorities (Examples Only)

Goals are designed for short-term (one year) and long-term (three years) planning periods as described previously. Improved care, effectiveness, efficiency, and cost reduction are anticipated features. Priorities include asthma, breast cancer, cardiovascular, colon cancer, diabetes, and pregnancy care.

Pediatric Asthma Care

Goal: to optimize the functional status and reduce the disease burden of asthma on the children and families enrolled in Health Plans.

Objectives

1. Provide appropriate, consistent, and ongoing patient and family, education to achieve the following:
   - Optimize adherence to effective treatment and care plans.
   - Define and maintain preventive health schedules for asthma.
   - Decrease children's exposure to secondhand smoke.
   - Reduce the number of asthmatic teens who smoke.

2. Implement a chronic disease model that incorporates the strengths of existing national, regional, and local models:

Outcomes Measured

1. Reduced:
   - emergency department visits,
   - hospital admissions and length of stay, and
   - unplanned clinic visits.
2. Appropriate use of medications.
3. Excellent patient and family (caregiver) satisfaction.
4. Optimal, improved quality of life and functionality.
5. Decrease morbidity.

1. Decreased emergency department visits and hospitalizations.

Objectives and Outcomes *(continued)*

- Improve care coordination.
- Target clinical outcomes for measurable improvement.
- Reduce direct and indirect impact of disease.

2. Improved functional status and quality of life.
3. Excellent patient and family (caregiver) satisfaction.
4. Optimal beta agonist and steroid therapy.
5. Fewer school and work days missed.
6. Reduced cost of care for this population due to decreased utilization of acute services and clinic visits.

3. Improve the identification and diagnosis of asthma and develop standardized language to describe asthma and asthma severity.
   - Select and develop consistent system coding.
   - Standardize language/definition to describe asthma.
   - Standardize language/definition to describe asthma severity.
   - Link to clinical outcomes.
   - Implement data analysis and reporting accuracy.

1. Referral to specialty care would be appropriate for defined level of severity.
2. Decreased morbidity.
3. Shorter hospital stays and reduced admissions.
4. Decreased emergency department visits.
5. Reduced clinic visits.
6. Excellent patient and family (caregiver) satisfaction.

Breast Cancer

Goal: to reduce the burden of breast cancer on plan members while finding cost-effective and innovative methods to provide care.

Objectives

1. Create a breast cancer screening program that provides appropriate, effective mammography screening and clinical breast exam to reduce disease state at presentation and improve survival.

Outcomes Measured

1. Decreased disease stage at presentation.
2. Increased screening rates (for the target population).
3. Excellent patient satisfaction.

Objectives and Outcomes *(continued)*

4. Decreased number of re-dos, re-takes, and duplication.
5. Increased provider counseling and recommendation for mammography.

2. Implement guidelines for indications (candidacy) and consistent management (reduce variation) of lumpectomy to ensure optimal clinical results.

1. Excellent patient satisfaction.
2. Reduced local recurrence rate.
3. Reduced microcalcification rate post lumpectomy.
4. Informed decision making as acknowledged by patients.
5. Decreased variations in candidacy and execution.
6. Reduced complications.
7. Successful cosmesis.
8. Appropriate patient selection.

3. Optimize the long-term care and follow-up of patients with breast cancer through the use of evidence-based standards and guidelines that manage functional status and quality of life.

1. Excellent patient satisfaction.
2. Excellent provider satisfaction.
3. Improved quality of life.
4. Decrease total system costs for this group of patients.
5. Improved functional status.
6. Increased percentage of patients on guidelines.
7. Communication of guidelines.
8. Percentage of providers following guidelines.

Cardiovascular Care

Goal: improve the lives of Health Plans' members by reducing the risk of having acute myocardial infarction (AMI) and by improving the outcomes of treatment for those who do experience an AMI.

Objectives

Outcomes Measured

1. All patients experiencing an AMI receive the following: beta blocker, heparin, aspirin; revascularization decision will be made within thirty minutes; and prophylactic use of lidocaine wil be eliminated.

1. Evaluate medical record to determine percentages.

Objectives and Outcomes *(continued)*

2. Provide appropriate assessment and decision making for treatment of all patients who present with symptoms of AMI.

   1. Compare and contrast all patients to establish baselines. Compare to local, regional, and national benchmarks.

3. Minimize time interval to return to full-function status.

   1. Measure by episode and compare to local, regional, and national benchmarks.

4. Reduce the time from onset of symptoms to identification.

   1. All eligible patients have lytics administered within six hours.
   2. One hour after onset of symptoms—patient presents to emergency department.

5. Optimize cost-effectiveness and evidence-based secondary prevention (risk reduction) to achieve:
   • symptom-free survival (cardiac and noncardiac sequelae), and
   • reduce recurrent events, including intervention.

   1. Compare and contrast all patients to establish baselines. Compare to local, regional, and national benchmarks.

6. Reduce postinfarction use of tobacco.

   1. Decreased pre- and postinfarction tobacco consumption.

Colon Cancer

Goal: to reduce the disease burden for colon cancer on the members of Health Plans.

Burden: morbidity, mortality, poor quality of life, lost productivity, and community costs.

Objectives

Outcomes Measured

1. Remove barriers to patient compliance with recommended screening and surveillance practices.

1. High screening rates for those for whom they are appropriate; measure against the identified potential number of appropriate candidates.

Objectives and Outcomes *(continued)*

2. High surveillance rates
   - There will be a subsequent increase in the incidence of colon-rectal cancer due to identifying cases.
3. Eventually, this will lead to a decrease incidence of death due to colon-rectal cancer.
4. Every new enrollee would receive a health risk assessment.
5. Every new clinic would know its screening rate for the appropriate population.

2. Link guidelines to resources for implementation of a screening process in a primary clinic setting.
   - Change financial incentives.
   - Focus on outcomes.
   - Link primary care and secondary care.
   - Provide incentives for "team effort."

1. Long term (greater than one year):
   - Lower colon cancer rate.
   - Lower mortality.
   - Increase detection rate at early stage.
   - Lower overall costs.
2. Short term (one year):
   - Higher screening rate, number of MDs performing the test.
   - Compliance for patients and clinic
   - Excellent patient satisfaction.
   - MD and nurse satisfaction: Do they see this as value-added versus another task?
   - Higher productivity.
   - Higher reimbursement.
   - Equipment available at site.

3. Identify and remove quality variance at each level of care (such as colonoscopy false negative rates).

1. Earlier stage at diagnosis.
2. Excellent patient satisfaction.
3. Improved survival rates.

Diabetes

Goal: improve the lives of Health Plans members through (1) early identification of diabetes, (2) by minimizing the progression of disease, and through (3) prevention of complications.

Objectives	Outcomes Measured
1. Attain a target for A_1C within 1.5 percent of upper limits of normal and measured at the appropriate frequency to reduce or delay the onset of complications of diabetes.	1. Identify baseline A_1Cs and monitor for statistically significant change in one to two years.
2. Optimize care and prevent morbidity. • Promote effective patient self-monitoring of blood glucose, and blood pressure, for all hypertensive patients. • Promote optimal foot care for all patients with diabetes to reduce known complications, infections, hospitalizations, and amputations.	1. Prevent or delay complications of diabetes: visual loss, renal failure, amputations, etc.
3. Identify all patients with diabetes and effectively track their care to promote optimal disease management and compliance. • Screen the membership at high risk. • Provide for documentation of health status and care management plans. • Ensure access to care.	1. Compare and contrast all patients to establish baselines. Compare to local, regional, and national benchmarks.
4. Provide appropriate diabetes education across the system to patients, members, families, and health care providers.	1. Implement education programs on a clinic-by-clinic basis. For employer groups, establish continuing education programs at the work site.

Pregnancy Care

Goal: to improve the care and outcomes for child-bearing women of the Health Plans, their infants and families. Rate of pregnant women who received prenatal care in the first trimester.

Objectives

1. Establish standards and implement strategies for pregnancy care that will reduce the incidence of low and very low birth weight infants and prevent early delivery. Address such issues as:
   - multigestational pregnancies,
   - identification and intervention for high-risk patients, and
   - identification of interventions and resources necessary to influence behavioral change that improves infant outcomes.

2. Promote the evidence-based forms of care for which effectiveness has been clearly demonstrated.

Outcomes Measured

1. Number of pregnant women who received prenatal care in the first trimester.
2. Number of pregnant women who are assessed for modifiable risk factors (e.g., smoking).
3. Number of women with high-risk status marked on chart.
4. Number of teenage pregnancies.
5. Number of C-Section deliveries.
6. Number VBAC deliveries.
7. Number of low/very low/extremely low birth weight babies.
8. Average length of stay for newborns/women in maternity care.
9. Number of infants with 1/2/3/4/5/6/ well child visits in the first fifteen months.
10. Cost PM/PM per live birth.
11. Number of eligible patients who rate satisfaction as excellent with:
    - overall care,
    - clear and understandable communication,
    - timeliness of communication, and
    - role and involvement of family.

1. Compare and contrast all patients to establish baselines. Compare to local, regional, and national benchmarks.

Objectives and Outcomes *(continued)*

3. Evaluate and implement an effective decision support system to serve providers as well as patients at the time of encounter and provide necessary information at all care settings.

   1. Compare and contrast all patients to establish baselines. Compare to local, regional, and national benchmarks.

4. Support effectiveness of care by eliminating unnecessary medical procedures (inductions and technologies) that add cost and increase morbidity.

   1. Induction(s), ultrasound, and fetal fibronectin:
   - Rate
   - Cost
   - LOS (hours of care)
   - Morbidity
   - Excellent patient satisfaction
   - Risk
   - Variance from appropriateness (MD induction profile)

   2. Ultrasound (additions):
   - Appropriate utilization
   - Screening for Type II; appropriate utilization and credentialing of personnel
   - Performance and interpretation

Service Quality Priorities (Examples Only)

1. Annually measure excellent care and service for all health plan members. Jointly develop and implement improvement plans with medical group and hospital providers.
2. Improve the rating of wait time of patients/members in primary care providers' offices between appointment time and when actually seen. Measure the degree of excellent care and services on Health Plans satisfaction survey.
3. Improve the rating of communication and interaction to excellent between members and providers as measured by the member satisfaction survey.
4. Reduce the number of provider claims inquiries per thousand members by ____ percent annually over the next two years.
5. Develop employer reporting package that meets short-term (one-year) and long-term (three-year) employer group needs as required by different market segments.

6. Improve usefulness of member benefit information as measured by decreased complaints/appeals and baseline benefit call inquiries.
7. Improve the quality of information provided to brokers and providers as measured by their satisfaction with the health plan's performance.
8. Develop a comprehensive broker strategy to enhance relationships and maximize profitable growth. Mutual measurable net revenue gain and excellent satisfaction are the measures.

SUMMARY

- Describe the organization's vision and mission. Are customer-focused activities a top priority? If not, think again—the ability to develop excellent care and services that offer customer choice and build commitment will be a critical factor for long-term success.
- What core values form the basis for customer-focused practice operations? Is the organization focused on prevention and health care improvement? Can progress toward health care improvement be measured? If yes, what are the targets? You must proactively plan and educate your patients and the interested public about the rising cost of care and what your group is doing about curbing costs. Technological advances aimed specifically at health care improvement and quality of life enhancements are going to be required and will increase costs. How will the medical group positively communicate this message?
- Competitive analysis requires diligent marketplace study. Over the course of the previous planning and budget cycle and in preparation for next year, document how market share of your priority care programs and services has changed within the organization and among your competitors. What strategies can be implemented to further increase market share for the organization? What cost benefit, return on investment, and/or level of effectiveness criteria will accompany increased market share?
- Was each priority target achieved during the last review of organizational performance? Have any FTEs been eliminated or refocused because their activity was not oriented toward priorities?
- It is important to define organization activities from a desired outcomes perspective. Continuous improvement and the ability to capitalize on change must be built into each plan at the grassroots level. How does the medical group incorporate continuous improvement into the daily operations that interface directly with the delivery of patient/consumer-oriented care and service?

Chapter 4

Aligning Focus, Measurement, and Outcomes

PROACTIVE CONSIDERATIONS

- Where do you want your provider group(s), hospital(s), and health plan(s) to be when they are appropriately positioned and effectively functioning? Whether your organization succeeds or fails should not come as a surprise. It is essential to optimize success through planning, predicated upon measurable outcomes management, to minimize error in the decision-making process.
- Planning has been described as a process used to guide the practice from where it is today to where it should be in the next one, five, ten, and fifteen years, and outcomes management is the structure used to keep the focus on achieving each priority target.
- The ability to forecast/predict the achievement of priority targets is a distinct competitive advantage. An initial requirement is the specification of desired quantifiable goals and objectives linked to each target. Once quantified, the value of each organizational service, product, and/or other contributing factor is analyzed to determine its rank-ordered importance toward one or more of the priorities, goals, and/or objectives.
- Management support, FTEs, and other resources are disproportionately focused on the four or five top predictors of each priority target. Flexibility is required as new potentially significant factors are identified and included. If noncontributing activities can be eliminated, value is added as a result of the cost reduction.
- Results of practice, service delivery, and/or other defined products are analyzed by comparing forecasted outcomes with actual findings. The discrepancy between predicted and actual results is decreased and/or eliminated by focusing attention and resources on the contributing elements responsible for the discrepancy. The law of re-

inforcement prevails: behavior and subsequent results are achieved in the direction for which reinforcement is provided.
- At least annually, a comprehensive evaluation is conducted of progress toward defined targets. Enhancements are made to those activities responsible for the top priorities—those for which less-than- desired performance was achieved. Results from one year are compared to the next to determine levels of success, complete with refinements, as needed. As advances continue in the electronic transmission of information (e.g., automated medical records, paperless bills), it is expected that immediate real-time monitoring/evaluation will provide the opportunity to make changes at the time negative occurrences and/or errors are identified or when the new opportunities present themselves.

INFERENTIAL MANAGEMENT AND CONTINUOUS IMPROVEMENT

The management technology applied to measurably guide the outcomes management process from the outset is referred to as the inferential evaluation model (IEM), originally copyrighted by the author in 1971.[1] The IEM is a mathematically based outcomes measurement and management tool that is used to forecast the achievement of quantifiable health care targets. Information processed through the model identifies strengths and weaknesses related to needed changes and/or new opportunities. As new or changing patterns are identified, "drill down" to the origin of each data source is applied to determine the nature of activity responsible for performance and the required enhancements. As a forecasting and validation tool, the IEM determines by percent of variance the relationship between a criterion variable (e.g., operating income) and one or more key indicator variables (e.g., health plan members, hospital admissions, outpatient visits, medical loss ratio, etc.). The IEM is used to predict desired outcomes (e.g., strategic targets associated with activities and functions of the health care system) by listing the most important indicators in rank order at preset levels of acceptable statistical significance. Management reports link information needs to their points of origin (e.g., service delivery units, malpractice insurance fund, medical loss ratio, net operating income, trend, membership, hospital admissions, average length of stay, emergency room use, pharmacy use, heart center activity, etc.). Electronic documentation software facilitates the communication of key indicator information between and among key decision makers.

Inferential management extends the decision-making process by providing the capability to match resources with planned measurable results.

Once priority targets have been identified through the planning process, the inferential model systematically provides decision makers with the information needed to successfully achieve the targets by focusing attention on the five or six key indicators most responsible for the results. This does not mean that other essential program and operational activity is not supported. However, it does mean that those factors most responsible for achieving success receive greater emphasis in both program plan and budget support.

Sequencing planning and inferential management activities is an initial requirement. Essential simultaneous steps are illustrated through a side-by-side comparison of model components as follows:

Planning	Required Interfaces	Inferential Management
Mission development and view of the current and future long-range goals (one, five, fifteen years) and priorities.	↓	Development of quantitative goals/objectives to define desired outcomes.
Operating plans and objectives of the participating organizations to achieve goals along with competitive positioning strategies.	↓	Measurement of the existing status/performance of defined goals/objectives, the competitive marketplace, and other factors that may impact desired outcomes.
Plans of departments and/or service centers, objectives, and budgets.	↓	Comparative inferential analysis of quantitative performance factors against desired outcomes, program plans, and budgets.
Systematic continuous improvement toward achievement of goals/ objectives.	↓	Enhance/adjust performance to eliminate discrepancies between desired and actual outcomes.

The process of continuous improvement (CI) is common to both planning and inferential management and is applied to monitor systemwide performance against targeted goals and objectives. At least annual evaluation of progress is required, although quarterly updates are recommended as midcourse outcome markers. The ability to capitalize on change or new opportunities is a significant strategic advantage. As CI data show new or changing strengths among key indicators and/or market conditions, it is important to analyze source information leading to those elements most responsible, that is identify resources to support new or different initiatives if warranted.

Alignment calls for inferential thinking in the very early stages of care, service, or practice management development when initial consideration is given to determining priority goals, objectives, practice standards, and evaluation methods, and to incorporating principles of continuous improvement (CI). The following example shows common interfaces.

Target Goal Development

Planning	Common Interface	Inferential Management
Target Goals: 1. Establish a vision and mission focused on meeting the health care needs of each defined consumer.	↓	Target Goals: 1. Use inferential management to align practice focus with key indicators of defined health care needs.
2. Define core values upon which to base the delivery of medical care and services.	↓	2. Understand the quantitative relationships between desired practice outcomes, planned goals/objectives, and budgeted resources.
3. Appraise marketplace environment by defining strengths, weaknesses, opportunities, and threats (SWOTs).	↓	3. Apply the inferential evaluation model (IEM) to your practice/organization and describe SWOT interrelationships statistically to eliminate subjectivity.
Objectives: 1. Specify key positioning strategies.	↓	Objectives: 1. Understand and apply each step of the IEM to your practice goals and objectives.
2. Outline goals, implementation strategies, objectives, and programs.	↓	2. Describe desired practice outcomes objectively within the strategic plan and budget.

3. Apply CI process to monitor performance and manage necessary enhancements to optimize desired outcomes.

Content:
Physician practice based upon clear vision and mission establishes planning context. Care, service, and business activities compose the practice structure. Budget development follows to support the achievement of measurable goals/objectives.

Evaluation:
Measurement of performance-based goals/objectives. Determine difference between desired and actual outcomes on at least an annual basis.

Continuous Improvement:
Monitor performance toward defined targets. Maintain appropriate activity and enhance performance determined to be less than adequate.

3. Analyze practice results and compare to desired outcomes to identify top predictors of success.

Content:
A multidimensional approach involving inferential statistics is well-suited to link vision, mission, quantifiable activities to results. Since a successful organization is based upon an appropriate mix of care and service delivered in a defined marketplace, it is necessary to determine the influence of market conditions both on the practice, as well as on competitors.

Evaluation:
Practice results are analyzed by comparing desired and actual findings. The variance between desired and actual results is decreased or eliminated by focusing activity and resources on the contributing elements responsible for discrepancy.

Continuous Improvement:
On at least an annual basis (preferably quarterly), a comprehensive evaluation of practice- and/or systemwide progress toward defined targets is made. Refinements are incorporated into those activities responsible for less-than-desired performance. Each set of results is compared to previous and desired outcomes to determine success levels and to identify areas for improvement. When possible, use local, regional, and/or national benchmarks to compare with practice results.

BEGIN WITH THE DESIRED OUTCOMES IN MIND

What results must be achieved? The focus of effort must be aligned to priorities with measurable outcomes that serve as defined targets. This means that each phase of the process will benefit from an identification (in measurable terms) of questions that must be answered to optimize success. Each phase of the planning process is enhanced by specifying expectations in the form of questions whose answers can be quantifiably documented. For example, the following illustration guides the process through decision points reflective of project outcomes associated with target goals.

Target Outcome Analysis

	Common	Inferential
Planning	**Interface**	**Management**

Target Goals:
1. Does the practice publish a defined vision and mission statement that includes the results a patient can expect to receive?

Target Goals:
1. How do plan and budget elements correlate with desired results? Can you identify and rank order resources (human and capital) for each priority practice activity?

2. List core values. Do they reflect commitment and strength underlying vision and mission?

2. Describe and list how your practice activities fit into the strategic plan and budget. Only documented priorities have a place in your plan and budget.

3. Rank order strengths, weaknesses, opportunities, and threats. How do they compare to your competition? What is the plan to correct weaknesses and optimize strengths?

Objectives:
1. Can you measure return on the investment of time, talent, and funds used to implement key positioning strategies? Are key positioning strategies in place for each priority?

Objectives:
1. Specify practice goals and objectives; describe procedures for pretest assessment, evaluation methodology, and procedures for posttest measurement.

2. Quantify progress/outcomes related to goals, implementation strategies, objectives, and programs.

2. Are desired practice outcomes clearly represented in the strategic plan? Are resources appropriately budgeted to realistically achieve targets?

3. CI enhancements must be measurable. What analysis can help identify elements to be enhanced?

3. How well did the practice achieve its predetermined results?

Content:
Outline vision, mission, core values, goals, and objectives of the practice. List new elements added to enhance last year's plan. Which activity was eliminated because it was no longer relevant?

Content:
Inferential thinking is to be operationalized into the way your practice does business. The process uses existing data.

Evaluation:
Define differences between desired and actual outcomes for each goal/objective. How will enhancements be considered for next year's plan?

Evaluation:
Various forms of evaluation can be helpful. Regardless of the type selected, each method should lead to answers for the following questions:
1. How did desired or expected results compare to actual?
2. Were desired targets clearly represented in the strategic plan and adequately supported by essential resources (human and capital)? How well was each target achieved? List top predictors of each target.

Continuous Improvement:
Do CI measures reflect increasing positive refinements? What progress measures are reported on a monthly, quarterly, and/or annual basis?

Continuous Improvement:
How will you build the necessary refinements into an environment that is constantly changing?

ESTABLISHING A BASIS
FOR HEALTH CARE DECISION SUPPORT

Key indicators are drawn from existing information sources present throughout hospitals, clinics, and health plans. Table 4.1 shows examples of the types of key indicators present in each setting. The inferential process uses information to cause change by focusing on the achievement of quantifiable targets. Performance measurement monitors progress and points out less-than-satisfactory results that, in turn, will warrant enhancement. The model is presented in four stages as follows:[2]

The Inferential Evaluation Model (IEM)

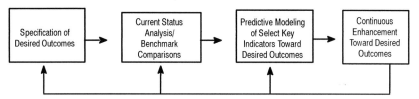

The IEM Process

Steps of the IEM process are shown with examples from both Group One: A Physician/Hospital Organization (1987-1994)[2] and Group Two: A Health Plan (1995-1997).[3,4]

Step 1: Specification of Desired Outcomes

• Group One: Increase the net revenue of a physician group and a hospital as a "combined/integrated" health care system.
• Group Two: Determine the most reliable and valid indicators (from key indicator report) of operating income for a health plan. Second, verify the status of each key indicator as an "actual" driver of the health plan's business and determine if other indicators need to be included.

Step 2: Current Status Analysis/Benchmark Comparisons

• Group One: Audited financial and business office data and patient activity statistics (inpatient and outpatient) comprised the database beginning in 1987. Annual comparisons were used for trend analysis and ongoing benchmarks.
• Group Two: The 1996 health plan key indicator list was accepted "as is" without validating each of the thirteen listed indicators. The list was composed by health plan senior management, who selected the indicators they believed would apply.

TABLE 4.1. Key Indicators for Physician Groups, Hospitals, and Health Plans

PHYSICIANS (expense/revenue, numbers)	HOSPITALS (volume/numbers/ expense/ revenue)	HEALTH PLANS (%/numbers)	COMBINED/INTEGRATED SYSTEM (expense/revenue/%, numbers)
• Executive office	• Licensed beds	• Employee satisfaction	• Combined clinic and hospital net revenue and expense (1) (C) (H) • OSHA reportable incidents
• Legal • Marketing and PR	• Beds in service • Avg. daily cens.	• Employee loyalty • Employee effectiveness	• Employee evaluation of information to do job
• Operations	• Percent occupancy	• Administrative exp. (2)	• Employee perspective of integrated values
• Med. directors off.	• Patient days (1) (H)	• Provider service avg. wait time	• Percent admissions to integrated facility
• Risk management	• Admissions (1)	• Provider service call abandonment rate	• Physician commitment to integrated system
• Human resources	• Avg. length of stay	• Claims adjustments	• Physician evaluation of information needed to do job
• Professional services	• Observation status pts.	• Pended claims (2)	• Days revenue in receivables
• Mgd. care/quality control	• Clinic/Amb. visits (1) (H)	• Customer service avg. wait time (2)	• Health plan's days/1,000 by product
• Business office —Accounting —Financial services —Credit and collections —MIS —Investment income —Fee mgmt. —Central registration	• ER visits • Deliveries • OR cases • Radiol. proc. • Lab procedures • Full-time equivalents • Inpatient referrals (1) (H)	• Trend (2) • Commercial members leaving by product • Medicare members leaving by product • Operating income percentage (2)	• Health plan's admits/1,000 by product

TABLE 4.1 *(continued)*

PHYSICIANS (expense/revenue, numbers)	HOSPITALS (volume/numbers/ expense/revenue)	HEALTH PLANS (%/numbers)	COMBINED/INTEGRATED SYSTEM (expense/revenue/%, numbers)
• Total bus. office expense	• Net patient revenue	• Medical loss ratio by product (2)	• Percent liability claims/ exposure by unit
• Med. dept. net revenue	• Other operating revenue	• Membership (2)	• Clinical indicator (sets) —Asthma —Breast cancer —Cardiovascular disease —Colon cancer —Diabetes —Geriatrics —Pregnancy care
• Med. dept. direct expenses	• Operating expense	Clinical indicators —Mammography —Immunizations —Pap tests —Percent health risk appraisals among members by product	• Patients willing to recommend
• Med. dept. net income avail. to cover corp. and direct exp.	• Income from operations (1)	• Year (length of study)	• Patient/member satisfaction by product
• Admin. O/H as a Percent of med. Dept. net revenue (1) (C)	• Prior year adjs.		• Percent members renewing by product
• Branch clinics	• Nonoperating revenue		• Percent disenrollment by product
• Contracts for physician services	• Excess of revenue over expense		• Percent members receiving services —integrated clinics —integrated hospitals

PHYSICIANS (expense/revenue, numbers)	HOSPITALS (volume/numbers/ expense/revenue)	HEALTH PLANS (%/numbers)	COMBINED/INTEGRATED SYSTEM (expense/revenue/%, numbers)
			—Home care
			—Pharmacies
• Contributions	• Operating fund cash		• Market share by product (2)
• Venture funds	• Depreciation fund cash		• Integrated net operating cash flow
• Workers comp. prog.	• PT accts. rec.		• Percent return on investment (ROI)
• Incentive plan	• Net land, bldgs. and equip.		• Year (length of study)
• Insurances	• Addns. to land		
• Corp. profit (loss)	• Bldg. and equip.		
• Other corp. costs	• Total assets		
• Total corp. costs	• Fund balance		
• Total corp. and admin. expense	• Cost per adjusted admit.		
• Net clinic revenues (1)	• Year (length of study) (1) (C) (H)		
• Clinic expenses			
• Corp. profit or (loss)			
• Physician salaries			
• Physician salaries as a percent of operating exp. (1) (C)			
• Clinic expenses per visit			
• Year (length of study) (1) (C) (H)			
Code key:			
(1) HealthPartners/Ramsey–1987- 1994 (C) = clinic, (H) = hospital (2) Allina Health System–1995-1996			

Source: Sommers, P. A. Internal study. Allina Health System. Minneapolis, MN, 1997-1998.

Step 3: Predictive Modeling of Select Key Indicators Toward Desired Outcomes

- Group One: Five variables were identified as the top predictors of net revenue, and including (1) time in integrated system, (2) inpatient hospital days, (3) inpatient referrals from outside primary care physicians, (4) outpatient/ambulatory care visits, and (5) physician compensation as a percentage of the clinic's expense budget.[2]
- Group Two: The top predictors of operating income selected from the key indicators for "drill down" included (1) health plan membership, (2) medical loss ratio of health plan products, (3) administrative expense, (4) trend, and (5) customer service wait time.[3,4]

Step 4: Continuous Enhancement of Desired Outcomes

- Group One: From 1987 to 1995 combined net revenue increased from $136 million to $250 million (clinic—$39 to $70 million; hospital $97 to $180 million).[2] Annually, the care and service activities related to each action plan were reviewed and enhanced in conjunction with medical and administrative leaders representing each department/caregiver/service delivery unit of the hospital and clinic. Each care and/or service identified as important to one or more of the top predictors received priority support in the capital and operating budgets to implement new or adjusted services that would further enhance performance.
- Group Two: Figure 4.1 which has been adapted from a version originally developed by the Harvard Business School in 1992, illustrates the Health Plan Excellence Pathway and 1996 key indicators.[4,5] Each indicator has been designated to occur at points from left to right across the pathway, with the ultimate outcome being health improvement. Table 4.2 shows the results of three predictive modeling applications aimed at determining the top predictors of operating income (R^2 coefficients were derived from simple pairwise regression analysis). Table 4.3 shows the "best fitting" multiple regression models to predict operating income (R^2 coefficients were derived by permitting multiple predictors to compete with one another for common variance and arrange themselves in rank order). Only predictors with p-levels of .05 or less were included.

FIGURE 4.1. Health Plan Excellence Pathway—1996 Key Indicators

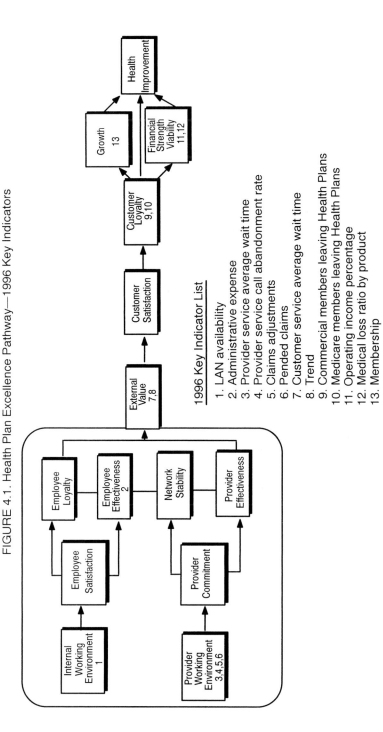

1996 Key Indicator List

1. LAN availability
2. Administrative expense
3. Provider service average wait time
4. Provider service call abandonment rate
5. Claims adjustments
6. Pended claims
7. Customer service average wait time
8. Trend
9. Commercial members leaving Health Plans
10. Medicare members leaving Health Plans
11. Operating income percentage
12. Medical loss ratio by product
13. Membership

Adapted from Harvard Business School, 1992, and Allina/Medica Health Plans Version, 1996.

117

TABLE 4.2. Top Predictors of Operating Income

1995		JANUARY-AUGUST 1996		1995, JANUARY-AUGUST 1996	
Predictors	R^2	Predictors	R^2	Predictors	R^2
Medical Loss Ratio	54%	Trend	76%	Membership	80%
Membership	44%			Medical Loss Ratio	71%
Commercial Customer Service Wait Time	42%			Administrative Expense	36%
Members Leaving Medicare	38%			Pended Claims Choice	23%
Members Leaving Commercial	37%			Trend	22%
Provider Average Wait Time	34%			Commercial Customer Service Wait Time	21%

Source: Sommers, P. A. Using Technology for Competitive Advantage in the Management of Integrated Health Care Services. Keynote address at SAS Institute World Headquarters Annual Health Care Conference, Cary, North Carolina, January 15-16, 1997.

TABLE 4.3. Best-Fitting Multiple Regression Models for Operating Incomes

1995		JANUARY-AUGUST 1996		1995, JANUARY-AUGUST 1996	
Predictors	R^2	Predictors	R^2	Predictors	R^2
Medical Loss Ratio	54%	Trend	76%	Membership	80%
Members Leaving Commercial	42%			Trend	5%
Provider Average Wait Time	2%			Commercial Customer Service Wait Time	4%
				Administrative Expense	4%
Total % of Variation Explained	98%	Total % of Variation Explained	76%	Total % of Variation Explained	93%

Source: Sommers, P. A. Using Technology for Competitive Advantage in the Management of Integrated Health Care Services. Keynote address at SAS Institute World Headquarters Annual Health Care Conference, Cary, North Carolina, January 15-16, 1997.

Results

Group One: A Physician/Hospital Organization (1987-1994)

Figure 4.2 shows an actual combined/integrated revenue and expense trend growth pattern from $136 million in 1987 to $250 million by the end of 1994. Table 2.6 in Chapter 2 p. 42 describes how the five key factors that consistently accounted for the prediction of net revenue were interpreted for discussions with leaders representing each needed action for inclusion in the annual strategic planning process. Budget resources were disproportionately allocated to support new and/or enhanced features of those clinic and hospital activities and functions responsible for needed action plans.

FIGURE 4.2. Combined Physician Group/Hospital Net Revenue Trend

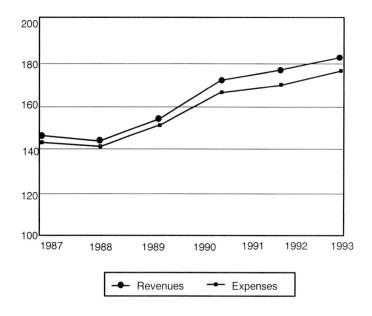

Source: Sommers Paul A., Luxenberg, M. G., and Sommers, E. P. CQI Longitu-dinally Applied to Integrated Service Outcomes. *Medical Group Management Journal,* 42(2): 50-54, 56-58; March/April 1995. Reprinted with permission from the Medical Group Management Association.

Group Two: A Health Plan (1995-1997)

Second-year results and those following need to be compiled. Monthly key indicator reports are routinely reviewed by management.

Next Steps

Group One: A Physician/Hospital Organization

The author joined Allina Health System in early 1996 and has not followed up on 1995-1996 results.

Group Two: A Health Plan

An SAS-based forecasting model using the key indicator data sets for analysis has been implemented and is being used by the health plan performance team as a decision support tool since 1997. Applications are being developed to address the following responsibilities:

- Recommending short- and long-term administrative and health care cost targets
- Creating action plans designed to meet identified cost targets
- Monitoring progress and ensuring completion of action plans
- Understanding and evaluating cost trends
- Ensuring analytic and data support for these efforts
- Providing support to the quality and strategic committee regarding return on investment and other cost-benefit analysis of prioritized clinical and service quality activities

Currently the IEM is providing investigative, auditing, and benchmarking functions for the health plan's performance team. Relationships are being tested between and among indicators and the "drill down" elements representing the origin of source data elements. Programming leadership has established an SAS-based Enhanced Data Support Methodology (EDSM)[5] for rapid access, analysis, interpretation, and reporting of information. A forecasting model is being field-tested. Forecasting attributes include: predictive modeling against preset targets, benchmarking, and comparisons of monthly, quarterly, and annual predictions with actual results to define progress. The results are being processed through the IEM to create change by focusing on the enhancement of activities accounting for the outcomes related to the indicators. The information provides decision support to the performance team.

OUTCOMES MANAGEMENT SYSTEM

A standard report of progress toward achieving priorities, goals, and objectives is needed to manage the achievement of outcomes. Criteria by which each activity should be judged/classified are based upon those categories that are most important to the organization. An example of one organization's approach is illustrated in Table 4.4. Each clinical quality and service excellence priority project or activity is included. Pediatric asthma is defined across each outcomes criteria as an example of how to incorporate each priority project.

On a quarterly basis, each staff member's progress is recorded and compared to desired, predefined expectations. Based upon measured differences between desired and actual results, more, less, or different resources may be called for to achieve the required performance. On an annual basis, organization-wide results are collected, analyzed, and used in the development of the next strategic plan and budget.

SUMMARY

- How well is the organization functioning? Can key indicators be listed in rank order based upon their importance for each organizational priority, goal, and objective? If they cannot be identified, an opportunity is being missed to enhance the achievement of organizational priorities, as well as the elimination of excess expense related to noncontributing activities.
- Does the budget support the top contributing programs, services and/ or other priority products? If not, were the financial, activity, and volume targets achieved from last year's efforts? Focusing efforts and resources on *only* priority activities will produce the desired outcomes.
- Is a formalized outcomes management system in place? It is important to monitor performance results against each activity to know whether it is producing what was intended. If an activity is not producing, then change the key elements to achieve results. If the activity is not essential to a priority—eliminate the activity. Return on investment (ROI) is a requirement for each target/priority outcome.
- Aligning focus, measurement, and outcomes requires defined measurable goals and objectives, that is targets. Once defined, the task is to compare desired outcomes to actual results. The discrepancy between desired and actual is identified. Focused actions are imple-

TABLE 4.4. Outcomes Management System

Project/Activity Name	Dept/Person(s) Responsible	Description of Activity/Target Population	Check Priority(ies) to which Activity Pertains					Quantified Outcome Measure(s) (Quarterly)	Baseline Data Collection/Type/Time	Intervention Implemented/Data Review Following Implementation/Time Interval	Final Clinical Outcome Analysis and Results (Short/Long Term)	Follow-up Action Plan Developed and Implementation/Time Line	Cost/Benefit Return on Investment (ROI) Resources Used/Value to Productivity	Next Steps/Required Resources	Final Report for NCQA File
			Strategic Plan	NCQA / Dept. Health	HEDIS 3.0	QI Work Plan	Others Specify								
Asthma Program	Performance Measurement	Develop & test a care management and educational process for MA pediatric members (new & current) 1. Severity measures test 2. Preferred outcomes 3. Referral providers to program 4. Educational - Alternative - Homecare Camp Super Kids	X	X		X		• Symptom Severity • Knowledge of medications & asthma claims $ • ER visits • In hospital admits.	• Baseline symptoms, severity, & self-reported ER/hospital utilization • Self & report knowledge at intake	Care management referred those eligible; follow-up up at 2 weeks & monthly after intervention	Preliminary results show significant reduction for small sample (30) in symptom severity, ER hospital utilization; and satisfaction with Camp	Presentation of these results at National Congress in February. Continue to enroll MAD members	Half FTE case management HC agency contract showed significant results! More FTE needed to expand program. Surveys show approx. $2,500 per member & savings to health plan.	• Continue enrollment • Communicate results • Continue follow-up to obtain one year • More FTE case managers	Expect this program to continue. Full Cost/ Benefit by year end

Source: Sommers, P. A. Internal study. Allina Health System, Minneapolis, MN, 1995-1996.

mented to enhance those activities responsible for the discrepancy. Routine measurements are taken to determine if the interventions are working.

- Continuous improvement toward desired outcomes is a dynamic process. Quarterly and annual evaluations are typically the formal periods for review. However, changes in planning or budgeting must be possible any time during an activity cycle in case an opportunity to advance the organization presents itself.

Chapter 5

Customer-Focused Care

PROACTIVE CONSIDERATIONS

- Clinical care, service quality, and operating systems must be enhanced toward meeting consumers' needs and desires. Consumer choice has evolved as a basic requirement in any competitive health care system. Changes should be based upon what it will take to define and meet all consumer expectations.
- Quality assurance and the accreditation agencies that support quality initiatives offer some help from a policy and procedure perspective. However, until providers voluntarily commit to providing excellent care and services, customer loyalty will remain less than optimal.
- Assess all aspects of the organizational structure and determine what it will take to change the focus toward the consumer. The ability to develop services and products that create consumer commitment will be a critical factor for long-term success, measured by retaining existing patients and expanding the patient/health plan member base.
- Consumers are continuing to require health providers and insurers to make changes in the way they deliver products and services. If the care and service is not packaged to provide excellent satisfaction and high-quality results at a low price, you may be forced out of business by your competitors.
- Determine the current status (and past trends) of quality of care, price, and satisfaction within the clinical service and operating systems of the organization. Many health care companies are rapidly endorsing new ways to market these critical factors to consumers.
- Manage outcomes toward excellence. Creating products and services that meet the consumers' demand for choice, convenience, accessibility, and superior results is becoming a key strategic marketing position.
- Measure the differences between consumers' expectations and actual results of care and service. Eliminate activity that is not consumer focused to reduce the variance and achieve satisfaction.

If the prices, outcomes, and quality of health care become similar, regardless of who the provider is, what will be left to allow consumers to choose between one or another? The answer, in no small part, will reside in consumer satisfaction with the care received and the services provided to them. Getting and keeping customers is a major goal of most health care providers. Understanding and applying consumer-focused practices in health care is management's prerequisite for knowledge-based decision making.

> In the past, medical professionals were able to function as a "service industry" without having to worry too much about addressing the issue of consumer satisfaction. The primary emphasis in medical care rested on the physician-patient relationship, with the physician generally held in high regard by the patient. Patients usually believed that a relatively equal—and high—standard of care could be received from almost all physicians. Very few patients gave much thought to comparative shopping. (p. 37)[1]

In recent years, however, patients have begun to ask for a greater voice in their own health care. They now see themselves as consumers of health care and, as consumers, have begun to question, along with their payers, both the quality they receive and its cost. The results have been a growing demand for care of good quality at less cost. That, in turn, has led to increased competition among providers of health care. The consumer revolution in health care is changing the way providers, insurance companies, and hospitals market themselves. The key to market success no longer lies just with the employers, purchasers, and physicians. Creating products and services that meet consumer demand for convenience, ease of use, and better results is an emerging new requirement for health systems, insurers, and providers. Internet-enabled applications are providing a wealth of information to consumers, and health systems are working to develop consumer-based commitment programs that provide coupons, discount cards, and services to fulfill the consumers' thirst for information, value, and convenience.[2]

In light of these trends, professionals in health care must change their old ways of doing business. Consumer satisfaction will play only a bigger and bigger role in medical practice, as patients and their families, referring physicians, and payers become more selective about determining which physicians will be getting their business. This principle stands out as a knowledge-based philosophy of the way business among all health care providers should be conducted. The focus of this chapter is intended to equip physicians and other decision makers in health care with the necessary tools to meet the growing demand for consumer satisfaction in medical practices. Using the tools described here must become a way of doing business if physicians, hospitals, and health plans are going to survive the economic changes projected for the health care professions.[1,3]

UNDERSTANDING THAT CONSUMER SATISFACTION IS THE ONLY WAY OF DOING BUSINESS SUCCESSFULLY

The practice of medicine has been a confidential and privileged relationship between physician and patient. The nature of the physician-patient interaction is embodied in the Hippocratic Oath, which outlines the duties and obligations of physicians. Therefore, when a physician enters the business of medical practice, he or she must run that business in association with high-quality medical care. Yet even high quality care can be delivered without consumer satisfaction, as indeed it often has been in the past. More and more frequently, however, medical professionals are recognizing the importance of providing high-quality service as well as high-quality care to their patients. They have found that such a consumer-oriented approach makes good business sense. It also goes a long way toward ensuring that the patient receives the very best care possible.[3]

Incorporating consumer satisfaction into a medical practice does not cost the typical physician any more than does the old, less service-oriented approach. Consumer satisfaction is a style, a total approach, a complete way to deliver health care. Cost is a nonissue because it does not cost any more to treat the consumer right the first time he or she comes into the hospital or clinic. In fact, *not* treating the consumer right can be very costly: first, all such complaints from patients must be documented and dealt with, which costs time and effort; second, some of those complaints may develop into expensive lawsuits for malpractice.[4,5] In addition, the dissatisfied consumer may go elsewhere for care, another costly problem. Albrecht and Zemke indicate that it takes five times as much money to attract a new customer as it does to retain an existing one.[6] By multiplying by five the annual value associated with *one* patient's outpatient and inpatient charges (including laboratory and X-ray charges), it is easy to see the loss of revenue from one unhappy consumer of health care.

Many providers of health care are unaware that their patients are dissatisfied with the care they are receiving because patients seldom complain directly to providers. In fact, research has shown that 96 percent of unhappy customers never complain to the people providing them with a service. They do, however, tell their families and friends. Research has also shown that each dissatisfied customer tells nine other people about their concerns, and 13 percent tell as many as *twenty* other people. Word gets around.[6]

Health care is primarily a physician-driven service. Without the commitment, leadership, and follow-through of physicians in the area of consumer satisfaction, little (if any) progress can be sustained. It is therefore essential that physicians take a leading and active role in identifying and implementing the changes that need to occur to make consumer satisfaction a way of doing business in hospitals and medical practices.[7,8] By caring enough about their patients to make these changes, physicians will find that their patients will remain loyal to them and will return to them whenever they have health care problems.

EXCELLENCE IS EVERYTHING

In the pursuit of excellence one must:

• Care beyond what others think is wise,
• Envision more than most feel is practical,
• Chance beyond what others see as safe, and
• Anticipate more than others think is possible.

Adaptive verse by M. R. Mittelstadt, 1990

Quality is the target of both clinical and service excellence in health care today. Although providers and related caregiving facilities, services, and programs have established standards of practice, the ultimate determiner of quality is a total voluntary commitment by providers to embrace patient-focused care. Combine this fact with the reality that it is the consumer's perception that totally determines the degree of excellence or quality.

Quality assurance organizations help to formalize policies and procedures for providers and health care systems. Accreditation requirements have added safeguards to ensure that the highest level of care and treatment is afforded to each patient. In this regard, a shift is occurring toward patient-focused systems founded on continuous quality improvement.[9] Accreditation by the Joint Commission (formally the Joint Commission on Accreditation of Healthcare Organizations or JCAHO) is gradually moving its focus from assurance of service of good quality to improvement of its quality.[10] Improvement of outcomes for the patient, the enhancement of organizational responsibility, and the implementation of principles for continuous improvement in quality of service are moving to the forefront of JCAHO activity. The Joint Commission is a nonprofit organization that performs accreditation reviews primarily on hospitals, other institutional facilities, and outpatient facilities. Most managed care plans require any hospital under contract to be accredited by the Joint Commission.[11]

The National Committee for Quality Assurance (NCQA) is a private nonprofit organization that assesses and reports on managed care plans on several levels. The information on accreditation that the NCQA provides is intended to enable purchasers and consumers of managed care to distinguish among plans based on quality. The NCQA is the leading accrediting body for managed care plans, as well as for some of the performance measures used today. [12] It evaluates how well health plans manage all parts of their delivery system—physicians, hospitals, other providers, and administrative services—to continuously improve health care for their members.

The Accreditation Association for Ambulatory Health Care (AAAHC) primarily accredits ambulatory surgery centers, although it has accredited several managed care plans using two groups of standards that are applied as appropriate. Core standards apply to and include rights of patients, governance structure, administration, quality of care provided, quality management and improvement (which includes peer review, quality improvement, and risk management), clinical records, professional improvement, and facilities and environment. [13]

QUALITY, CONSUMER SATISFACTION, AND THE PRACTICE OF MEDICINE

Cast aside what is thought to be the patient's need and instead ask the patient about his or her expectations. Once the expectations have been defined, it is up to the physician and supporting staff to fulfill them. [7] Best defined as perception, consumer satisfaction is a style, a total quality experience, a voluntary commitment by providers to deliver health care and achieve excellence.

Patients Differentiate Quality by the Nature of Care and Treatment Received

For physicians to thrive, instead of just survive, in the contemporary marketplace for health care, traditional approaches to achieving excellence in medical practice will have to change. Quality assurance through adherence to accreditation standards is part of the success formula and a basic requirement for every health care system. However, excellence can only be attained on a patient-by-patient level. All consumers must believe that they are receiving personalized care that is totally focused on meeting or exceeding their defined needs.

The attitude one takes to address excellence in patient care and treatment is often just as important as the technical skill used to treat the specific health care conditions.[9] Without clear and distinct leadership and proactive participation by physicians at each level within the universe of health care as it is defined today, health care and health products-related services will be less effective, and both the clinical and service quality of the care provided will be less than excellent.

MYTHS AND OTHER MISUNDERSTANDINGS ABOUT MEDICAL PRACTICE

For physicians to excel in the current health care marketplace, traditional approaches to cost-effective medical practice will have to change. Like it or not, physicians will have to reexamine—and then discard—the following myths and outdated beliefs about what the practice of medicine is going to be like during the twenty-first century.

Myth #1: Solo practitioners and independent practices will dominate the practice of medicine.

With increasing frequency, independent physicians are going to find it advantageous to consider some form of affiliation with another physician, a group, or a consortium. Such affiliations will benefit independent physicians by helping them insure against potential suits for malpractice, negotiate with insurance carriers and HMOs, share patients within defined specialties, and reduce duplicate overhead costs, including those associated with incorporating consumer satisfaction into the practice.[14]

Myth #2: Medical practice will remain an entrepreneurial small business.

In the past, many medical practices functioned as entrepreneurial small businesses, but that was before the government, the insurance industry, and other third-party payers declared the 1990s to be "the decade of containing physician costs," much as the 1980s were a watershed for significant cost-containing changes in hospitals. Payers and regulators of health care are fed up with uncontrolled costs for health care and are doing something about it by directing patients to medical practices that are both quality oriented and cost conscious. As a result, reimbursement will decrease for all physicians, which in turn will force practices to de-escalate their costs while keeping standards for quality high. To hold down medical and administrative costs while enhancing revenues, physicians will need to think and act more collectively.

Myth #3: "Curing" patients is all that is needed for consumers to feel satisfied with the care they receive.

In the past, physicians had the luxury of practicing medicine without too much concern about how the service was perceived by the patient. In many cases, it was presumed that the patient was just grateful for whatever medicine or related care was received. Indeed, most people perceived "service" as something they received at a gas station, restaurant, or hotel, but not at a doctor's office.

Times have changed. The medical practices of physicians who have no other competition in their specialty in a particular geographic area may survive the changes forecast for the next ten years, but they will probably not thrive—unless those physicians make consumer satisfaction a way of doing business. Of course there will be always be exceptions—"one of a kind" medical practices such as those performing organ transplantations—but even those physicians will benefit (as will their patients) from offering consumer-oriented services. As a service industry, the practice of medicine is fast becoming as market driven as those which serve travel, banking, hotels, and a myriad of other industries. Consumers expect high-quality service from all physicians. Their perception of service received is predominant in swaying consumers when they evaluate a physician.[15]

Myth #4: Implementing a program to provide consumer satisfaction in a practice takes too much time and money.

Actually, it will be costly not to implement such a program, because patients will simply go elsewhere. The specific cost of a program toward consumer satisfaction depends on how it is implemented—the number of personnel involved in surveying patients, for example, and how surveys will be conducted (by mail, telephone, focus groups, or a combination of these). Physicians whose practices are currently in an area without noteworthy competition would be wise to become consumer-oriented now, before the competition arrives. Doing it now will be less expensive than doing it while dueling with other physicians for patients.

Myth #5: Once a physician has referred a patient to another physician, he or she will continue to refer patients to that physician.

A physician who receives a patient referred from another physician should not expect that he or she will receive further referrals from that source. Thus, referring physicians need to be treated as consumers. After being provided with a high-quality consultation, the referred patient should be returned to the referring physician in a timely fashion, along with a clear, concise report aimed at making it easy for the referring physician to incorporate the information into his or her planning for that patient's future needs for health care. Physicians should call referring physicians a day or two after sending their report to see whether they have any questions or concerns.

Myth #6: Consumer satisfaction is more important in some medical settings than in others.

Too often, less-than-satisfactory service is rationalized because of an erroneous belief that in some specific settings, meeting the consumers' high expectations for service is not all that important. This is not true. Consumer satisfaction should be the goal of all medical practices, no matter where nor under what circumstances the care is provided—whether inpatient or outpatient, for example, or in a hospital or private practice.[16] Physicians need to take the lead in being committed to consumer-oriented medical care, for it offers the greatest potential in attaining consumer satisfaction. Once physicians take the lead, other medical support staff will follow.[17]

Myth #7: A program toward consumer satisfaction can replace programs in risk management and quality assurance.

Wrong. Through its emphasis on making patients and members of their families well-informed and active participants in their medical care, a consumer-oriented service can help minimize the risk of suits for malpractice. It does not, however, take the place of a carefully thought-out program of risk management or quality assurance.

Some medical professionals worry that asking consumers to respond to any kind of questions about their medical care, even ones related only to service, will cause them to focus on what they did not like about the care, rather than what they did like. Some even worry that this may lead to more lawsuits for malpractice, as consumers begin to think that something must have been wrong with the care since the physician is quizzing them about it. This concern is unmerited. For medical practices to stay competitive, they must find out what their patients do not like, as well as what they do like. Only when problems have been clearly identified is it possible to design and implement modifications in service to correct them. The goal is to determine what is wrong, not just what is right. When consumers are convinced that their input is really valued and that the goal in gathering that input is to improve medical services, they will become willing and generally supportive participants.

Myth #8: Attaining consumer satisfaction requires simple techniques such as "smile training."

Establishing a consumer-oriented approach to medical care requires more than superficial techniques. Physicians, support staff, and volunteers alike must be truly committed to improving their relationships with consumers. They must learn how to become good listeners and how to ensure each patient's needs are met. More often than not, these skills are not recognized as being important, even crucial, in health care.

Yet they are crucial. The St. Paul Fire and Marine Insurance Company has demonstrated that although about one of every hundred hospitalized patients could legally bring an action for negligence against his or her provider of medical care for failing to act or for acting improperly, less than 10 percent of those who could actually do. Why? The company reported that the answer can be found in the relationships patients have with their providers of health care. The more positive and satisfactory the patients perceived those relationships to be, the less likely they were to initiate a lawsuit.

Myth #9: Providing consumers' satisfaction is outdated and too expensive.

Although it has been discussed for some time, consumer satisfaction has yet to be fully integrated into modern practices in health care as a way of doing business. Some physicians believe that they have enough to worry about—especially worries about shrinking reimbursement from Medicare and other payers—without spending time and money developing consumer satisfaction programs for their practices. By putting all their efforts into counteracting government-initiated measures toward cost containment, however, physicians are often overlooking the bottom-line benefits to their business of a program for customer satisfaction.

Physicians do not have to go overboard to become service oriented. Large expenditures are not needed, either for development of satisfaction surveys or for the purchase of systems to do the mailing, telephone calls, and collecting and analyzing of data. What is most needed in becoming consumer oriented is a commitment—a commitment to begin thinking about the consumer first. Whether a consumer arrives at a medical facility as a result of a marketing campaign, an ad in the Yellow Pages, or a referral from another professional, the fact remains that the care and service he or she receives at the facility will determine whether he or she returns. Furthermore, each satisfied consumer will tell at least five other people, one of whom is quite likely also to choose to use the service or facility.

LOOKING AT HEALTH CARE
FROM THE PATIENT'S PERSPECTIVE

Good health is perhaps the most primary desire among humans, along with food, sleep, sex, and the need to feel important. Healthful living has been idolized and sought, from time immemorial. Kings, queens, and other luminaries have quested for perpetual life as far back in history as records have been kept. A belief in the importance of attaining and maintaining good health is almost universally shared by the world's societies. Thus, it is not surprising that efforts toward public health have been financially supported by government-run social, educational, and health-oriented agencies and by hundreds, possibly thousands, of volunteer and lay organizations throughout the world.

Annually, billions of dollars are spent on programs to promote health care and related services. In most cases, the consumer has had little to say in the evaluation of those services. That is now changing. Given the current climate of spiraling medical costs and the intense discussions now underway about a national program of health insurance in the United States, the need to involve those who benefit from health care—consumers—in the process of evaluating it has become more evident. Although the concept of asking consumers their opinions about the system for delivery of medical care is not new, it has not been addressed consistently by many providers of health care.

So what must be done to ensure that patients are more satisfied with their service in health care? To begin with, professionals in health care need to start examining the services they provide from the patient's viewpoint. Take the office visit, as an example. Only 10 percent of the time a patient spends at a doctor's office is directly related to the health care sought. Most of the patient's time is spent waiting, filling out forms, or moving from one station to another. The amount of time actually spent with a doctor or nurse— whether it be for a physical evaluation, a laboratory test, or information about treatment options—is usually quite limited. Patients have basically resigned themselves to the fact that most trips to the doctor are a waste of time, except for the few minutes they spend with the doctor or nurse.

Because patients have, for the most part, quietly endured long waits at their doctors' offices in the past, some practitioners have come to believe that it is now permissible to let patients sit in their waiting rooms well beyond the time for which their appointment was scheduled, without even giving them an explanation for the delay. Consumers are becoming increasingly intolerant of such treatment. Indeed, clinicians who fail to give patients and their families appropriate consideration will soon find themselves losing many of their patients to their competitors. Shopping for medical services is now commonplace, and people will not hesitate to travel an extra fifty to seventy-five miles for satisfactory services.

Examining the System for Delivery of Service

Delivery of health care is designed around the doctor's schedule. Patients must fit their concerns—their working hours, the hours their children are in school, the distance they must travel from home or work site to the doctor's office—into the doctor's schedule. Most medical practices try to assist the patient in finding a convenient time, but doing so is not considered a priority. If an appointment can be scheduled at a time that does not greatly inconvenience the patient, fantastic. If not—well, perhaps the patient will have better luck next time. In the new competitive climate, however, this type of attitude is not going to be tolerated much longer.

Medical practices could learn a lot about meeting consumers' needs from studying other businesses that count on consumer satisfaction for their livelihood—motels, hotels, and restaurants, for example. All these businesses are considered service industries, as are the providers of health care. These services, however, have routinely developed short checklists of questions to ask consumers when they call to make reservations—checklists that help the provider of the service better meet the needs of consumers. The business thus accommodates the consumer, rather than the other way around. Why can't providers of health care do the same?

Hotels, restaurants, and other businesses conduct frequent and thorough surveys of consumers to make sure their customers are happy with the services provided, while at the same time identifying accommodations to make their next trip even more enjoyable. Medical practices need to do the same. Although some medical organizations conduct periodic surveys to examine patient satisfaction, relatively few establish and maintain a routine system of such evaluations. The market for health services is highly competitive. To maintain ratings for accreditation, hospitals need a certain number of patients to occupy their beds, and, to balance their budgets, all medical facilities need a certain number of patients walking through their doors. One would therefore think that providers of health care would place greater emphasis on the development of a complete consumer-oriented approach to the delivery of care.

Aligning Services with Patients' Needs

By placing oneself in the patient's shoes, it is possible to gain a better understanding of what leads a patient to feel frustrated and dissatisfied with the medical care he or she receives. Too often, for example, patients are expected to follow rigorous directions and procedures. Written orders and paperwork handed to them may be far too complex and detailed. Patients may be given pills for very good reasons, but some fail to understand adequately why they must strictly comply with the recommended dosage and schedule. Patients also frequently fail to understand the need for filling out a seemingly endless and often redundant stream of forms and applications.

All current activities and demands made of patients should be examined, and if one is found to impede favorable service, it should be eliminated, if possible, or at least modified. These include not only activities at the nurses' station and the appointment desk but also procedures in the physician's examining room, and even paperwork aimed at patients that originates in offices doing billing or insurance processing. *Is medical service being provided with an eye on consumers' needs?* Such a question must be asked about all parts of the system.

Too many executive meetings aim discussions at one subject—the need to see a certain number of patients on a daily, weekly, monthly, or yearly basis. Yet it is often forgotten that office budgets, profits for practitioners, and the financial strength of progressive hospitals and physicians' service organizations (1) exist to provide better health, and (2) depend on consumer satisfaction. Few providers of health care manage to design services appropriately for the consumer. The organization that does will soon provide services truly appreciated by its patients.

One of the best ways to help employees in health care to see their services from a patient's viewpoint is through training. Employees, as well as volunteers, could be given training in such areas as "techniques in serving patients," "listening to patients' problems and then solving them," "turning patients' complaints into routine requests," and "developing a consumer satisfaction approach in your department." Only after the entire staff—doctors, nurses, medical assistants, administrators, nurses' aides, insurance clerks, financial counselors—everyone—makes a commitment to be consumer-oriented will the organization actually realize an increase in consumer satisfaction. Making such a commitment can also lead to higher morale among the staff itself, as employees begin to feel more appreciated by their satisfied customers (and as salaries increase to reflect the increase in business).

Some Points to Remember

- Everyone needs and deserves satisfactory services for their health—such services are more available now than ever before.
- Health services would not be needed without patients. Why don't producers of health care more carefully consider patients' needs in the planning, delivery, and evaluation of services provided to patients (consumers)?
- National health insurance has been supported for implementation by many. If enacted, it will cover charges incurred by consumers of health care, so that they may go just about anywhere to have their health needs met. Patients will eventually become very selective in seeking these services.
- Consumers have a tendency not to complain openly about problems or poor service. Instead, they leave the doctor's office without informing anyone of their concerns, making it impossible to correct the problem. (Of course, the patient's business is lost, along with the business of everyone else who comes in contact with that patient.)
- Both positive and negative information about one's practice should be sought from patients. It is extremely helpful to obtain negative information, since problems (or just poor service) can be improved only after being identified.
- One way to influence a consumer is to talk in terms of what he or she wants. Patients seem to be developing an ever-increasing attitude favoring "shopping for health care" and are willing to drive past locally available doctors if they believe better care is available at another location.
- Examine the system for delivering services. Focus attention in the system on those needs determined by the *patients* to be important.
- Implement a consumer-oriented approach to health care. Train members of your staff and volunteers to become consumer oriented.
- Satisfied patients will inform others about good services. Not only will "new" referrals increase but so will morale among your staff, because of appreciation shown them by these patients, and because of increases in their salaries related to increased profits in the practice as a business.

MAKING CONSUMER SATISFACTION
A WAY OF DOING BUSINESS

The Service Isn't Right Until the Consumer Says So

Adopting a Consumers' Bill of Rights

To be successful in today's competitive marketplace for health care, every medical practice must acknowledge that the recipient of its services is a consumer, one whose rights must be observed. No matter how large or small a medical practice—whether it has one or more than a thousand physicians—it must embrace the opportunity of assuring each consumer the following rights:[18,19]

Every Consumer Has the Right to High Quality Health Care

- The consumer deserves health care of the highest quality that money can buy.
- The consumer deserves the kind of care that will enable him or her to live a long, productive life.

Every Consumer Has the Right to Long-Term Protection of His or Her Health

- The consumer deserves the security of knowing that he or she is receiving the best possible return on investment for his or her dollars spent for health care.
- The consumer deserves to receive health care consistent with high standards required by the Hippocratic Oath.

Every Consumer Has the Right to Friendly Evaluation and Competent Treatment

- The consumer deserves to be treated as a person in need of health services, not just as a checkbook.
- The consumer deserves to do business with providers of health care who are interested in his or her needs, not just in the wants of the providers.

Every Consumer Has the Right to Information

- The consumer deserves to understand clearly the condition of his or her health and how to maintain and/or improve it.

- The consumer deserves to know the truth about the status of his or her health.

Every Consumer Has a Right to Address Grievances

- The consumer deserves to be heard. Physicians cannot be expected to be perfect in their interactions with patients, but an uncaring response to a patient's concern is inexcusable.
- Consumers deserve to have their concerns listened to and addressed by the health care professionals who serve them.

Every Consumer Has the Right to Satisfaction

- The consumer deserves more than just a thank-you.
- The consumer deserves to feel totally satisfied with the treatment he or she received. This includes feeling satisfied with the attitude of the health care provider during treatment, as well as with the quality of care.

Suggestion Box for Identifying and Following Up on Less-Than-Satisfactory Service

- Ask your consumers how satisfied they were with the services provided. You can do this in person, by telephone, or by mail, after the visit to the office.
- Invite groups of patients and/or their families to quarterly meetings to address complaints about less-than-satisfactory service and to offer suggestions that might help resolve the problems.
- Send a follow-up letter to each patient or the patient's family after an evaluation or treatment to let them know the status of the patient's health, what needs to be done to improve it, and what questions need to be answered before further treatment can proceed.
- Provide educational opportunities for patients and their families. These could include classes or support groups where they could learn more about their particular medical concerns or conditions and possible courses of treatment.
- Provide friendly, helpful assistance with insurance claims and billing.
- Encourage patients to call you at your expense—toll-free or collect—with questions or concerns about their treatment plan or if they need help with insurance claims.
- Establish a definition of consumer satisfaction that acknowledges that consumers' needs and desires are to be fulfilled, concerning quality of

both clinical care and service. Make sure everyone in your practice understands the meaning of consumer satisfaction and his or her role in implementing it.

- Ensure that consumers receive appropriate and timely information regarding the status of their health.
- Design a process that promotes a continuing relationship between physicians and consumers. For example, send out periodic newsletters, announcements of changes in staff, or notices of new programs or expanded hours to all consumers who use your medical facility.
- Give all consumers access to videotapes and libraries that provide medical information in lay terms.
- If practical, establish closed-circuit televised programming for consumers, so they can view special programs regarding their interests in health care.
- Draft a formal "Bill of Rights" for patients. This sets the stage for patients—and their families—to participate fully in their care and in follow-up treatment.[17]

BECOMING CONSUMER ORIENTED

Health care is a competitive business and, as such, part of the free-enterprise system. Its product is service of high quality. The quality of service that a patient receives while under treatment by a health care professional is what he or she will remember longest. Quality care will bring the patient back to the practice when further care is needed. Providers of health care must therefore emphasize individualized, patient-oriented service to keep their current patients and to enjoy success in recruiting new ones.

Consumer satisfaction in health care settings can be measured objectively.[20,21] Medical practices already measure, either by time or by function, the services they provide. These measurements can be found in fee schedules and other accounting practices. Consumer satisfaction with the quality of service can similarly be measured at each stage of service delivery. For example, asking consumers to fill out a short questionnaire after a visit to your clinic or hospital can provide valuable tips on how to improve services. A suggestion box should be available for recommendations. By encouraging patients' feedback on services and then acting on those suggestions, providers of health care can give patients the opportunity to participate actively in planning their own health care. As service improvement recommendations are implemented, it is important to communicate results to the patients who made the recommendations.

Active participation by patients in planning their own health care is the hallmark of a successful program for consumer satisfaction. Once the patient believes that a health care professional is sincerely interested in his or her opinion about the care being received, a visible change in the patient's attitude can be seen. Patients become much more open about their feelings and concerns. Most important, this information then helps the attending physician or other health care providers to improve the ways they meet the patient's medical needs. Patients and clinicians alike benefit from these partnerships: patients receive care directly related to their individual needs, and providers watch their practices thrive and grow, as word gets around that they are patient oriented.

Without a strong partnership between those providing and those consuming health care, consumer satisfaction happens only randomly. Yet, for too long, even in the most respected medical centers and physicians' offices, the patient's role in health care has been of secondary concern. Only recently have providers of health care realized the importance of attaining partnerships with their patients and of including them in their own care.

Tips for Becoming Service Oriented

1. Remember that your medical practice is a competitive business; treat it accordingly.
2. Keep in mind that many patients consider the quality of service they receive to be as important as the end result of that service.
3. Devise ways to measure the quality of service in your practice.
4. Build partnerships with your patients. Their attitudes toward you will become more positive when they know that you value their opinions about the care they receive.
5. Remember that a patient-oriented practice grows and thrives.
6. Recognize patients whose suggestions for improving service have been implemented.

In your medical practice, you can make consumer satisfaction a way of doing business by (1) establishing standards that define, measure, and monitor consumer satisfaction; (2) increasing support from the involvement of managers; (3) using tools for quality assurance; and (4) improving relations with patients, physicians, and employees in a manner acceptable to the patients, physicians, employees, administration, board of directors, and community. Here are some recommendations:[18,20,21]

Recommendation #1: Define consumer satisfaction.

Adopt a definition of consumer satisfaction that incorporates the views of physicians, employees, patients, and administrators.

A Sample Definition

> Consumer satisfaction is the perception held by consumers inside and outside of the organization that their needs and desires concerning health care have been fulfilled and that a high quality of both treatment and services is being received.

Defining the consumers in your medical practice is essential. Considerations should include:

- Patients
- Regulatory agencies of compliance
- Families of patients
- Contracting parties such as groups that use your lab, radiology, and services of consulting physicians
- Physicians
- Nonphysician staff
- Payers (government, HMOs, other third parties)
- Other producers/users related to the medical practice

Recommendation #2: Develop written surveys of patient satisfaction.

The surveys can be mailed to patients either at or after their discharge from the hospital, or on completion of their treatment. Questions in the survey should cover such matters as the staff's concern for the patient, the quality and quantity of medical and nursing care, the quality of information supplied to the patient, the friendliness of the staff, the promptness of service, and prices and billing procedures. Be sure to encourage patients to sign the forms in your survey to allow for follow-up calls to clarify areas of low satisfaction. You should also ask for demographic information and about any other needs they may have that concern health care.

Recommendation #3: Develop scheduling procedures that recognize and value each patient's time.

Conduct studies to identify scheduling procedures that would maximize physicians' time yet not inconvenience patients.

Recommendation #4: Establish focus groups of consumers.

Invite five or six discharged patients and perhaps one member of each family to a focus group meeting to discuss their perceptions of the service they received while at your medical practice. Be sure to provide all participants with a free lunch and parking. An experienced facilitator should lead the meeting, making sure that patients feel comfortable about expressing their opinions of the quality of service received from your medical practice. The facilitator should write a summary of positive and negative comments that emerge from the focus group. These comments should then be organized according to the department they affect, and the complete summary should be sent to administrators and middle managers. To ensure that all points brought up in the meeting are thoroughly understood and acted upon, the meeting should be videotaped. Departmental or physician representatives should be encouraged to view the video, and it should be discussed at departmental meetings. The confidentiality of testimonies from patients should, of course, always be honored.

Recommendation #5: Place consumer satisfaction on the agenda for meetings on planning.

Both physicians and managers need to make consumer satisfaction the "way of doing business." Thus, consumer satisfaction should be discussed as an item on the agenda at joint meetings of committees on planning for your hospital and medical clinic. It should be directly included in all plans for the medical practice.

Recommendation #6: Encourage top physicians and managers to have direct contact with patients.

All members of top management should introduce themselves to at least one consumer each week. The manager should ask the consumer about his or her visit to the medical practice. Administrators should also take turns assisting staff in areas where large numbers of patients wait for service. They should wear their name tags at these sites, so that patients can clearly identify them.

Recommendation #7: Make consumer satisfaction part of all evaluations of employees' performance.

Standards for consumer satisfaction should be incorporated into all evaluations of employee performance, including those of physicians. Such standards should also become part of the guidelines for the office, handbooks, and personnel policies for both physicians and other employees.

Recommendation #8: Make consumer satisfaction a routine subject for discussion at meetings for your office or department.

Physicians and managers should clarify the priority given to consumer satisfaction within your medical practice. Nurses and physicians should provide input, feedback, and follow-up. Routine reports on progress in resolving identified problems with consumer satisfaction should be scheduled at subsequent meetings.

Recommendation #9: Train head nurses and physicians in management to serve as role models for appropriate interpersonal and communication skills.

Leading physicians and managers must ensure that nurses and staff physicians are provided with the necessary education and training to create consumer satisfaction within the medical practice. The development of interpersonal skills and the ability to communicate effectively with staff members is essential.

Recommendation #10: Solicit opinions from employees.

Employees should be asked for their perceptions about the working environment and about problems in performance of services.

Recommendation #11: Recognize "heroes" in quality of service with dramatic awards.

To provide a meaningful incentive to changing their behavior, award employees with days of vacation or cash bonuses for their efforts in improving consumer satisfaction. Name a "Pro of the Month." Employees should be "caught being good" and should be rewarded for it!

Recommendation #12: Make criteria for performance on consumer satisfaction part of every employee's job description.

These criteria should also be a substantial part of reviews of performance and of considerations for raises in pay for all employees.

Recommendation #13: Tailor sessions for training in consumer satisfaction specifically to each service unit and/or department.

Although all employees should receive such training, the sessions should focus on employees in positions with high levels of public contact, such as nurses, receptionists, and patient account representatives. Make participation in training sessions mandatory. Also, be sure to emphasize that the performance of skills learned in those sessions will be included in future job reviews. Nurses, chief technicians, and/or departmental managers should be trained first, so that they can encourage and reinforce a consumer-oriented attitude among other employees.

Recommendation #14: Implement a formal program of patient education.

Through a formal education program, both patients and their families can receive information about their condition and options for its treatment. Special classes on common medical conditions should also be made available to all consumers of health care. Personal letters should be sent to all patients following treatment. The letters should explain what happened during the visit, answer all questions that might have arisen from the visit, and restate instructions given to the patient regarding medication or therapy.

Recommendation #15: Provide patients with assistance in processing billings and insurance claims.

Designate a person from the billing or insurance department to be available to answer questions from patients and families. Distribute to patients a telephone number so they can get quick and easy answers to their questions. Many medical practices have an 800 number for this purpose.

THE PHYSICIAN'S ROLE IN DEVELOPING A CONSUMER-ORIENTED INITIATIVE

Physicians must take steps now to improve the quality of service they provide their consumers. Because of the physician-oriented nature of the health care marketplace, it is up to physicians to take positions of leadership in this effort. Such an initiative should be:

1. integrated with current programs for improving quality, managing risk, and managing care;

2. consumer driven, with leadership by physicians; and
3. designed as an ongoing process that will result in fundamental operational changes.

The initiative must improve the quality of service in ways consistent with other key factors for success—quality of medical care and cost-effectiveness.

When a program for consumer satisfaction is initiated, discrepancies can be anticipated between administrative goals for the program and physicians' acceptance of those goals. Physicians are usually more focused on patient outcomes, while administrators typically emphasize the process of delivery. Medical and administrative goals can be integrated, however, by having the two groups work together in the planning and implementation of the program. Issues that are likely to emerge between physicians and administrators include:

- lack of information regarding the necessity for consumer satisfaction;
- lack of incentives related to consumer satisfaction;
- lack of agreement on the meaning of consumer satisfaction; and
- lack of agreement on the business value of consumer satisfaction.

Physicians must be specifically trained on the merits of incorporating consumer satisfaction into the conduct of their practices. Most physicians do not receive any formal training on this subject during medical school, residency, or experiences in fellowship. The process of convincing physicians to accept this idea begins with education. Here are some recommendations.

Recommendation #1: Get physicians to take leadership in the establishment of a program for consumer satisfaction.

Historically, the practice of medicine has been "physician driven," although, in response to measures aimed at cost containment in recent reforms of health care, nonphysician medical professionals are increasingly being used to deliver certain medical services. Yet only physicians can admit patients to a hospital, and only physicians—or their appropriate designees—can prescribe related medications. Therefore, for a system for consumer satisfaction to work, it must be physician driven or physician directed. Physicians must take the lead in establishing a program for consumer satisfaction and, by their own example, set the standards in this area for others in the practice to follow. Good administrative support is, however, necessary for physicians to take such a lead; it allows physicians to focus on physician-to-physician communication about consumer satisfaction, an essential element in making any program work.

Recommendation #2: Educate physicians by demonstrating the importance of consumer satisfaction to the successful operation of a medical practice.

The long-term economic success of a medical practice rests on a steady or slightly increasing number of patients. Due to the current trend of decreasing reimbursement from third-party payers, it has become more difficult to attain revenues in excess of expenses without significantly increasing the number of paying consumers. This situation will be further tested, under the "captitation system" in which HMOs will pay providers a set amount for a certain number of patients. If providers find they need to spend more than that amount to take care of their designated patients, they will have to do so out of their own pockets. Thus, under the captitation system, providers must be able to attract and keep as many healthy patients as possible to nullify the financial impact of those patients who need more care.

A practice built on consumer satisfaction is assured "return appointments." Satisfied patients and their families also bring in new patients through word of mouth. Physicians, however, have been taught in their medical training that to satisfy consumers, all they need to do is provide competent patient care. Thus, they do not feel a need to be educated about consumer satisfaction—something they think they are already providing. Research shows otherwise. Studies have revealed that no significant connection exists between patient satisfaction and physicians' perceptions of patient satisfaction.

Physicians must therefore be educated on the importance of patient-physician interactions and on how such interactions relate directly to the economic success of their practice. Studies have found that the conduct of a physician, as perceived by patients and their families, is clearly the most important factor determining whether consumers feel satisfied with the care they have received. Other factors—accessibility, availability of other specialists, completeness of the facilities, and continuity of care—also contribute to consumer satisfaction, but not as much as the conduct of the physician. In one study that looked at why families change pediatricians, the determining factors that parents cited concerning whether they felt satisfied with a particular pediatrician's care were all related to the personal qualities of the physician—communication skills, clinical competence, and apparent level of concern for the child. Parents' dissatisfaction was also a result of personal qualities such as the attitude and demeanor of the physician during treatment.

Recommendation #3: Incorporate standards for consumer satisfaction into evaluations of physicians' performance.

Responses from surveys of patient satisfaction should be included in evaluations of each physician's performance—along with indicators of the physician's productivity and ability to meet his or her obligations on the staff. Some medical groups encourage involvement of physicians in service to the community and activities in volunteer organizations such as serving as physician for a high school's athletic team or working for charitable organizations. Such outside involvement demonstrates a physician's interest in the community and is often considered by committees on compensation when they evaluate salary adjustments. Surveys of patient satisfaction can be coded by specialty, by program, or by individual physician. The surveys would thus become a database for evaluating the performance of each physician. Once the first set of results has been collected and analyzed, these become a basic measurement against which it can be determined whether any progress has been made toward correcting less-than-favorable results.

Recommendation #4: Provide head nurses and physicians with education and hands-on training in management and budgeting, as well as in interpersonal and communication skills.

A broadened awareness of, and involvement in, the management of a medical practice will increase the probability that a physician will embrace a consumer-oriented approach to doing business. Each member of the medical and supporting staff needs to have a stake in the management of consumer satisfaction. A "team approach" to the issue will have a greater impact on the achievement of consumer satisfaction than will one or more members of the staff acting as individuals.

Recommendation #5: Measure physician satisfaction through questionnaires for employees.

If physicians are not satisfied with their working environment, it is unlikely that their supporting staff or their patients will be pleased either. Harmony and disharmony are contagious. It is therefore important to identify and rectify less-than-harmonious relationships among staff before the negative side effects of those relationships detract from the quality of services being offered consumers. Employees, including physicians, should be given questionnaires periodically to find out what they do or do not like about their working environment. Areas of dissatisfaction should be discussed at medical staff meetings, and appropriate solutions or responses should be developed to increase physician satisfaction. Other steps that can be taken include:

- telling physicians whenever positive comments about their care appear in the surveys of patient satisfaction;
- decreasing patients' rate of "no-shows" by instructing ancillary staff to make reminding telephone calls to patients twenty-four hours before their scheduled appointments; and
- fostering good relationships between physicians and supporting staff by planning shared lunches, parties, and other get-togethers.

Recommendation #6: Reward behavior by physicians that demonstrates competence, caring, and good use of communication skills.

Develop a special award such as "Pro of the Month," or other ways to recognize physicians for excellence in service to consumers. The "Pro of the Month" could be chosen from the entire pool of employees or from separate groups for physicians and for other employees. Each year, award the physician who received the most positive responses in surveys of patient satisfaction with a meaningful memento such as a gold pin, a pen, a trophy, or an ornament for the desk. Develop a system of monetary rewards for physicians who exhibit excellence in enhancing consumer satisfaction, as demonstrated by the surveys of patient satisfaction. The system should be linked to basic compensation or to incentive/bonus pay.

Recommendation #7: Provide physicians with education on how to continue the emphasis on consumer-oriented service.

The results of each consumer satisfaction survey should routinely be shared with physicians and their supporting teams. Past performance should be compared to current trends to determine the effects of any changes that have been made to improve less-than-satisfactory services. This is the time to refocus efforts and to emphasize the changes called for by consumers. Successful strategies would include the following:

- Providing, for viewing at meetings of medical staff, videos of patient focus groups in which patients are shown discussing problems and suggesting changes
- Involving physicians in activities for marketing and public relations—those aimed at referring physicians as well as at patients
- Offering seminars for physicians on the topic of enhancing consumer satisfaction, led by outside consultants

• Making the concept of consumer satisfaction part of the orientation of physicians new to the practice

HOW CONSUMERS SELECT AND EVALUATE PHYSICIANS

To develop an effective marketing message for their practice, health care providers must first understand the factors and criteria that consumers use when selecting and evaluating their physicians (see Table 5.1). In March, 1987, Ramsey Clinic, St. Paul, Minnesota hired Nelson Research Services, Inc., to conduct a study on how people living in the area served by the clinic select their primary physicians. A scientific sample of 240 people were interviewed for the study, some in person, others on the telephone. Findings of the study offer some important information about

TABLE 5.1. Factors Considered by Consumers When Selecting a Physician

Major Factors	Principal Components
Personal relationships	Willing to talk on the telephone
	Good communication skills
	Involves patient in decisions
	Spends time, doesn't rush
	Kind, considerate, caring
	Willing to refer patient
	Letter/phone follow-up
Convenience	Time spent in waiting room
Practicality	Length of time to schedule an appointment
	Hours
	Physician's fee
	Availability of parking
	Location
Technical	Affiliation with a teaching facility
	Affiliation with a research facility
	Physician's medical school
	Size of group (number of physicians)
	Referred by referral service
	Affiliated with large group of specialists
	Clinic has physicians in wide range of ages

Source: Nelson, A Consumer Satisfaction Evaluation Study of Ramsey Clinic Services. Internal study conducted by Nelson Research Services, Inc., Minneapolis/St. Paul, Minnesota, 1987. Reprinted by permission.

consumers of health care and the factors they consider when selecting their physicians. Here is a summary of the findings of that study:[22]

1. Three-fourths of consumers in the five-county area served by the Ramsey Clinic have a personal physician. People living in rural areas and people sixty years of age or older were more likely to have a personal physician, while men and adults under thirty were less likely.
2. Most primary care physicians are general practitioners. Very few specialists (other than family practitioners and internists) function as primary care physicians.
3. About three of every ten consumers in the five-county area have been with their current primary care physicians for at least ten years. Long-term relationships with physicians are especially common in rural areas and among consumers sixty years of age or older. This suggests that these rural and older consumers are least likely to switch to a different primary care physician.
4. The most important factors consumers use when choosing a primary care physician are qualities exhibited by his or her staff. In this survey, consumers cited the following specific factors as being most important:
   • The physician's skill at communicating—listening, asking questions, and explaining medical matters in understandable language
   • The physician's diagnostic and problem-solving skills
   • The physician's willingness to refer the patient to another physician for specialty services or perhaps for a second opinion
   • The physician's ability to project a kind, caring, and considerate manner to the patient
   • The physician's willingness to involve the patient in making decisions about treatment and care
   • The physician's availability for consultations by telephone
   • The attitude and manner of the physician's staff
5. On the other hand, many factors played little or no role in selection or evaluation of a primary care physician by a consumer. These included the following:
   • The physician's gender, age, and mode of dress
   • The medical school the physician attended
   • The physician's affiliation with a teaching or research facility
   • The size of the medical group
   • Whether the patient was referred to the physician by a referral service
   • The availability of parking at the physician's office or clinic
   • The physician's fees

6. Several other factors fell somewhere in the middle, being of some importance to consumers when selecting a physician. These are listed here in order of importance:
   - Length of lead-time required to schedule an appointment with the physician
   - Whether the physician expressed a friendly interest in the patient beyond his or her immediate health problems
   - Length of the wait in a waiting room (most consumers judge a twenty-minute wait to be acceptable, although men, consumers in upper-income brackets, and residents of the metropolitan area are less patient than others, but all consumers are agreeable to waiting twenty minutes—if given a good reason)
   - The reputation of the clinic
   - The location of the office or clinic
   - The physician's previous work experience
   - The physician's practice of offering follow-up, by letter or telephone
   - The availability in the clinic of a wide variety of specialists
   - The hours the clinic is open
   - The physician's affiliation with a large group of specialists
   - Recommendation of the physician by a friend
7. Interestingly, the overall ranking of factors used to pick a primary care physician was similar for all segments of people surveyed, regardless of area (rural or metropolitan), gender, age, income, or insurance coverage.

From another perspective, analyses of findings of this study place consumers of health care in the area served by Ramsey Clinic into three basic categories:

1. Consumers to whom interpersonal skills are key factors in choosing and evaluating a physician; 89 percent fall into this group.
2. Consumers who are practical, oriented to convenience, and choose their physicians accordingly; 8 percent do this.
3. Consumers who assign a high value to technical considerations; only 2 percent of consumers are of this type.

Therefore, the technical competence that distinguishes the Ramsey Clinic from its competition—its affiliation with a teaching and research facility and its expansive multispecialty network of physicians—influences only 2 percent of people in the area served by the clinic when it comes time to choose medical care. Furthermore, it is important to note that respondents to the survey indicated that they do not consider it particularly difficult to find physicians who offer the benefits they seek. This finding emphasizes how intensely competitive the health care industry has become in this five-county metropolitan area.[22]

In a 1997 study, Allina Health System/Medica Health Plans identified key customer requirements for its four major customer groups:[2]

1. Patient Requirements:
   - Communication
   - Respect
   - Emotional and physical comfort
   - Involvement
   - Quality of care
   - Financing of care
   - Access to care

2. Member Requirements:
   - Continuity/choice of physician
   - Access
   - Cost
   - Service/ease of use
   - Quality of care
   - Coverage relative to perceived need

3. Employer Requirements:
   Concerning the health plan
   - Choice of physician
   - Access
   - Cost containment
   - Service/ease of administration
   Concerning the delivery group
   - Single bill
   - Patient involvement
   - Prompt return to work

4. Physician Requirements:
   - Communication
   - Collaboration
   - Systems

THE ROLE OF MANAGEMENT IN DEVELOPING A CONSUMER-ORIENTED INITIATIVE

Implementation of a program for consumer satisfaction will typically encounter some roadblocks among the nonphysician staff as well as from physicians. Although administrators are usually highly supportive of the concept, clinicians and members of the supporting and ancillary staff frequently have had no consistent experience in making consumer satisfaction part of their day-to-day performance on the job. Furthermore, they are likely to perceive consumer satisfaction as a separate, compartmentalized function of the medical practice rather than as an integral aspect of the job of each staff member.

Many factors appear to be responsible for these misconceptions. Consumer satisfaction may not have been made a priority within the practice. The practice may also lack clear guidelines and expectations for employee performance of services to consumers. A systematic procedure for rewarding excellence in service also may not be in place. How then can the leadership of a medical practice persuade its clinicians and supporting staff to participate actively, to support and implement effectively, a program for consumer satisfaction? Here are some recommendations:

Recommendation #1: Develop a practice-oriented mission statement that clearly defines service to consumers as a key element in the mission of the practice; then develop a campaign to publicize the statement.

A clear, concise, and highly visible statement of mission communicates a strong and focused message to employees as well as to consumers. Through such a statement, both groups will have an improved understanding of the expectations of the organization regarding service. A strong mission statement can also become a "guiding light" for the organization, defining the culture of the practice. The revision of a mission statement is, ultimately, the responsibility of the partners in the practice, its shareholders, or its board of directors. Administrators, however, can assist this process, ensuring that the concept of consumer service becomes a clear and concise element of the statement.

After the statement is revised, the next challenge becomes increasing its visibility. One way of doing this is to publicize the mission statement itself. Posters can be placed at strategic locations throughout the organization. The statement can also be included on the letterhead and prominently featured on all the brochures and publications for the organization. To further increase the visibility of the mission statement—and the concept of consumer satisfaction as a way of doing business—a promotional campaign can be initiated within the organization. The campaign should have a theme or promotional slogan developed as an outgrowth of the statement, such as "You're Special at the Doctor's Clinic." The slogan could then be promoted through posters and publications. It could even be embossed on buttons worn by employees or included on their name tags.

The revised mission statement, the organizational emphasis on consumer satisfaction, and the promotional campaign can be presented to employees through a series of in-service programs. For these programs to be effective, all employees must be involved, no matter how much actual contact they have with patients. Employees must understand that it is important to treat one another, as well as patients, as consumers. Poor relationships among employees of an organization will have negative effects on the relationships of employees with consumers. Be sure that all physicians and administrators take part in the in-service programs; their presence lends credibility to the endeavor and provides evidence of administrative support. However, to avoid the perception of criticism, physicians and administrators must be sure to communicate to the rest of the staff that they believe the employees are already doing a good job. They must also stress the importance of incorporating the principle of consumer satisfaction into the very fabric of the medical practice.

Recommendation #2: Develop or revise job descriptions for nonphysicians on the staff; clearly state the expectation by the organization so that employees will incorporate the concept of high-quality service and consumer satisfaction into their day-to-day performance on the job.

Job descriptions in medical practice typically emphasize the clinical aspects of care, almost to the exclusion of everything else. Descriptions should be revised to include expectations concerning service to consumers. To permit quantitative evaluation, these expectations should be specifically defined and stated in measurable terms. In addition, programs for employee orientation should routinely devote time to the subject of consumer satisfaction. An employee's initial orientation should also be regularly followed by continuing on-the-job training that reinforces the updates, concepts, and techniques learned for consumer satisfaction. Once standards for performance have been established, supervisory and rank-and-file employees can more appropriately work on concerns aimed at attaining the desired results.

To consistently incorporate into day-to-day job performance the concept of high-quality service to consumers—as well as other aspects of the mission statement—the organization should clearly outline its expectations of each employee in each job description. Rather than serving as a tool for pointing out poor performance, the job description should provide clear expectations of performance. It therefore serves as an instructional device and should specify the behaviors it expects of the employee as concretely as possible. A focus group of supervisory and nonsupervisory personnel could be formed to get this process started. The objective for such a group should be to specify at least three measurable key behaviors for each job classification.

For a receptionist, for example, the key behaviors could include the following:

1. Answers the phone in two to three rings, using proper identification of the organization, the department, and its name
2. Acknowledges a patient's presence promptly with eye contact, a courteous hello, or if on the phone, some nonverbal signal such as a nod or a smile
3. Gives the patient undivided attention and uses effective communication techniques—empathy, confirming information, eye contact—to allow the patient to express his or her concerns or questions
4. Returns to calls on hold within thirty to sixty seconds while assuring waiting patients of continued attention to their needs

Recommendation #3: Use the criteria of consumer satisfaction in evaluations of job performance.

Key indicators developed for job descriptions can be incorporated into evaluations of performance. This sets the stage for open dialogue between the employee and supervisor concerning the concept of consumer satisfaction and how its measurable aspects will be considered in performance review. The employee receives important feedback concerning definable outcomes in this area, while the supervisor reemphasizes that consumer satisfaction remains a top priority for the organization. The evaluation of performance also enables supervisors to identify substandard performance and to develop individual plans of action to correct the situation. Routine, ongoing monitoring of outcomes related to the plan of action enables employee and employer to chart results that will form bases for the next evaluation.

Recommendation #4: Develop a "Pro of the Month" award, to recognize employees for outstanding performance in "living the mission statement."

Programs for recognition of employees, such as a "Pro of the Month Award," are based on the proactive concept of "let's catch the employees doing it right." As noted in the section for physicians, "Pro of the Month" can include both physicians and nonphysicians, or a separate monthly designation can be made for each group. The award sends a clear message throughout the organization that efforts by employees are highly valued.

As part of the award, the employee should receive personal notification by leaders of the organization, special recognition in the form of flowers and perhaps a lunch or dinner with the leaders, prominent coverage in in-house newsletters and on posters located in common areas throughout the organization, and the addition of the employee's name to a plaque honoring "Pros of the Month" in a central corridor of the organization. The award should provide recognition that is positive and highly visible. The committee selecting for these awards should be presented as a recognizable and respected group of physicians and nonphysicians. The purpose of the selecting committee is to establish the standards for qualification and to solicit recommendations and applications for nominations each month from the staff at large and then to select the most worthy member of the staff from among those nominated.

The "Pro of the Month" award offers a systematic and positive way of reinforcing the mission of the organization to provide outstanding service to consumers. Thus, criteria for the award should clearly correspond to a mission statement. The award should send a nonambiguous message to all employees and to the community that the recipient of the reward is being acclaimed for "living the mission statement" of the practice.

Recommendation #5: Routinely monitor the results of surveys of consumer satisfaction.

Routinely administered surveys provide a basis for monitoring the quantitative effectiveness of the consumer satisfaction program. The surveys should be longitudinally charted to ensure that the program is doing what it was designed to do. When measuring outcomes, it is most important to focus on less-than-satisfactory performance. Although it is also important to acknowledge and reward employees for what is going right, it is extremely important to identify and correct unsatisfactory services. Routine review of the outcomes will identify the elements responsible for the problems that necessitate changes, leading to an improvement of the service or services in question. Each plan for remediation that is implemented to correct a service problem must be closely monitored to ensure the desired outcomes.

THE ROLE OF NONPHYSICIAN STAFF IN MAKING A CONSUMER-ORIENTED INITIATIVE WORK

The managing staff of most medical practices are usually aware that a high level of consumer satisfaction is necessary for the continued success of the practice. In some cases, however, managers who recognize the importance of high-quality service to consumers find themselves working with a staff who have not yet experienced the same recognition. Consumer satisfaction has not yet become the way of doing business in those practices; it has not yet become part of the culture of that organization.

Difficulty in communicating to staff the message about consumer satisfaction can be traced to two basic causes:

1. The widely diverse training and experience among individuals within a typical practice
2. Problems related to the structure of a medical practice

The following recommendations for making a consumer-oriented initiative work.

Recommendation #1: Treat physicians and nonphysician staff as consumers.

Experts say that cultural acceptance is essential for the successful implementation of any major initiative in an organization. Using education to develop that culture is not enough. Change in organizational values must also occur, and one way of initiating that change is to expand the traditional definition of consumer to include fellow physicians and other staff. Satisfying these "internal customers" should be given the same priority as satisfying external ones, and it should occur on both the interpersonal and the interdepartmental levels. The manner in which one member of the staff treats another is contagious; it will influence how the staff treat patients and other outside customers. As one expert in management has suggested, "the employee's capacity to provide quality service to other employees and customers will be directly related to the quality of service they receive as internal customers of the organization's day-to-day management."[18] By improving employee satisfaction, an organization will likely see improvements in patient satisfaction as well.

Both physicians and other leaders must become role models for the "ethic of consumer satisfaction." Managers may have little contact with external customers on a day-to-day basis, but they have many opportunities to show exemplary consumer-oriented behavior in their service to one another and to those they supervise, which they can demonstrate by "walking their talk." In fact, administrative job descriptions and incentive plans should be modified to include criteria that measure the level of consumer satisfaction they provide to intraorganizational consumers (other employees). Criteria should be included that measure how well they provide to the employees they supervise a role model for the "ethic of consumer satisfaction." Leadership is the key to initiating cultural change within organizations.

Recommendation #2: Change those organizational values that hinder the successful implementation of a program for consumer satisfaction.

The most important element of any attempt to make an organizational change is ensuring that the change becomes so internalized and so much a part of the everyday workings of the organization that it will last long after the initial incentives to implementing the change have gone. Consumer satisfaction must become a routine way of conducting business in the health care industry. Changing organizational norms is, however, extremely difficult. In *Management of Corporate Culture,* Kilmann suggests the following approach.[23]

- Work with groups of employees to elicit lists of the norms of the practice—both positive and negative (such as whether most people arrive to work on time). This process is designed to allow employees to see the counterproductive "directives" they have imposed on one another.
- Work with staff to establish new norms. This step in the process should include discussion of where the organization is headed—its mission, vision, core values, goals, and objectives. From these discussions, employees should be able to develop an acceptable list of norms that fit with the goals of the organization.

Silversin and Kornacki have listed the following as values often found among employees working in organizations with a commitment to service:[24]

- Respect for each other
- Acknowledgment of the mission to service
- Universal accountability for behavior—everyone is expected to obey the rules
- Participation in decision making and discussion
- Teamwork
- Superior quality of service to consumers

Identify gaps between existing norms in the practice and the new, desired norms. Close the gaps. Having a list of new organizational values is not enough. Those values must be put into practice. This can be accomplished in a variety of ways. Some of the most important include:

- role modeling by physicians and other leaders;

- clear communication of the values through changes in job descriptions and mission statements; and
- ceremonies to award recognition upon reaching certain milestones.

By being included as active participants in the creation of the new norms, the staff will feel an important ownership of them. Members of the staff will be more likely to encourage one another to adhere to the new values and let go of the old.

Recommendation #3: Implement the program for consumer satisfaction on a service-by-service basis. Also, work to create a model program that can serve as an example to be replicated by others.

Individual leaders among physicians and other staff should be made responsible for implementation of the program in their own services. This recognizes that different services make changes at different rates. It will also allow leaders to focus on specific problems related to each of their services. The creation of a model service provides an example for other services to emulate and a chance for managers to demonstrate the benefits of a program in consumer satisfaction. Using members of the staff from that service as trainers for other services will facilitate expansion of the program throughout the organization. They will have become the experts and will appear credible when training people to do the same jobs as they do. Appropriate recognition should be given as each service reaches designated milestones in the implementation of its program for consumer satisfaction.

Recommendation #4: Hold educational seminars on the subject of consumer satisfaction and/or include the topic as part of other presentations on service in the delivery of health care.

The goal of the educational process should be to inform staff of progress made toward the attainment of goals and objectives in consumer satisfaction and of ways this information is related to the medical practice. Ideas that have proven beneficial for certain services should be discussed and adapted for implementation by other providers of service. The following are some general suggestions for which specific examples could be drawn and presented at educational sessions:

- Point out that, to survive, the practice must attract consumers and that a high level of consumer satisfaction is one way of doing so. Show the correlation between the number of returning visits made by patients and their levels of satisfaction.

- Note that consumer satisfaction is the life blood of most service industries. Service of high quality motivates us to shop at certain stores; why should it not motivate us when selecting the place where we receive our health care? Show examples in which low levels of patient satisfaction led to an erosion of the patient base.
- Stress that consumer satisfaction can make the medical practice a better place to work. Such a program has very good potential to improve employee satisfaction on the job, once the staff begin to treat one another as they would like to be treated themselves.
- Demonstrate that it is already working. Allow past "Pros of the Month" and other employees who are pleased with the program to give testimonials and teach others about its merits.
- Show clips of taped comments, both critical and complimentary, from consumer focus groups. These should show the significance consumers place on such things as having the practice staff answer phone calls promptly and getting friendly help with questions about billing.
- Results from past and current surveys should be discussed to demonstrate quantifiable outcomes and to associate key findings with patient activity and financial benchmarks.

Recommendation #5: Expand the definition of consumer to include employees as well as patients.

Staff should be required to serve internal consumers—fellow employees—with the same commitment as when serving external consumers. Studies confirm the positive, contagious nature of the "self-fulfilling prophecy" of treating others as you would like to be treated yourself. Once in motion, this aspect of behavior will be shared with all people with whom an employee comes in contact—staff and patients alike. Furthermore, such commitment should be recognized; staff should have a uniform way of rewarding those within the organization who serve one another well. Employees of Federal Express, for example, use special stickers that can be placed on memos or paperwork to recognize those who serve them well within the organization or who are doing a good job in general.

Recommendation #6: Develop a satisfaction survey among the staff.

These should be similar to the satisfaction surveys for external consumers, given to patients. Through these internal surveys, satisfaction with service within the organization can be measured and evaluated. The results of these surveys should also be used in evaluation of employee performance and for setting new goals for service.

Consider establishing written internal customer service agreements to ensure that all participating parties understand and agree to defined expectations (see the following sample review and agreement).

Once established, the agreement of understanding is used as a baseline set of expectations against which to compare ongoing performance. By reducing expectations to writing, misunderstandings can be avoided. As new projects or activities arise, they can be formally added to the agreement under "New Priority Needs."

Recommendation #7: Modify administrative and managerial job descriptions and performance evaluations to include criteria on consumer satisfaction.

The criteria should be based on employees' service to those they supervise (internal consumers) as well as on their service to patients. Administrators should be evaluated for how well they serve as role models for the "ethic of consumer satisfaction." Leading physicians and administrators should review the program for consumer satisfaction at regular intervals. Routine review, at least annually, is required to ensure the program remains on course and is still applicable. Employee feedback from surveys should prove a useful tool in evaluating the program.

FROM INITIAL CALL FOR APPOINTMENT TO BILLING: TREATING THE PATIENT RIGHT

When patients arrive at a hospital or a physician's office, they are there for help. Whether they are merely seeking information about a new insurance plan, or checking in for surgery on their gallbladder, they have come for one reason: to get assistance with a problem.[17] The quickest way to create dissatisfied patients is to treat them poorly during this initial contact, but unfortunately, it is done all too often. Instead of showing an interest in their patients' needs, medical facilities usually insist that patients deal first with the bureaucratic demands of the organization, asking them, for example, to fill out forms or having them first check in at the desk that handles insurance to make sure the bill will be paid, or embarrassing them by indicating they are too early or too late for their appointment.

Before the Appointment

In anticipation of the patient's visit, whether to a doctor's office or a hospital, several considerations should be addressed to make the visit

Sample:

INTERNAL CUSTOMER SERVICE REVIEW AND AGREEMENT OF UNDERSTANDING

Date:_____ Department:_____

Contact:_____Telephone Number:_____Mail Route:_____

I. Review of current/continuing project needs:

Project Name	Staff Involved and Responsibilities	Strategic Priority Focus

II. New priority needs:

Activity	Strategic Priority Focus

III. Preferred method(s) of communication from production staff about projects:

_____In person   _____CCmail

_____Telephone   _____Other (please specify)

IV. What **ONE** service element about meeting the needs defined above is **MOST IMPORTANT** to your department?

_____

_____

_____

_____

V. Do you propose any specific action to meet your defined needs?

_____

_____

satisfying and efficient. Some patients may find it advantageous to schedule all appointments on the same day, ending with a meeting of the staff to summarize all findings. Other patients, to avoid exhaustion, may appreciate appointments coordinated over more than one day. In the past, many specialists accepted referrals only from other physicians, but most medical practices today are quite open to accepting appointments for patients who have demonstrated insurability, whether or not they were directly referred by another physician. It should be pointed out, however, that most plans from an HMO will limit and/or direct their referrals to specialists and will almost always permit such referrals only after the patient has been evaluated by a primary care physician viewed by the HMO as a "gatekeeper."

Many patients find it helpful to receive written brochures or other literature describing a particular program or service at a hospital or clinic. Such background information can help set the patient and family at ease about going to a doctor whom they have never met before.

Service on questions of fees, insurance, and financial needs should be brought up as the plan for evaluating satisfaction is developed. Too frequently, patients are not given clear answers to their questions about costs and, as a result, remain unaware of the financial impact of their care until a bill is received. Since patients are responsible for paying their bills, they should know approximately how much the charges are going to be before treatment begins. If the patient has insurance, staff should help verify the extent of his or her coverage prior to the service; every insurance policy is different, and the cost to be covered by the patient may vary considerably. This may require that the staff do some searching, and perhaps telephoning, to secure the information, but such duties are required of a consumer-oriented business. Patients who appear embarrassed about the matter of paying their bill should be quickly befriended by the staff, and an effort should be made to find out what outside financial resources might be considered in setting up an installment plan, based on ability to pay, for low-income patients.

Establishing Rapport

If patients are treated poorly during the first few minutes after their arrival at a medical practice, chances are quite good they will not return. A more appropriate way of greeting newly arrived patients is to smile and welcome them into the setting with a cheerful "hello" or "good afternoon." Such common pleasantries establish a friendly and informal, yet businesslike, attitude. Staff should also be encouraged to offer a kind compliment or two to the patient, if appropriate, on what he or she is wearing, or perhaps to make a comment about the weather or about parking difficulties. Such personalized pleasantries are easy to make and will help patients relax and feel that the staff is interested in them as people, rather than just "health cases."

Members of the staff should identify themselves to the patient by name and briefly indicate who they are (nurse, doctor, receptionist). They should then describe to the patient how they plan to help. Here are two examples of beginnings for such a dialogue:

> Hello. My name is Sally Jones. I am a patient coordinator, and I am here to help you today. Do you have any questions before we begin? First, I would like to outline what you can expect to happen at each of your appointments.

> Good morning. I am Doctor Smith. I am a pediatrician. My special training is in pediatric cardiology, and I will be giving your son a physical examination. This examination will be used to determine whether it will be necessary to do additional testing of his heart. My procedure will involve . . .

This open and easygoing communication pattern between the patient and members of the staff should continue throughout the appointment. Each dialogue sets in motion a clear, meaningful relationship with the patient. Briefly outlining what will be taking place during the appointment allows the patient to prepare, both physically and mentally, for what will follow.

Defining the Patient's Needs and Wants

Always talk in terms of what the patient wants. In a friendly way, convince the patient that you are going to do everything reasonably possible to make sure his or her needs are met, but that to accomplish this, you must have the patient's total cooperation. Ask yourself, "How can I encourage him or her to be cooperative?" Demanding cooperation of people seldom works. Rather, you must plan an approach that encourages the patient to see that his or her needs can best be met by cooperating with you.

When confronted with an uncooperative patient, it is natural to react defensively. All members of the staff must learn, however, to exert as much willpower as necessary to resist responding with a similarly abrasive attitude. The only way to come out ahead in an argument is to avoid the argument in the first place. So even if the patient is clearly wrong, avoid debating the point. One argument may lead to another, creating an even more uncooperative patient.

You also have the patient's health to consider. Arguing with patients who are ill, especially those with dangerously high blood pressure or other serious conditions, might exacerbate their health problems. Remember Murphy's Law: "Anything that can go wrong, will go wrong." Instead of arguing, concede to the patient that you are wrong. It will do absolutely no good to lose control of your temper. A patient who believes he or she has been neglected or mistreated will never be won over by an out-of-control argument.

Instead of reacting defensively, train yourself to let the "hot air go in one ear and out the other," and listen for a comment from the patient or a pause in the conversation that you can use to find common ground. The ability to listen quietly and stay focused on a patient is a difficult but essential skill. Openly acknowledge that the patient may be right and you may be wrong. Offer to reexamine the facts. Chances are quite good that some of the facts associated with the case may have been overstated, either by you or the patient. After the patient has finished describing the problem, politely ask questions rather than pointing out all the places where the patient's statement of the facts was in error. By gently asking questions, the patient will most likely be able to see the errors on his or her own. This enables the patient to save face—and calm down.

Remember that the goal of a consumer-oriented approach requires you, as a provider of health care, to put yourself in the patient's place. When in doubt, the rule of thumb becomes one of treating the patient as you would want to be treated, if you exchanged roles.

Solving Problems

Complaints are inevitable. If a complaint does not surface from time to time, perhaps the service being provided is not worth complaining about. Remember, however, that each problem or issue between two or more individuals can be viewed from several different perspectives. Be prepared to uncover these divergent viewpoints as you receive and review complaints from patients.

Do not go looking for problems, but be alert for warning signs that indicate areas of potential conflict. Obvious complaints—such as an error in the billing statement—will surface quickly and will not be difficult to identify. Many patients, however, indicate their dissatisfaction much more subtly, through statements such as "I have obtained information from another doctor that may be worth considering," or "Here are some facts about my history that I trust you will not lose sight of," or "The other doctor said . . ." When a patient criticizes or challenges you, it is important that you remain calm and refrain from taking the criticism personally. Avoid allowing patients to transfer their anger onto you. Becoming angry yourself may cause you to overlook important information that can help resolve the situation more quickly and quietly.

Angry patients often need a lot of time to express fully what is bothering them. Try not to interrupt. Let them continue until they have finished. Then tell them you appreciate their point of view and acknowledge that you know how important this issue is to them. Probe all aspects of the case, and assure them that all matters will be cleared up to their satisfaction. This technique will quickly remove the "wind from their sails," and angry patients will find themselves unable to continue their harassment. It is not important that the issue be totally resolved then and there. What is important is that patients feel they are being heard. Any disagreement, however, should be followed up with proper corrective action—and patients should always be notified of what has been done to resolve the problem.

Patients also often complain about the amount of time and attention they receive—or rather, do not receive—from medical professionals, particularly their physicians. Doctors should heed these complaints and change their behavior accordingly. The patient-doctor relationship may be the most crucial factor in determining patient satisfaction. Patients who feel that their physicians listen to their concerns and complaints tend to rate their health care service higher than those patients who feel they have little say about their own care.

Turning Complaints into Routine Requests

Let the patient talk. Listen carefully with an open mind. Ask polite and meaningful questions about background essential to this patient's history and related problems. When patients become convinced that you are genuinely interested in their welfare, they will also become convinced that the care they are receiving is highly satisfactory.

To make a lasting impression, go beyond just letting patients talk; engage them in meaningful conversation about their health needs. You will soon learn how to judge the needs of each patient and thus when and how to end each conversation appropriately. Some people can talk and talk without saying too much, while others can provide a lot of information with only a few words. The ability to listen and subsequently to guide patients through these very important conversations will improve over time and with practice. Even if only a few minutes can be given to a patient, that time should be spent in a friendly, caring exchange of information rather than in a brisk, one-sided rush that implies, "I'm too busy and am only going to give you the facts about your health."

Possibly one in one hundred patients will protest a correct bill. Perhaps the patient believes a second X-ray or laboratory test was unnecessary, or perhaps the patient did not fully understand the need for a certain procedure and, when billed for it, refused to pay. Most medical practices follow a standard procedure with an unpaid bill: they repeatedly send a bill to the patient over a period of months; if the bill remains unpaid, it is turned over to a bonded collection agency or an attorney for legal action. This process can be avoided, and a great deal of time and expense saved, if an effort is made simply to discuss unpaid bills with patients.

When entering into such a discussion, treat the patient with respect. It should be assumed that the patient is sincere, honest, and responsible and that he or she would like to arrange payment or find an acceptable alternative for a debt justly incurred. Begin by explaining why the particular service was provided and that no attempt was made to overcharge, double bill, or conceal charges. Then listen attentively to the patient's response. After exploring together all facets of the case, turn the focus to the specific charges listed in the bill. Give the patient a copy and explain each entry in detail. Acknowledge that as the recipient of the services, the patient knows more about them than anyone else—and that he or she is likely to agree to a payment plan out of a sense of fair play. Patients treated in a personal yet businesslike fashion will, in all likelihood, also return to the practice for future medical services.

Making the Job Easier for Providers of Health Care

A surefire way to make your job, as a provider of health care, easier is to find convenient methods of helping patients have their needs met. All aspects of the medical practice should be as streamlined as possible, while still providing comprehensive care. One place to start is with the avalanche of paperwork that often greets patients as soon as they arrive in a medical facility. Avoid duplicating similar bits of information on different forms. A review of most medical records and registration forms reveals much duplicated information. In hospitals, this problem is often compounded by having the patient fill out similar forms in each department. By consolidating a patient's history and the forms with associated information into one concise set, the burden on the patient—and on the staff—is greatly reduced.

When talking to patients, begin by discussing matters on which you agree. By emphasizing points that are mutually agreeable, you convey the idea that you are both interested in achieving the same outcome. As a result, you are more likely to have a positive conversation. If a difference of opinion arises later in the conversation, stress that the conflict is over the way things are being done, not over the purpose of doing them. Providers of health care need to take an adequate amount of time to explain why certain requirements exist and what has to happen to resolve the issues. When patients understand the need for doing something, whether it is filling out a form or taking a medication, most issues can be resolved to mutual satisfaction.

Make it your goal to alleviate the patient's immediate need, no matter how minor you believe it to be. If you treat a patient's problem on the basis of your perception of the importance of the issue, rather than on the patient's perception, you are headed for significant difficulties in communication. No one should have to prove his or her need for health care before receiving prompt and courteous service. Of ten typical patients seen in the doctor's office, at least eight will have average complaints, concerns, and expectations. All deserve the empathy of the medical staff. Patients should not need to justify why they have sought care. Instead, they should all be treated with an equal concern for their health needs and an understanding of their apprehension of the medical process.

Only through such appreciation and understanding of the reasons patients seek medical attention will it be possible to deliver consumer-oriented care. Although taking a few extra minutes to empathize with the patient will usually not significantly alter the provider's decisions on medical treatment, it will alter the patient's perception of that treatment. By first approaching each individual who comes into their clinic as a person and only after that as a patient, physicians and other professionals in health care will find that such a person will then leave the clinic as a more satisfied, informed, and compliant patient, who will then return as the need arises.

Helping the Referred Patient

All aspects of case processing and associated details should be handled by a staff member of the receiving physician following the referral. This task should not be left to the patient, nor to the referring physician. Forms to authorize the release of information should be signed by the patient, which permits the staff of the receiving physician to acquire previous records and reports that may better explain that patient's health problem and help avoid duplication of tests. Forms for collecting information on the patient's history should be sent directly to the patient's home, along with a telephone number (preferably toll-free or collect), so that the patient can call if there are questions. All forms and requests for information should be accompanied by a stamped, self-addressed envelope, to make them more convenient for a patient to return.

Be sure to include a form that gives your agency the right to share any information obtained with significant people such as other physicians, nurses, and school personnel. If a child is being seen by a doctor because of a learning problem, for example, it would be helpful if the child's school psychologist, teacher, or principal could receive a copy of the medical report. Vocational rehabilitative agencies or other regional, state, or federal groups may need a copy of a doctor's report for purposes of instituting financial, social, or training services on behalf of the patient. A patient may also be eligible for assistance to buy a motorized wheelchair through the Muscular Dystrophy Association or other agency. Before this can be determined, however, a copy of the medical report will need to be sent to that group. Once forms have been signed by the patient or his or her representative authorizing release of medical records, the staff providing health care can expedite the necessary follow-up services.

TIPS FOR PROVIDING HIGH-QUALITY SERVICE

- Remember that each patient you see today is there because he or she needs help.
- Listen intently, pay attention to the patient, and be eager to help.
- Go out of your way to greet each patient in a friendly yet busineslike way. Without being asked, identify who you are and what services you will be providing. Remember: The first impression you make will set in motion an attitude about all the services that the patient can expect to receive.
- Talk to the patient about his or her needs. Convince the patient that you will be working to ensure his or her satisfaction.
- Assume the position that the patient is never wrong. Whether this axiom is true is not important; what is important is that you evoke a patient-oriented attitude when trying to resolve problems.
- Remember that the only way to come out ahead in an argument is to avoid the argument in the first place. Even if you are clearly right and the patient is clearly wrong, do not argue! You will not change the patient's opinion by doing so.
- Do not go looking for problems, but do learn to be a good listener. Probe for all factors related to the patient's problem; most can be solved by identifying the issues and engaging the proper services and resources.
- Keep a friendly attitude when confronted by an angry patient; strive to find common ground that will help you both resolve the problem.

- If a disagreement arises, convince the patient that you are both after the same results. Make sure the disagreement focuses on methods, not purpose. Methods can be renegotiated; purposes should stay intact.
- Find ways of making it easier for you to provide good service to patients.
- Before being seen by the physician, each patient should be instructed to develop a list of questions he or she would like the physician to answer. This process will ensure that patients receive answers to their main concerns about health.
- Let patients talk about their problems and concerns and even vent their anger. Only then can you develop a complete picture of the problem and guide the patient ever so gently to resolution.
- Do not hassle patients about their bills. Treat them as you would expect to be treated, with respect, patience, and understanding.

Follow Up on Good Service

Many cases requiring the attention of health care providers are resolved at the time of the office visit. Others need to consider long-term treatment. In both instances, it is important to make follow-up contact with the patient after the visit. Such contact will enable monitoring of that person's health status. It will also promote a continuing linkage between the patient and the provider and will facilitate the consumer's satisfaction with the service.

Patient satisfaction is one aspect of health care that is frequently overlooked or taken for granted. A "halo effect" appears to surround providers of health care, particularly physicians: this involves a perception that the doctor can do no wrong and that once care has been given, no questions need to be asked. Yet despite the extensive and excellent training and experience received by physicians, they are human and, thus, fallible. Questions about the adequacy of health care services must therefore be asked of patients as well as of doctors, if improvement in that care is to occur.

Medical services have generally been assumed by consumers to be of high quality, but this assumption has not been adequately tested.[1,21] Only recently has the Joint Commission on Hospital and Ambulatory Care Accreditation, for example, begun focusing its efforts on clinical outcomes and the development of parameters for a practice to judge appropriate quality.[25,26] Patient satisfaction is a very reliable indicator of successful medical practice. It must be continually assessed, if services perceived by patients as relevant and meaningful are to be offered.

Effective Forms of Follow-Up Service

Effective follow-up services for patients can take a variety of forms. Patients should be asked to write out questions they wish the doctor to answer about their health problems. For their convenience, a place to list these questions should be included on the forms used for obtaining a history, which patients fill out upon their arrival at the medical facility. Health care personnel should still encourage patients to ask their questions orally, but putting questions in writing can provide added insight into patient expectations. In addition, the questions can serve as benchmarks for comparison, when a determination is being made about whether the patient's expectations of care were met.

If a patient is seen by more than one staff member during the process of evaluation, each person who sees the patient should review with him or her the evaluation results. Every visit should also be followed up with a letter, telephone call, and/or report. Research has shown that such follow-up has a strong and positive influence on how patients feel about the care they received, yet it is all too often neglected. Providing a letter summarizing and explaining the physician's findings and recommendations for care is one of the most meaningful services that can be offered to a patient. It proves "closure" to the patient's questions. It indicates problems that were either ruled out or confirmed during the examination. The summary also provides a record of the current status and recommended direction of treatment. The summary report should be sent to the patient within ten working days after an appointment.

Follow-up may also include telephoning the patient to check on his or her medical progress. This technique is especially valuable after surgery or in cases for which medications have been prescribed; it can help determine whether the surgery or medications have had the desired results. Telephone follow-up also establishes a personal link between the doctor and the patient. If the initial treatment does not appear to be working, the physician can prescribe an alternative treatment and/or request that the patient return for another appointment. Some practices ask the patient to call the doctor at specified intervals or whenever the need arises, but this approach to follow-up service has been found to have a low rate of compliance. At the very least, the organization should provide a toll-free or collect telephone number to make calls more convenient for the patient.

Return appointments also fall into the category of follow-up service. Many health problems that require therapy or frequent checks on medication necessitate periodic appointments. Scheduling patients on a weekly, biweekly, monthly, quarterly, semiannual, or annual basis sets up a systematic avenue of communication between doctor and patient. Such scheduling should always be done with the patient's needs in mind. When patients believe their needs are being met, they will remain undaunted in their trust and support of their health care provider.

Monitoring how well follow-up services are provided will prove to be a valuable asset to management when called on to reflect organizational commitment to consumer satisfaction. When an administrator is asked, "How satisfied are your patients with the services provided?," it will be possible to refer to current outcomes and discuss specific changes made to enhance services to patients. Only through systematic patient participation in the evaluative process can health care professionals really know whether their patients are pleased with the services they have received.

Evaluators of health care often recognize the need to include information from consumers in their assessments—whether, for example, the consumer felt a physician answered all questions or whether the consumer received a follow-up report. But those same evaluators often fail to include in their assessments consumers' specific likes and dislikes about the medical care and service received. Many doctors neglect to assess objectively any aspect of their patient's satisfaction with services. Others collect information so sweeping that it cannot be used except in a most general way. Still others ask the wrong questions, leading to the collection of useless information. One must:

> Cast aside what is thought to be the patient's need and instead ask the patient about his or her expectations. Once the expectations have been defined, it is up to the physician and supporting staff to fulfill them. (p. 5)[7]

Only by focusing on those activities which patients state are important to them can a consumer-oriented system be built that will meet the needs of both patients and providers.

Involving Patients and Their Families in the Evaluative Process

Patient participation in the evaluative process is valuable on at least two levels: (1) it improves care for individual patients, and (2) it makes it possible to compile data on the opinions of large groups of patients, thus showing ways of improving care for all patients. Through such compilations of data, researchers have learned that what patients often remember best about their medical care is whether they were given opportunities to ask questions of their physicians, how their appointments were scheduled, and what kind of follow-up care they received. Research and experience have also shown that several other steps can be taken to enhance a patient's experience at the physician's office.

A good index of patient satisfaction involves comparing what kinds of services the patient expected to receive with what he or she felt was actually received. This requires thinking about services from the consumer's point of view. For example, what could a patient expect to hear when calling for an appointment? Would the patient's schedule at work be considered? Could multiple appointments be scheduled for different services on the same day? This technique would not only save time and perhaps make the visit easier for the patient, but it would also reduce the risk of duplicating laboratory tests, X-rays, and such, thus lowering costs.

Patient participation must continue far beyond the hospital or the doctor's office.[10] What happens to the patient after the appointment is all-important. Now the question becomes: Do the medical services resolve the patient's problems? If the answer is "no," or worse yet, if a medical facility does not know the answer, the potential for a malpractice lawsuit exists, and for good reason.

The follow-up process may involve referring the patient to a specialist. Most patients are usually unaware of the services of specialists, so it is up to the examining physician, usually a primary care provider, to inform them of those services. In fact, most HMOs require authorized referral by a primary care provider before they pay for the specialist's services. Matching a patient to the right specialist is an important part of providing high-quality service. Once the specialist has evaluated the referred patient, it is important that the results of the evaluation be sent back to the primary care physician. This ensures a continuity of care that is in the patient's best interest.

Getting Consumers Actively Involved

Providers of health care often recognize the need to include information from consumers in an assessment of their services, yet they fail to conduct the systematic evaluations needed for such assessments. If an organization wants to provide patients with satisfactory services, then it must take the necessary steps to assess how well their needs are being met. Active consumer participation in this process is essential, and a variety of ways exist to encourage this activity. For example, consumers can be placed on advisory boards, committees, or task forces considering health care.[15]

Such appointments make consumers full participants in the development of policies and procedures for the organization. Some health organizations have mandated that a certain number of appointments to, or positions on, a committee be reserved for members of the public. These organizations can clearly state that their services and methods have developed with full participation by consumers. Similarly, many federal, state, and private grant-giving agencies require the participation of consumers on governing bodies of all health care organizations applying to them for funds. The funding agencies believe such a requirement ensures that the public's opinions about health care and its delivery will be heard.

Unfortunately, what typically happens with this form of consumer participation is that the organization appoints, elects, or recruits its own "friends." Such action defeats the purpose of seeking unbiased input from consumers to help assess patient satisfaction. Effective efforts toward participation by consumers must go far beyond the token involvement of friendly appointments. If a health care organization truly wants to accurately estimate how satisfied its consumers are, it must involve its patients—and not necessarily just its "friendly" ones—in the evaluative process.

Assuming the organization does provide services that are capable of meeting patients' needs, the first step in the process of assessment is rather routine: ask the patients what they thought of the services, either through questionnaires, follow-up phone calls, or focus groups. Some health care providers believe that this form of participation by consumers actually places the patient in a position of judgment over the provider. It does, and rightly so. The patient should be the judge of how well his or her needs have been met, particularly since the patient is the one responsible for the final bill and the one who must live with the functional results in his or her personal health.

Only with direct participation by patients does the evaluation of services become a valid process. It is patients who are qualified to determine whether their doctors gave them enough time to ask questions, or whether their appointments occurred at the times scheduled, or whether they noticed any progress in their health after their visit. The people receiving medical services—the patients, not the providers—can assess these questions. What providers can and should do is measure the results of the patients' evaluations and then modify their services to improve any weaknesses identified during the process.[1,21]

Hints for Follow-Up Service

- We often recognize the need to involve patients in the delivery of services for their health, yet fail to conduct evaluations to determine how successful our efforts are.
- Many forms of patient involvement are possible. Search for those most meaningful to the goals and objectives of your organization.

- Are the actual services being provided perceived as adequate by your patients? If not, why not?
- Patient involvement in the delivery of services will help you identify what improvements need to be made.
- Do consumers want to participate? Ask them; this is the only way to find out.
- Anticipate what your consumers expect from their visit to the doctor's office, and then make sure they get it.
- Patient satisfaction is that aspect of health care which is often taken for granted or overlooked. Make sure each patient receives answers to all questions, and actively involve them in an evaluation of the system responsible for delivery of their care.
- Services to consumers go beyond their visit to your office. Follow-up communication after the visit is needed to ensure patient satisfaction.

CONSUMER SATISFACTION: AN OVERVIEW

- Everyone needs and deserves satisfactory service in caring for their health. That is available now more than ever.[17]
- Providers of health care must be more careful in considering patients' needs in the planning, delivery, and evaluation of their services. Customer evaluation of business performance helps to balance a scorecard traditionally composed of financial measures.[27]
- Universal health insurance, or an equivalent result of current activity to reform health care, will allow consumers to go just about anywhere to have their health care needs met. Patients will eventually become very selective in seeking this service.
- Consumers have a tendency not to complain openly to their providers about problems or poor service. They usually leave the doctor's office without informing anyone of their concerns, thus making it impossible for the physician to identify or correct the problem.
- Patients should be asked for both negative and positive comments about the service they received. Negative information is extremely helpful because a problem (or just poor service) can be improved only after it has been identified. Positive comments support the ongoing allocation of financial resources so that the organization can maintain and perhaps enhance those satisfactory elements of the service system.
- One way to provide good service is to think in terms of what the consumer wants. Patients are shopping around for health care more than

ever before and are quite willing to forsake local doctors if they believe better service is available elsewhere.

- Examine the system that delivers services; focus on those needs deemed important by patients.
- Implement a consumer-oriented approach to health care. Train staff who provide health care so that they become consumer oriented.
- Satisfied patients will inform others about the good service they received. This increases the number of new referrals to the practice and increases the staff's morale, as employees receive appreciation from patients and higher salaries due to the increased business.

SUMMARY

- Have all aspects of the practice (clinical, service, and operational) been reviewed to focus on consumers? Eliminate any element in the practice not essential for operations to meet consumers' needs.
- How has voluntary commitment toward excellence in patient care and service been embraced by the practice? What is being done to instill voluntary commitment into each staff member's mind as the way we do business?
- What measures were used to determine consumer satisfaction with medical care and the delivery of services? Compare results to peer groups by physician, by specialty, and from clinic to clinic.
- Can the results differentiate between excellent and nonacceptable levels of care and service? How was the lack of information from nonrespondents followed up on?
- Were outcomes defined to focus on ways to improve less-than-satisfactory care and services? Can you identify which components of medical care and service were most important to consumers? What interventions were implemented to enhance less-than-excellent performance?
- List satisfaction results that represent measures of quality of care, cost of service, access, and communication. How do current outcomes compare to those from the last evaluation (if one was done)? How do the results compare to benchmarks throughout the community, region, and nationally?
- Did the results meet preestablished expectations, or were your surprised? What evidence can you point to that shows how well clinical care, service, and functions of the operating system were received by consumers?

- Do you know which indicators account for the most success toward achieving growth in net revenues, retained patients, and new patients? How does consumer satisfaction relate to compensation and retention of physicians? Could any aspect of the practice be eliminated because it had no relationship to customer-focused care and service?

Chapter 6

Special Applications

PROACTIVE CONSIDERATIONS

- Certain circumstances require specialized applications. A variety of outcomes management examples that have proven to be helpful are presented here. Many more options exist in the marketplace, and the reader is encouraged to seek them out through related literature, by attending topic-specific seminars, and/or by taking classes. The ultimate goal is continuous health care practice enhancement.
- To sustain practice success, it is important to stay a little in advance of the times. Oftentimes, an advantage can be gained by the application of one or more innovative improvement techniques to enhance on a continuous basis or at the right point in time (i.e., when it is needed most). Regardless of the procedures selected, their use must be guided with the end in mind (i.e., the application is managed to produce the desired outcomes).
- Although the outcomes management applications presented to enhance alignment are by no means the only ones available, each activity has successfully impacted the practice of health care and continues to be used to achieve competitive advantage.

CONSUMER SATISFACTION REDEFINED

Consumer satisfaction will play an increasingly important role as more is learned about the effects of health care reform and managed competition. However, more than general knowledge is needed about the consumer's (patient, payer, referring professional, etc.) perception of how well care and service should be provided. If one expects to eliminate the difference between what the consumer expects and services actually delivered, it is important to design a consumer satisfaction program that measures results at the department/service/caregiver level.

This may mean that the needs of every consumer must be systematically addressed. To accomplish such a comprehensive program, consumer satisfaction must become a business priority. The voluntary commitment by each physician, support staff, and rank-and-file employee to achieve excellence through the care and service provided each patient will be required to differentiate your practice from the competition. All staff and employee performance evaluations must reflect expectations and responsibilities for consumer satisfaction performance. Incentives must be changed to reinforce the production of desired consumer satisfaction levels, which, in turn, will create a need to restructure the existing organization and service delivery network into a patient/consumer-centered care system.[1]

Consumer Satisfaction Analysis

From 1990 through 1993, a physician-hospital organization conducted direct mail, paper and pencil surveys to assess patient satisfaction with services received. On an annual basis, satisfaction with outpatient and inpatient care activity was measured by asking general and specific questions about services received of randomly selected patients from each service location.

Results were reported to each department responsible for the service and to the boards of directors for both the medical center and clinic. The intent of sharing this information with the service departments was for purposes of identifying the areas in need of improvement. Once identified, the department would be expected to eliminate those aspects accounting for less-than-satisfactory service ratings and/or comments. Results of corrective action were formally measured during the next year, with the goal of improved satisfaction for each service element originally identified as in need of improvement, as well as satisfactory performance on all other service aspects addressed in the survey.

The boards of directors received a general overview of results that could be used to judge overall satisfaction. Table 6.1 illustrates overall satisfaction and willingness to recommend other patients to the physician-hospital group. The outcome satisfaction ratings remained at acceptable levels over the four-year study period, ranging from 92 percent to 96 percent. However, a problem was perceived with the way satisfaction was being measured and reported at the department level.

TABLE 6.1 Physician-Hospital Patient Satisfaction

	1990	1991	1992	1993
Physicians' Clinic				
Total on-campus outpatient clinics (excluding Psychiatry*)				
Overall satisfaction	96 %	94 %	94 %	94 %
Willingness to recommend	95 %	93 %	93 %	93 %
Sample size	1,892	1,864	1,633	1,614
Hospital Total inpatient units (excluding Psychiatry*)				
Overall satisfaction	94 %	92 %	93 %	94 %
Willingness to recommend	93 %	93 %	92 %	94 %
Sample size	434	520	538	509

Source: Sommers, P. A. Internal study. Ramsey Clinic, St. Paul, MN, 1994-1995.

* Psychiatry department data were omitted from analysis since the patients surveyed were not randomly sampled.

Each department received the satisfaction ratings and related comments from a representative sample of patients who received care from that department's physician, nursing, and ancillary service staff. Plans were assembled by the departments to address activities receiving less-than-satisfactory ratings and/or negative comments. From the department viewpoint, results were not acceptable due to the general way information was being collected and interpreted. Although the survey instruments and the sampling approach were valid and reliable according to scientific measurement standards, the type of patient satisfaction information being collected was not helping service providers at the department level focus on the correction of specific service weaknesses for purposes of improving satisfaction.

This finding led staff to recommend that the current patient-consumer satisfaction program needed to be changed. More appropriate ways to obtain and use information at the department/service level would be a basic requirement of the new program.

Psychometric Analysis of Satisfaction Surveys
and Pilot Testing of Department-Specific Approach

Psychometric analyses, including factor analysis and reliability analysis were performed to develop homogeneous scales from the items on the collated satisfaction surveys. Statistical analyses, including multiple regression and analysis of variance, were also performed. Stepwise multiple regression analyses were used to determine how the various satisfaction scales related to overall satisfaction rating between departments and clinics and within each year of the study. Overall regressions were then performed across department and year. Analysis of variance techniques were used to compare years, clinics, and departments on average satisfaction scale ratings.

This analysis confirmed that valid and reliable measures of consumer satisfaction were being obtained and had remained consistent across the study period. High ratings with overall satisfaction and willingness to recommend others to the physician-hospital organization (ranging from 92 to 96 percent, as noted in Table 6.1) were strong indicators that the delivery of services was perceived by patients as generally acceptable. However, the analysis did not adequately provide staff with appropriate information that could be used to correct specific department-level service activity.

It is at this point in many consumer satisfaction studies that management concurs that the current levels of satisfaction ratings are adequate. In fact, it is quite possible that the ratings may not go much higher due to the law of diminishing returns. The problem with accepting the results, although appropriate in many instances, is that they are not generalizable at the department-specific service level. Thus, the survey methodology needs to be examined, and the evaluation approach reconstituted, to accurately reflect service-specific findings that can be used to measure department performance. With department-specific information, staff can design and implement programs to eliminate the difference between what the patient expects and the service actually delivered.

The physician-hospital approach to address this issue began following a review of the psychometric results. The departments of surgery, pediatrics, and internal medicine agreed to participate in a pilot study in 1994 that would incorporate alternative patient satisfaction measurement processes. Interviews were conducted with each department's staff to get feedback on the existing patient satisfaction and to gain input about the following:

• Pilot studies will be carried out in both the inpatient and outpatient units, although they may vary in scope and design.

- The results of the pilot study will be used to develop an organization-wide patient satisfaction measurement system for the physician-hospital group.
- The pilot studies will be completed by the end of 1994, and recommendations will be made for a new satisfaction measurement system to begin in 1995.

Recommendations Made to, and Approved by, the Physician-Hospital Organization Board That Were Implemented in the Fall of 1994

- Develop a program of one-on-one interviews which would be administered on-site and which would use an instrument designed with input from all, or a cross-section of, employees at the pilot sites.
- The pilot sites will include the outpatient components for the departments of internal medicine, pediatrics, and surgery. Other sites may be added as the study progresses.
- Staff of the pilot sites will be trained in the interviewing technique and will administer the interview instrument to patients as they visit the pilot site.
- The interview instrument will solicit not only input on satisfaction but also suggestions for improvement and patient exceptions.
- The pilot site will incorporate the development of a parallel instrument for the non-English-speaking population.

Results from the pilot programs indicated a need to address satisfaction at the department/clinic-specific level if changes were needed at the caregiver/provider level. General overall ratings on the clinicwide level were not appropriate to judge provider performance.

RANK ORDERING CLINICAL PRIORITIES

Establishing priorities among many worthy clinical quality initiatives is frequently a challenging exercise among physicians and nonphysician health care leaderships. When return-on-investment criteria are applied to clinical quality definitions, the task of rank ordering can be enhanced by determining whether the return period is a short- or long-term opportunity. If short term is desired, then you would rank contributing factors ahead of long-term activities for annual planning and benefits.

For illustrative purposes, a process used by a physician-led health plan to rank order its 1997-1998 clinical quality priorities is used as an example. All clinical activity occurring in 1996 that passed through the health plan's claim processing service provided the database composed of 800,000 to 950,000 members.

Step One: All clinical categories were arranged by frequency and volume using both inpatient and outpatient codes (including pharmacy, lab, diagnostic imaging, and other ancillary services).

Step Two: Each category was screened to eliminate redundancy, while grouping related measures (e.g., breast cancer and mammography, etc.).

Step Three: A knowledgeable work group of physician, nursing, and administrative staff was asked to develop priority criteria by which each category could be evaluated in an objective manner.

Example

The work group agreed upon a scaled weighting approach (1 through 5, with 5 being the highest priority and 1 the lowest). Priority criteria (e.g., clinical action groups [CAGs], HEDIS, NCQA, Public Health, etc.) were developed, reviewed, defined, and scored by the group. Mean average weights ranging between 1 and 5 were determined as follows for each criteria (rank ordered):

- HEDIS = 5.0
- High use/high cost = 5.0
- Regulatory/compliance = 4.8
- CAGs (clinical action group) = 4.4
- Employer/purchaser preference = 4.2
- Public health = 2.3
- ACE (medical record review instrument) = 2.2
- MD priorities = 1.4
- QI work plan = 1.0

Table 6.2 shows the analysis grid with clinical categories down the left margin and priority criteria across the top. NCQA could be applied to each category since it is not category specific. Table 6.3 adds the effects of weighting, which changes the rank order (e.g., asthma moves from 1 to 4; diabetes moves from 6 to 1; breast cancer moves from 2 to 5; etc.).

TABLE 6.2. Clinical Priorities/Rank Ordering Grid

	CAGs	HEDIS 2.5/3.0	Public Health	Regulatory Compliance	High Use/High Cost	ACE	MD Priorities (Provider)	1996 QI Work Plan	Employer/ Purchaser Preference	Total Points
Weighted Mean	4.4	5.0	2.3	4.8	5.0	2.2	1.4	1.0	4.2	
Diabetes (eye)	X 4.4	X 5.0	X 2.3	X 4.8	X 5.0	X 2.2		X 1.0	X 4.2	28.9
Cardiovas-cular Disease	X 4.4	X 5.0	X 2.3	X 4.8	X 5.0	2.2		X 1.0	X 4.2	26.7
Preventive Care	X 4.4	X 5.0	X 2.3	X 4.8		X 2.2	X 1.4	X 1.0	X 4.2	25.3
Asthma (Peds.)	X 4.4	X 5.0	X 2.3		X 5.0	X 2.2		X 1.0	X 4.2	24.1
Breast Cancer	X 4.4	X 5.0	X 2.3		X 5.0			X 1.0	X 4.2	21.9
Pregnancy Care	X 4.4	X 5.0	X 2.3		X 5.0			X 1.0	X 4.2	21.9
Otitis Media		X 5.0		X 4.8	X 5.0			X 1.0		15.8
Tobacco		X 5.0	X 2.3		X 5.0	X 2.2				14.5
Mental Illness		X 5.0			X 5.0				X 4.2	14.2
Colon Cancer	X 4.4		X 2.3		X 5.0			X 1.0		12.7
Cervical Cancer		X 5.0				X 2.2			X 4.2	11.4
Geriatrics	X 4.4	X 5.0						X 1.0		10.4
Violence								X 1.0		1.0
Nonusers of Care								X 1.0		1.0

Source: Sommers, P. A. Internal study. Allina Health System, Minneapolis, MN, 1997-1998.

TABLE 6.3. Weighting Priorities and Rank Order Implications

	CAGs	HEDIS 2.5/3.0	NCQA (all applied since NCQA does not specify)	CHIAC	Medfor- mation/ Nurse- line**	Regulatory Compliance	High*** Frequency	High Cost***	Preventive Care Guidelines	ACE	MD Provider Priorites	1996 QI Work Plan	Employer Purchaser BHCAG other	Total Points
*Asthma (Peds)	X	X	X				1	2	X	X		X	X	
*Breast Cancer	X	X	X				3	2	X			X	X	
Colon Cancer	X		X				3	2	X			X		
*Pregnancy Care	X	X	X				1	1	X			X	X	
Cardiovascular Disease	X	X	X				1	1	X			X	X	
*Diabetes (eye)	X	X	X			X	1	1	X	X		X	X	
Tobacco		X	X	X			1	1	X	X				
Violence			X	X			3	3				X	X	
*Immunizations	X	X	X			X	1	2	X			X	X	

	CAGs	HEDIS 2.5/3.0	NCQA (all applied since NCQA does not specify)	CHIAC	Medtor-mation/ Nurse-line**	Regulatory Compliance	High*** Frequency	High Cost***	Preventive Care Guidelines	ACE	MD Provider Priorites	1996 QI Work Plan	Employer Purchaser BHCAG other	Total Points
Geriatrics	X	X	X				1	1	X			X		
Pap		X	X				3	2	X	X			X	
Otitis Media		X	X				1	3			X			
Mental Illness		X	X				1	1				X		
Demand Mgmt (e.g., ER Urgi Care/After Hours)		X	X				1							
Nonusers of Care			X				-	1						

Source: Sommers, P. A. Internal study. Allina Health System, Minneapolis, MN, 1997-1998.

*Core clinical areas currently in place.
** 70,000 calls for first half of 1996 (150,000 annually); 64% from females; 36% from males: 16% about injury/poisoning; 15% digestive system; 14% ENT, Respiratory; 12% "other," 21% pertaining to ages under 1; 16% ages 1-10; 10% ages 11-20; 29% ages 21-35; 12% ages 36-45; 6% ages 46-55; 3% ages 56-65; 4% over 65.
*** Rank order.

The clinical categories can be viewed another way: [2]

- Tobacco is a number-one priority because it is linked with the following:
  1. Asthma
  2. Cardiovascular disease
  3. Diabetes
  4. Cancer
  5. Pregnancy (high risk)
- Geriatrics is a number-one priority because the frequency of cancer, cardiovascular disease, and diabetes is higher among people sixty-five and older.
- Mental illness is a number-one priority because of high pharmacy costs.
- Otitis Media is a number-three priority in terms of cost. This is because otitis media has a very small amount of inpatient cost. It does, however, have significant physician office visit and outpatient cost.
- Cancer would be a number-one priority in terms of cost if all cancers were combined. When looking at them separately, however, the costs are not as significant as diabetes or cardiovascular due to the small number of cases.

Table 6.4 combines weighted averages with return on investment and offers an option for the allocation of resources. Each clinical category has features that yield the best alternatives for long- and short-term return on investment.

BENCHMARKING: THE SEARCH FOR BEST PRACTICES

Benchmarking is the process of discovering and implementing best practices that result in excellent performance. The goal of benchmarking is to define the target of interest, determine the difference between actual and desired performance, and close the gap. Results that can be directly influenced by benchmarking include:[3,4]

- improved quality of care,
- reduced expenses,
- saved time, and
- improved patient, physician, and staff satisfaction.

Table 1.2 in Chapter 1, p. 12 shows national performance across managed care indicators for 1993, 1994 and 1995. The indicators are benchmarks for comparisons by health plans across the United States and other managed care marketplaces.[5,6] In this example, concern should be focused

TABLE 6.4. Adding Return on Investments and Related Implications

1997 Clinical Quality Priority Grid (Rank Ordered Goal Areas)

	CAGs	HEDIS 2.5/3.0	Public Health	Regulatory Compliance	High Use/High Cost	ACE	MD Priorities (Provider)	1996 QI Work Plan	Employer/Purchaser Preference	Total Points	Weighted Rank Order
Weighted Mean	4.4	5.0	2.3	4.8	5.0	2.2	1.4	1.0	4.2		
Geriatrics	X 4.4	X 5.0						X 1.0		10.4	11
Cardiovascular Disease	X 4.4	X 5.0	X 2.3	X 4.8	X 5.0			X 1.0	X 4.2	26.7	2
Asthma	X 4.4	X 5.0	X 2.3		X 5.0	X 2.2		X 1.0	X 4.2	24.1	4
Breast Cancer	X 4.4	X 5.0	X 2.3		X 5.0			X 1.0	X 4.2	21.9	5
Colon/Rectal Cancer	X 4.4		X 2.3		X 5.0			X 1.0		12.7	9
Tobacco/Lung Cancer		X 5.0	X 2.3		X 5.0	X 2.2				14.5	7
Otitis Media		X 5.0		X 4.8	X 5.0			X 1.0		15.8	6
Pregnancy Care	X 4.4	X 5.0	X 2.3		X 5.0			X 1.0	X 4.2	21.9	5
Preventive Care	X 4.4	X 5.0	X 2.3	X 4.8		X 2.2	X 1.4	X 1.0	X 4.2	25.3	3
Diabetes	X 4.4	X 5.0	X 2.3	X 4.8	X 5.0	X 2.2		X 1.0	X 4.2	28.9	1
Mental Illness		X 5.0			X 5.0				X 4.2	14.2	8
Cervical Cancer		X 5.0				X 2.2			X 4.2	11.4	10
Violence								X 1.0		1.0	12
Nonusers of Care								X 1.0		1.0	12

TABLE 6.4 (continued)
Return on Investment/Recommended Allocations

LifeSmart (ROI) 15% cost/savings by/or across categories	UHC Best of Practice (ROI)	Impact Analysis UHC = (UHC) LifeSmart = (LS)		Allocation of Resources Two Pools: (1) = 30% (Regulatory/Compliance) (2) = 70% (Best Bet)
#1	#4	Greatest opportunity (LS)	(2)	Low compliance/highest cost (LS) Needs specification (UHC)
#2 Specifically: congestive heart failure, myocardial infarction, revascularization	#1	Great opportunity (LS)	(2)	Focus on three areas initially. Avoiding 10%of heart disease would reduce costs by additional $6.9 million annually (LS/UHC)
#3	#2	Quick Impact (UHC)	(2)	By ensuring adequate use of medication (UHC)
#3	#3	Quick Return (LS)	(2)	Early detection may save lives but not decrease overall costs (UHC)
#4	#5	Quick Return (LS)	(2)	Compliance = early detection/lower costs (LS)
N/A	#3		(1)	Avoiding 25% lung cancer by $1.8 million annually (LS)
N/A	#4	Minimal to moderate cost saving	(1)	Outcomes may improve but cost impact will be minimal to moderate (UHC)
#5	#4		(1)	Preventing preterm deliveries (UHC). Avoiding 10% of high-risk pregnancies will reduce expenses by $4.4 mil (LS)
N/A	#5	Long-term ROI (UHC) Will add expense initially	(1)	Specific definitions/ interventions needed (LS/USC)
#5	#5	5-7 yr. ROI (UHC) May add expense initially	(1)	Long-term disease mgmt. plan (UHC)
N/A	#5		(1)	Pharmacy/drug costs utilization can be managed to decrease cost
N/A	#6			Unlikely cost driver (UHC)
N/A	#6			Little impact on expense (UHC)
N/A	#6			Unlikely cost driver (UHC)

Source: Sommers, P. A. Internal study. Allina Health System, Minneapolis, MN, 1997-1998.

on the fact that although HMOs continued to ratchet down inpatient days per 1,000—from a median of 275 days in 1994 to 253 days in 1995—their medical expense loss ratios increased from $80.68 PMPM in 1994 to $82.93 PMPM in 1995. Premiums, on the other hand, fell from $48.3 million in 1994 to $45.7 million—a reduction of more than 5 percent in a single year.[6] Such a national trend has become a wake-up call for HMOs and other health care organizations. It is not business as usual. Health plans are being required to demonstrate their value more than ever before. In fact, purchasers and physicians alike have often wished they could skip the insurance companies and have health care provided directly to whomever needed it.[7] Direct provider contracting has been endorsed by a variety of employer-based purchasing groups who have formally organized and are dealing directly with providers.[7] In many of these purchasing organizations, the desired benchmarks, or performance outcome standards, are being set internally, and interested providers are invited to participate on the employer purchasing group's terms.

Designing and/or Using Existing Benchmarks to Meet Defined Needs

Physician, hospital, and health plan needs vary by location, amount/nature of competition, growth potential, and marketshare, to name a few. Each organization must select comparative measures that, when achieved, will lead it toward the predefined targets specified in the strategic plan. Available information can be identified upon which to base a group's performance standards. However, such a process requires up-front determination of those marketplace components most important to the organization. A variety of measures to consider follows.[5]

Per Member Per Month (PMPM) Expense Rates for Physicians, Hospitals, and Health Plans

- Utilization rates and trends
- Physician panel sizes
- Clinician staffing ratios
- Stop-loss attachment points and premiums
- Premium allocations by specialty
- Withhold percentages
- Profit ratios
- Physician performance measures
- Physician incentive plans
- Outcomes data
- Economic profiling

Actual Rates and Data Used to Reflect a Variety of Practice Settings

- Hospitals
- Physician hospital organizations (PHOs)
- Multispecialty groups and IPAs (RVUs)
- Primary care physicians (PCPs) (RVUs)
- Specialists (RVUs)
- Ancillary providers (RVUs)
- Commercial plans
- Medicare plans
- Medicaid plans

Financial and Accounting Reports and Procedures Under Capitation

- Reserve funding and allocation
- Actual versus expected expenses, visits
- MD performance measures
- Income statements
- Claims lag reports
- Referral costs
- Enrollee risk adjustment
- Factor impact analysis
- Stop-loss tracking
- Disenrollment analysis

Management Tools

- Models and templates for tracking incurred but not reported (IBNR) claims
- Forms for comparing capitation revenue with fee for service (FFS) equivalents
- Tools for calculating per member per month (PMPM) expense rates
- Spreadsheets for settling physician incentive plans
- New payment trends, emerging risk contracting markets, and changing contract structures that are reflected by:
  — Capitation payments
  — Member enrollment
  — Satisfaction levels
  — Utilization trends
  — Stop-loss insurance
  — Staffing ratios

Establishing Managed Care Readiness Benchmarks

Examples follow that show the process which health plans go through to establish PMPM benchmarks and targets for various practice elements.

National actuarial firms provide updated benchmark information from across the states to match practice elements on a loosely, moderately, or tightly managed care basis. Information is available to fit the practice into the range of established benchmarks. For monitoring budget purposes, a "target" is selected from which the organization can manage provider performance toward preset budget targets. Routine comparisons are made to determine the amount of variation between the targets and the comparable benchmarks. The goal for the health plan is to meet (or exceed) each target to stay on budget.

Physicians Incorporated is a multispeciality medical group that instituted the following measures to establish fiscal targets for its managed care business.

Lab

PMPM	Physicians Inc.	Loosely	Moderately	Tightly
Hospital Outpatient	$ 0.81	$ 1.30	$ 1.00	$ 0.40
Physician	$ 4.05	$ 4.77	$ 4.34	$ 4.00
	$ 4.86	$ 6.07	$ 5.34	$ 4.40

Lab Fee Savings	$(0.84)
Net	**$ 4.02 OK for 1997 target**

Target
 • Set the target at $4.02 for now.

Comments
 • Benchmarks for laboratory will be reconsidered once more information is available about further potential PMPM reduction possibilities.

Action Plan
 • The $4.02 target should be achieved with the fee changes.

Radiology

PMPM	Physicians Inc.	Loosely	Moderately	Tightly
Hospital Outpatient	$ 3.33	$ 3.70	$ 3.23	$ 1.13
Physician	$ 4.14	$ 6.30	$ 5.80	$ 5.00
	$ 7.47	$10.00	$ 9.03	$ 6.13

Expense Reduction Savings	$(0.20)
Net	**$ 7.47 OK for 1997 target**

Target
 • 1997 target was set at $7.47 due to fee schedule change and expense reduction activity.

Action Plan
- Promote savings through expense reduction activity and unit price/ appropriateness changes through fee review.

Diagnostic Testing

	Physicians Inc.	Loosely	Moderately	Tightly
PMPM	$ 1.96	$ 1.24	$ 0.96	$ 0.77

Fee schedule savings $(Not yet determined)
Net **$ 1.24 OK as 1997 target**

Target
- The target for 1997 was set at $1.24.

Action Plan
- Outside consultant believes that $0.75 - $1.00 can be reduced from the $1.96 by focusing providers on lower utilization options.
- Consider precertification requirements on high-frequency/high-cost tests.

Pharmacy

	Physicians Inc.	Loosely	Moderately	Tightly
PMPM	$15.56	$16.43	$14.19	$13.75 /

(Use as long-term goal/benchmark)
Cost Savings $(0.28)
Net   **$15.28 OK for 1997 target**

Target
- $15.28 set as target for 1997.

Comments
- Limited by legislature to 25 percent copay (approx. $9.00).

Action Plan
- Pharmacy Committee will be developing further action plans.

Emergency Room Facility

	Physicians Inc.	Loosely	Moderately	Tightly
PMPM Total	$ 2.79	$ 1.92	$ 1.58	$1.15
ER	$ 2.79+			
Cost Savings	$(0.87)			
Net	**$1.92 OK for 1997 target**			

Target
- $1.92 was set as 1997 target for now.

Comments
- Outside consultant believes that close to $1.00 PMPM can be eliminated with improved utilization.

Action Plan
- Results of previous ER use analysis will be combined with current results to develop an action plan.

Outpatient Surgery Facility

	Physicians Inc.	Loosely	Moderately	Tightly
PMPM	$ 6.27	$ 6.17	$ 5.47	$ 5.01

(Use as a benchmark)

Cost Savings	$(0.14)
Net	**$6.27 OK for 1997 target**

Target
- Target was set at $6.27 for 1997.

Comments

- Use $6.27 as 1997 target, but reduce utilization to reduce PMPM by at least $0.40.

Action Plan
- Share utilization reports with physicians. Can more be done on an outpatient basis if adequate equipment and "back up" staff are available?

Physical Therapy

	Physicians Inc.	Loosely	Moderately	Tightly
PMPM	$ 1.09	$ 0.92	$ 0.77	$ 0.61

(Use $0.60 as a benchmark)

Expense Reduction Savings	$(0.08)
Net	**$1.09 OK for 1997 target**

Target
- Target for 1997 was set at $1.09.

Comments
- Need to reduce PT prescriptions by 30 to 40 percent to approach desired benchmark.

Action Plan
- Focus on expense and utilization reduction through alternative therapy approaches.
- Review per unit cost for potential adjustment.

Inpatient Facility (Excluding Drug, Alcohol, and Psychiatric)

	Physicians Inc.	Loosely	Moderately	Tightly
PMPM	$ 22.80	$ 29.14	$ 21.10	$ 14.12

(Use as a benchmark)

Cost Savings	$(0.33)
Net	**$22.80 OK for 1997 target**

Target
- $22.80 was the figure set as 1997 target.

Comments
- Outside consultant believes at least $3.75 can be eliminated from the PMPM.

Action Plan
- Utilization will be managed to reduce PMPM by at least $3.00 in the next seven months. Education and use of social workers, psychologists, and clinical nursing staff will be emphasized.

Total Physician

	Physicians Inc.	Loosely	Moderately	Tightly
PMPM	$ 14.47	$ 17.33	$ 15.36	$ 13.47

(Use as long-term goal/benchmark)

Fee Schedule Savings	$(0.64)
Net	**$15.36 OK for 1997 target**

Target
- $15.36 was set as target for 1997.

Comments
- Consider switching to a single conversion factor.

Action Plan
- Determine the results of recent fee changes. Determine next fee analysis steps.
- Move to single conversion factor and measure the results.

Physicians Inc. uses a summary report to show comparisons between actual performance, benchmarks, and targets (see Table 6.5). This type of report has multiple applications:

1. The variance from "actual" Physicians Incorporated PMPM to target and benchmark represents an estimate of cost savings if the variance can be eliminated. In this example:
   Target = $2,660,000
   Benchmark = $33,440,000
2. On an ongoing basis (monthly preferred), the reporting of the information serves as a monitoring tool from an outcomes management perspective. If the desired target PMPM estimates are not consistently achieved, reanalysis of the factors associated with the production of each target's results needs to occur. Drill-down procedures are used to determine which elements are causing the PMPM to miss the target. Once determined, corrective action is taken to adjust each contributing element to the desired level. Without active management, the PMPM will randomly fluctuate, thus inhibiting the achievement by each target.

Clinical Quality Benchmarks

National average benchmarks were composed from 1995 to 1996 through the National Committee for Quality Assurance (NCQA).[8] Included is information from the Quality Compass ™ reporting system with a focus on Health Plan Employer Data and Information Set (HEDIS)® measures. Data was collected and summarized from 250 health plans in 1995, and over 300 in 1996, from throughout the United States.*

Categories	National Average Member Rate of Compliance/Utilization	
	1996	1997
Childhood Immunization	78.6%	65.3%
Mammography	69.1%	70.4%
Pap	73.7%	70.4%
Prenatal Care	87.5%	84.5%
Diabetic Eye Exam	37.3%	38.4%
C-section Rate	19.6%	20.6%

*Reprinted with permission from the National Committee for Quality Assurance; *Quality Compass ™ Version 1.1;* Copyright©1996 and 1997 by NCQA.

TABLE 6.5. PMPM Comparisons to Benchmarks and Targets

Services		Benchmark	Target	Actual Physicians Inc. PMPM	Actuarially Determined Managed Care Market			Variance from Benchmark	Variance from Target
					Loosely	Moderately	Tightly		
Lab									
	Outpatient Physician	$1.00		$0.81 4.05	$1.30 4.77	$1.00 4.34	$0.40 4.00		
	Total		$4.02	$4.86	$6.07	$5.34	$4.40	$3.86	$0.84
Radiology									
	Outpatient Physician			$3.33 4.14	$3.70 6.30	$3.23 5.80	$1.13 5.00		
	Total	$7.02	$7.47	$7.47	$10.00	$9.03	$6.13	$0.45	-0-
Diagnostic Testing		$1.17	$1.24	$1.96	$1.24	$0.96	$0.77	$0.79	$0.72
Pharmacy		$13.75	$15.28	$15.56	$16.43	$14.19	$13.75	$1.81	$0.28
Emergency Room		$1.88	$1.92	$2.79	$1.92	$1.58	$1.15	$0.91	$0.87
Outpatient Surgery (facility only)		$5.47	$6.27	$6.27	$6.17	$5.47	$5.01	$0.80	-0-
Physical Therapy		$0.60	$1.09	$1.09	$0.92	$0.77	$0.61	$0.49	-0-
Inpatient Facility (Excluding alcohol/drug abuse/psych)		$21.10	$22.80	$22.80	$29.14	$21.10	$14.12	$1.70	-0-
Total Physician		$15.30	$15.36	$14.47	$17.33	$15.36	$13.47	$(0.83)	$(0.89)
Total Variance								$8.8	$.7
Member Months								3,800,000	3,800,000
Estimated savings if variance eliminated								$33,440,000	$2,660,000

Source: Sommers, P. A. Internal study. Allina Health System, Minneapolis, MN, 1997-1998.

Each of the participating health plans and other plans with similar interests compare their results across categories to the Quality Compass™ data, which will show whether the utilization and preventive aspects of your organization are on or off track. Departures of scores by a health plan's provider group below these national benchmarks warrant analysis and follow-up intervention, with action plans aimed at meeting or exceeding the national average.

Cross-Plan Comparisons

The following tables (6.6, 6.7, and 6.8) show 1995 HEDIS performance published by the Minnesota Department of Health for different competitive health plans from the same marketplace.[9] Oftentimes state, federal, and employer purchasing organizations want to know about perceived quality differences between and among health plans before they recommend one or more plan options to the employees they represent.

Based upon what the purchasing group believes to be important, performance standards are built into specific contracts with physicians, hospitals, and/or health plan providers. Payment is tied to performance. Both withhold dollars and incentive dollars are paid to providers only after the agreed-upon targets have been achieved.

Using Relative Value Units As Standard Measures for Medical Groups

Data on medical groups can be used successfully to measure and compare their productivity. Data on their RVUs can also provide a baseline for calculating capitated rates. Relative value units can only be determined

TABLE 6.6. 1995 HEDIS Quality Measures

Health Plan	Childhood Immunization (chart review) Hybrid	Prenatal Care in First Trimester (chart review)	Mammography Screening (2-year rate) Females 52-64	Pap Smear Screening (3-year rate) Females 21-64
#1	0.0%	0.0%	0.0%	0.0%
#2	92.1%	97.0%	79.8%	81.7%
#3	86.2%	97.4%	77.1%	79.9%
#4	82.4%	92.4%	75.0%	76.1%

Source: Minnesota Department of Health, St. Paul, Minnesota, 1996.

TABLE 6.7. 1995 HEDIS Ambulatory Measures

Health Plan	Member Months Total Male and Female	Emergency Room Visits	Visits/1000	Outpatient Medical Services Visits	Visits/1000
#1	594,109	7,252	146.5	153,143	3,093.2
#2	1,313,201	6,376	58.3	425,979	3,892.6
#3	3,487,846	19,604	67.4	783,639	2,696.1
#4	5,252,503	52,223	119.3	1,585,881	3,623.1
Aggregate	10,647,659	85,455	96.3	2,948,642	3,323.1

Source: Minnesota Department of Health, St. Paul, MN, 1996.

TABLE 6.8. 1995 HEDIS Inpatient Measures

Health Plan	Medical/Surgical Days /1000	Admits /1000	LOS	Maternity Days /1000	Admits /1000	LOS	Complex Newborn Days /1000	Admits /1000	LOS
#1	185.6	44.4	4.2	38.8	16.0	2.4	16.4.	0.7	23.2
#2	138.2	35.3	3.9	32.9	12.2	2.7	16.0	0.7	21.6
#3	134.0	34.4	3.9	42.7	17.5	2.4	23.0	0.9	26.2
#4	157.6	37.1	4.2	35.0	16.8	2.1	15.2	1.0	15.5
Aggregate	149.0	36.4	4.1	37.5	16.4	2.3	17.9	0.9	19.9

Source: Minnesota Department of Health, St. Paul, MN, 1996.

by establishing frequencies of use for each procedure. An RVU is the measure used by the federal government as the basis for calculating physicians' payments for services.[10] Other payers also use the RVU method of determining such payments. Other than office visits by patients, the most frequently performed procedures typically involve drawing blood, performing hemograms, analyzing urine and tissue, and handling specimens, according to data from medical group practices (see Table 6.9). Together, these activities account for very high frequencies of tasks performed.

TABLE 6.9 The Most Common Procedures of Medical Group Practices

Procedure	Relative Frequency per 10,000 Procedures	CPT-4 Code*
Office/Outpatient Visit, Est., Level 2	1,352.5	99212
Office/Outpatient Visit, Est., Level 3	1,126.9	99213
Drawing Blood	507.3	36415
Automated Hemogram	454.1	85025
Post-op Follow-up Visit	414.1	99024
19 or More Blood/Urine Tests	386.2	80019
Automated Hemogram	327.6	85024
Urinalysis with Microscopy	300.2	81000
Tissue Exam by Pathologist	249.3	88305
Tissue Exam by Pathologist	249.3	8830526
Tissue Exam by Pathologist	249.3	88305TC
Mammogram, Screening	248.2	76092
Automated Hemogram	223.4	85022
Urinalysis Nonautomatic w/o Scope	211.4	81002
Prothrombin Time	204.2	85610
Specimen Handling	198.1	99000
Office/Outpatient Visit, Est., Level 1	197.2	99211
Office/Outpatient Visit, Est., Level 4	193.2	99214
Automated Hemogram	189.7	85027
Assay Thyroid Hormone	166.8	84443

Source: Reprinted with permission from Medical Group Management Association. *CRAHCA Physical Services Practice Analysis Comparison: 1993 Medians.* Author: Englewood, CO, 1994.

* CPT-4 codes over five digits designate a professional or technical component of the CPT-4 code.

Example of RVU information applied:

Activity Summary
(Medians for Six Months of Procedures)

FTE Physicians/Group Practice	28.76
Patients/Group Practice	45,488
Procedures (six months)	96,099
RVU Count	115,779.30

Procedures/Patient	3.04
Procedures/FTE Physician	3,530
Patients/FTE Physician	1,301
RVUs/Procedure	1.10
RVUs/FTE Physician	4,310.60
RVUs/Patient	2.67

Comparisons of Productivity

Study of the office visit profiles of RVUs performed by medical specialty enables group practices to compare their activities and productivity to those of a national sample of medical groups, using the resource-based relative value scale developed by the Health Care Financing Administration. The RBRVS was developed to establish a new relationship between cognitive and procedural services for purposes of reimbursement.

Rates of Reimbursement per RVU

The following standard conversion factors are not geographically adjusted:[11]

$35.42: primary care services
$40.80: surgical services
$34.63: other nonsurgical services

Group practices may develop an individualized RVU comparison using activity reports generated internally by their own practices and coupling those with software developed to calculate RVUs per physician per month, by specialty. Two examples of RVU calculations are provided to allow comparisons within similar specialties and to familiarize readers with methodology in using RVUs. See Table 6.10 and Figure 6.1.

Relative value units provide a unique view into a medical specialty by focusing on procedures consuming the most resources, either by the frequency with which they occur or by the complexity of the procedures. For example, a total knee replacement in an orthopedic practice has an average RVU per month of 76.05, with an RVU per occurrence of 53.35, as is seen in studying the value schedule published by the government. This equates to an average of 1.43 procedures of this type per orthopedic surgeon per

TABLE 6.10. Procedure Code Profile by Specialty

Allergy/Immunology (17.55 FTEs)

CPT-4 CODE	Description	RVUs*
95117	Immunotherapy Injections	62.08
95115	Immunotherapy, One Injection	49.18
99213	Office/Outpatient Visit, Est.	43.46
99214	Office/Outpatient Visit, Est.	24.33
99244	Office Consultation	22.82

Noninvasive Cardiology (29.83 FTEs)

CPT-4 CODE	Description	RVUs*
93307	Echo Exam of Heart	129.03
93015	Cardiovascular Stress Test	56.26
99213	Office/Outpatient Visit, Est.	54.51
9330726	Echo Exam of Heart	47.16
99254	Initial Inpatient Consult	26.83

Family Practice (115.113 FTEs)

CPT-4 CODE	Description	RVUs*
99213	Office/Outpatient Visit, Est.	139.64
99212	Office/Outpatient Visit, Est.	67.58
99214	Office/Outpatient Visit, Est.	34.06
59410	Obstetrical Care	23.01
99215	Office/Outpatient Visit, Est.	22.92

Invasive Cardiology (30.17 FTEs)

CPT-4 CODE	Description	RVUs*
92982	Coronary Dilation	118.49
93307	Echo Exam of Heart	68.65
93325	Doppler Color Flow	61.14
99213	Office/Outpatient Visit, Est.	38.14
99231	Subsequent Hospital Care	23.72

Diagnostic Radiology (37.85 FTEs)

CPT-4 CODE	Description	RVUs*
71020	Chest X Ray	94.53
76700	Echo Exam of Abdomen	29.25
76090	Mammogram, Both Breasts	17.84
76805	Echo Exam of Pregnant Uterus	17.38
76091	Mammogram, Both Breasts	5.14

General Surgery (49.170 FTEs)

CPT-4 CODE	Description	RVUs*
19120	Removal of Breast Lesion	22.97
49505	Repair Inguinal Hernia	22.42
99212	Office/Outpatient Visit, Est.	18.11
44140	Partial Removal of Colon	14.47
19240	Removal of Breast	13.82

TABLE 6.10 (continued)

Hematology/Oncology (41.1 FTEs)

CPT-4 CODE	Description	RVUs*
99214	Office/Outpatient Visit, Est.	61.89
99213	Office/Outpatient Visit, Est.	51.35
96410	Chemotherapy, Infusion Method	30.33
99215	Office/Outpatient Visit, Est.	18.79
99231	Subsequent Hospital Care	13.86

OB/Gyn (62 FTEs)

CPT-4 CODE	Description	RVUs*
59400	Obstetrical Care	313.54
59510	Cesarean Delivery	101.57
59410	Obstetrical Care	90.63
99213	Office/Outpatient Visit, Est.	71.66
59515	Cesarean Delivery	53.83

Orthopedic Surgery (89.397 FTEs)

CPT-4 CODE	Description	RVUs*
27447	Total Knee Replacement	76.05
29881	Knee Arthroscopy/Surgery	65.16
27130	Total Hip Replacement	46.61
29877	Knee Arthroscopy Surgery	26.68
63047	Removal of Spinal Lamina	17.13

Internal Medicine (203.5 FTEs)

CPT-4 CODE	Description	RVUs*
99213	Office/Outpatient Visit, Est.	83.41
99215	Office/Outpatient Visit, Est.	29.06
99212	Office/Outpatient Visit, Est.	28.68
99232	Subsequent Hospital Care	12.29
71020	Chest X Ray	7.93

Ophthalmology (28.8 FTEs)

CPT-4 CODE	Description	RVUs*
66984	Remove Cataract, Insert Lens	235.78
92014	Eye Exam and Treatment	88.75
99213	Office/Outpatient Visit, Est.	51.76
67210	Treatment of Retinal Lesion	39.15
99202	Office/Outpatient Visit, New	4.18

Pediatrics (80.44 FTEs)**

CPT-4 CODE	Description	RVUs*
99213	Office/Outpatient Visit, Est.	97.31
99212	Office/Outpatient Visit, Est.	63.97
99214	Office/Outpatient Visit, Est.	7.95
99203	Office/Outpatient Visit, New	4.42
99202	Office/Outpatient Visit, New	3.53

Source: Reprinted with permission from the Medical Group Management Association. CRAHCA Physician Services Practice Analysis Comparison: 1993 Medians. Author: Englewood, CO, 1994.
* Represents mean RVU per FTE physician per month.
** Pediatrics excludes subspecialty pediatrics such as pulmonology, neurology, gastroenterology, and endocrinology.

FIGURE 6.1. Procedure Code Profile—Internal Medicine

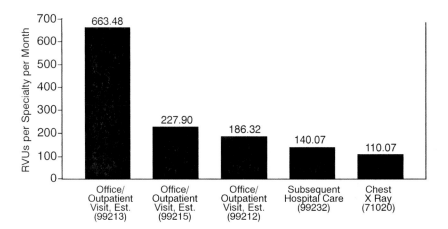

Source: Reprinted with permission from Medical Group Management Association. *CRAHCA Physician Services Practice Analysis Comparison: 1993 Medians.* Author: Englewood, CO, 1994.

month (76.05 divided by 53.35, or 53.35 multiplied by 1.43). The conclusion to be drawn is that knee replacements consume large amounts of resources in orthopedic physicians' work and overhead. For pediatricians, the top procedure by RVU in that specialty is an outpatient office visit with an established patient, consuming 97.31 RVUs per physician per month—just under one hundred occurrences of this procedure. Each office visit has a low relative value, as published in the federal schedule, but their high frequency indicates that these procedures consume a large amount of resources for this specialty.

Production Trends Used to Calculate RVUs per FTE Physician

The frequencies and total numbers of procedures/encounters performed in group practices are used to determine the total RVUs, RVUs per specialist, and RVUs per procedure. Table 6.11 shows, for each specialty, the percentages of total encounters or procedures for the ten most common types of office visits. Sixty-two percent of total encounters and procedures for family group practices were reported among these ten office outpatient procedures. Conversely, 38 percent of total encounters for family group

TABLE 6.11. Procedure Frequency per Specialist per Month*

CPT-4 CODE	Invasive Cardiology (30.17 FTEs)			Noninvasive Cardiology (29.83 FTEs)			Family Practice (115.113 FTEs)		
	Freq/Mo/FTE	% of Total	% Freq.	Freq/Mo/FTE	% of Total	% Freq.	Freq/Mo/FTE	% of Total	% Freq.
99201	0.17	—	0.2	0.53	0.033	0.5	2.99	0.338	1.0
99202	0.44	—	0.5	0.53	0.100	0.5	8.74	1.477	2.9
99203	1.41	0.184	1.7	0.73	0.133	0.7	4.50	0.963	1.5
99204	1.97	0.287	2.4	1.30	0.077	1.2	1.70	0.318	0.6
99205	2.43	0.436	3.1	2.21	0.398	2.1	.74	0.139	0.2
99211	1.32	0.218	1.6	4.64	0.387	4.4	5.51	0.791	1.8
99212	14.76	1.298	18.1	8.24	1.051	7.7	100.11	22.391	33.7
99213	39.92	8.648	48.3	56.17	6.193	52.7	140.09	29.364	47.2
99214	17.77	2.458	21.8	25.64	2.356	24.0	22.87	3.676	7.7
99215	1.79	0.149	2.3	6.56	0.310	6.2	9.74	2.233	3.3

CPT-4 CODE	General Surgery (49.17 FTEs)			Hematology & Oncology (41.1 FTEs)			DEFINITIONS OF CPT-4 CODES
	Freq/Mo/FTE	% of Total	% Freq.	Freq/Mo/FTE	% of Total	% Freq.	
99201	3.02	0.716	3.4	0.12	0.048	0.1	99201: Office/outpatient visit, new, Level 1
99202	3.50	0.822	3.9	0.63	0.038	0.5	99202: Office/outpatient visit, new, Level 2
99203	1.29	0.464	1.5	1.73	0.143	1.2	99203: Office/outpatient visit, new, Level 3
99204	0.27	0.063	0.3	1.18	0.248	0.9	99204: Office/outpatient visit, new, Level 4
99205	0.29	0.084	0.3	1.04	0.153	0.7	99205: Office/outpatient visit, new, Level 5
99211	24.25	3.708	27.5	18.63	2.177	13.4	99211: Office/outpatient visit, established patient, Level 1
99212	30.89	9.671	34.9	13.97	0.831	10.0	99212: Office/outpatient visit, established patient, Level 2
99213	22.30	5.394	25.2	52.94	6.532	38.0	99213: Office/outpatient visit, established patient, Level 3
99214	2.19	0.211	2.5	41.26	8.146	29.6	99214: Office/outpatient visit, established patient, Level 4
99215	0.41	0.042	0.5	7.93	1.776	5.6	99215: Office/outpatient visit, established patient, Level 5

CPT-4 CODE	Internal Medicine (203.5 FTEs)			OB/Gyn (62 FTEs)			Ophthalmology (28.8 FTEs)		
	Freq/Mo/FTE	% of Total	% Freq.	Freq/Mo/FTE	% of Total	% Freq.	Freq/Mo/FTE	% of Total	% Freq.
99201	1.25	0.221	0.7	1.72	0.164	1.1	0.89	0.250	0.9
99202	3.43	0.636	1.9	4.44	0.434	2.8	2.79	0.985	2.9
99203	2.95	0.869	1.7	3.60	0.590	2.3	5.20	1.085	5.5
99204	2.23	0.408	1.2	2.30	0.213	1.5	3.90	0.284	4.2
99205	2.68	0.279	1.5	.55	0.049	0.4	0.07	0.033	0.1
99211	3.62	0.595	2.0	6.99	0.812	4.5	6.45	0.000	6.9
99212	42.18	6.837	23.6	51.45	8.436	32.8	22.51	9.229	23.6
99213	88.74	17.067	49.7	73.87	8.403	47.2	42.24	11.916	44.1
99214	19.13	18.26	10.7	8.49	1.303	5.4	10.19	3.755	10.7
99215	12.26	2.400	6.9	3.22	0.377	2.0	0.92	0.050	1.1

CPT-4 CODE	Orthopedic Surgery (89.397 FTEs)			Pediatrics (80.44 FTEs)**		
	Freq/Mo/FTE	% of Total	% Freq.	Freq/Mo/FTE	% of Total	% Freq.
99201	10.19	0.534	6.0	1.65	0.658	0.7
99202	16.88	4.879	10.2	2.78	0.974	1.2
99203	12.70	1.349	7.7	2.54	0.665	1.6
99204	1.85	0.341	1.2	1.73	0.181	0.8
99205	1.04	0.252	0.7	.36	0.087	0.1
99211	10.39	2.890	6.3	5.93	1.579	2.7
99212	70.45	12.835	42.6	94.08	23.205	43.1
99213	32.04	5.217	19.4	100.32	29.264	46.0
99214	7.59	1.467	4.6	5.30	1.747	2.3
99215	2.19	0.430	1.3	3.32	0.423	1.5

WHAT THIS DATA MEANS

Freq./Mo.: The median number of procedures per physician per month. **Example:** For orthopedic surgery, Procedure 99201 occurred 10.19 times per month per physician.

% of Total: The percentage of all procedures per month. **Example:** For orthopedists, Procedure 99201 occurred 10.19 times and was 0.534% of all procedures for that specialty. This field will not add up to 100%; only the top 10 codes are shown.

% Freq.: The percentage each procedure represents of the 10 procedures shown. **Example:** For orthopedists, of the 10 procedures, 6.0% were office outpatient visits (99201). The percentages add up to 100% for this column.

207

TABLE 6.11 *(continued)*

RVUs per FTE, by Specialty

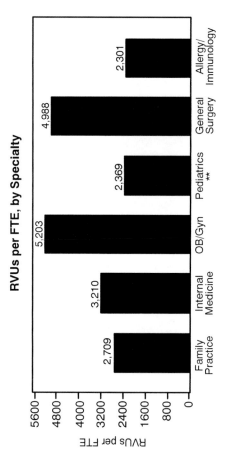

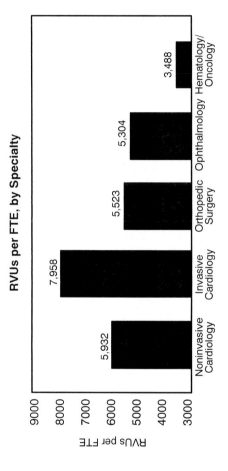

RVUs per FTE, by Specialty

Source: Reprinted with permission from Medical Group Management Association. *CRAHCA Physician Services Practice Analysis Comparison: 1993 Medians.* Author: Englewood, CO, 1994

*   All numbers are medians for all groups for six months, January through June 1993.
** Excludes pediatric subspecialties such as pulmonology, neurology, gastroenterology, and endocrinology.

practices were not codes for office visits. Pediatric group practices experienced a pattern of very high volumes of office visits (59 percent of total procedures). Total RVUs for family practice groups were 26,611.97 for office visits, resulting in 2,709.41 RVUs per FTE physician. (Some data are not shown.)

Groups Can Use RVUs per FTE to Compare Their Productivity

Total RVUs for each specialty comprise the frequency per month for each procedure or office visit and the total FTEs in each specialty. The total RVUs for a group practice are indicators of the complexity of procedures and of case intensities. Case intensity is a measure of the difficulty of a patient's case and of multiple problems. This explains why the RVUs per FTE physician of 7,958 RVUs for invasive cardiologists are so much higher than the 2,709 RVUs per FTE for family practitioners. The conclusion to be drawn is that cardiologic procedures are roughly three times as complex as procedures in family practice.

Combining Fee-for-Service and Staff Model HMO Cardiology Practices Using Benchmark Information to Address Compensation Issues

Flexibility to judge physician performance will become extremely important as various groups determine the need to link up. Leverage through larger and broader-based medical groups is inevitable. An example of how a fee-for-service group developed a process to integrate with a staff model HMO follows. For demonstration purposes, one group of specialists, and the process used to address their collective needs, is used for this example. The specialist group is cardiologists:

> Goal: To integrate two different cardiology groups into one. One group is predominately fee for service based and the second group is part of a staff-model HMO.

> Objective: Improve integration, quality of care provided, and physician group practice development. Use compensation-sensitive guideposts throughout the process.

> General Remarks: The first two decision points in this process are (1) to establish operating principles for the compensation plan and (2) to determine which factors should be considered when determining individual compensation (compensation drivers). An integration

committee composed of cardiologists had the task of recommending operating principles.

Guideposts were derived through analysis of a specialty-by-specialty breakdown of base and total compensation, as well as comparisons of compensation and productivity, by specialty, to market benchmarks. Information sources included a twenty-five-clinic survey and an MGMA annual survey, as well as estimates for bonus redistribution to bring all physicians in line with, or equal to, market benchmarks. This preliminary information was reviewed with senior management and the cardiology integration committee to determine the most appropriate variables and comparison benchmarks.

Example of Operating Principles

The objective of the cardiology compensation committee was to develop a common compensation plan that met the needs of the integrated group:

1. Compensate physicians for the work effort and value they bring to the Cardiology group and through "equal pay for equal work."
   * the compensation strategy was based on group performance and team accomplishments, but also recognized outstanding individual contribution.
2. Provide market competitive compensation for work that will allow the group to retain and recruit high-caliber individuals.
3. Facilitate operations integration and appropriate coverage for all work activities by coordinating professional effort and encouraging collaboration among physicians. The compensation plan contribution measurements will support:
   * coordination of professional effort (collegial practice) that results in operations integration for cardiology services,
   * high-quality and efficient patient care for health plan and community patients,
   * medical best-practices development activities and preventive care,
   * medical education and research, and
   * efforts that produce business growth and market share retention.
4. Contribution measurements will include both quantitative and qualitative factors, and performance will be communicated formally to each individual by the program director.
5. The compensation plan was flexible to change and responsive to the buyer marketplace.

6. Physician understanding and communication was highly valued during the development and subsequent modifications of the plan. Timely results reporting occurred on an ongoing basis.

These operating principles were used to guide and assess the development of the new group. The next step included the process of describing and prioritizing the factors used to determine individual compensation within the combined group. The collection of this information and feedback from management on factors critical to business success were combined to develop the criteria to guide physician compensation.

Example of Survey Used to Solicit Physician Input
on Both Definitions and Priority Factors

Cardiology Compensation Plan Development
Valued Activities and Compensation Drivers Survey

From time to time throughout the compensation plan development process, we will request your thoughts and creative ideas on various issues critical to plan development. At this time, we are requesting you to provide both a prioritized listing of currently valued professional activities as well as creative ideas about other, not traditionally measured, activities or characteristics that reflect an individual's or group's contribution to the professional practice. Space is provided on the following page to list or describe five ideas for the three questions listed below. We expect this effort to take you approximately ten minutes to complete. We appreciate your time and effort in responding to these requests on this important project.

Realizing that physicians contribute to the operations and success of professional practices in many different ways:

1. Please list and prioritize the five most important factors you would consider when determining individual compensation levels.
   Examples: 1. Patient care access
   2. Tenure
2. What activities or characteristics, not traditionally measured, best determine an individual physician's contribution to the group practice?
   Examples: 1. Communication with patients and colleagues
   2. Staff or colleague training
3. Which work activities do you believe will be critical to the clinical and business success of the combined cardiology practice?
   Examples: 1. Cost performance improvement initiatives
   2. Medical best-practices development

Sample Results of Cardiologist Responses

(Those responses that supported the integration of the two groups, quality of patient care, and the successful development of a unified medical practice, were valued/weighted at a higher level.)

Valued Activities and Compensation Drivers Survey Results

Number of Surveys	Weighted Number of Surveys	**Compensation Drivers**
7	31	• Clinical Work Load/Work Effort/Productivity (amount of call time)
5	18	• Seniority/Tenure (commitment to the organization)
4	14	• Prior Training or Special Skills
4	14	• Consumer and Customer Satisfaction (primary care physicians and patient evaluations)
3	7	• Administrative and Other Nonclinical Responsibilities
2	7	• Peer Evaluations
2	6	• Ability to Collaborate (flexibility, willingness to adapt)
2	6	• Ability to Problem Solve and Be Part of Team Problem Solving
1	5	• Accountability in the Delivery of Outstanding Service
1	3	• Recruitment of Business (from primary care and outside)
1	2	• Program and Practice Development
1	1	• Leadership

Number of Surveys	Weighted Number of Surveys	**Contribution to the Group Practice**
4	19	• Availability/Accessibility
4	17	• Referring Physician Satisfaction
5	16	• Collegiality/Teamwork
3	13	• Quality of Care Delivered
4	13	• Diversity of Skills
3	9	• Administrative Contribution
2	6	• Patient Satisfaction
1	3	• Outreach/Business Growth
1	3	• Continuing Education and Advancement of Skills
1	1	• Continuing Education Delivered to Group
1	1	• Research Accomplishments
1	1	• Leadership

Number of Surveys	Weighted Number of Surveys	Clinical and Business Success Factors for the Institute
6	20	• Community and Primary Care Physician Recognition of Cardiovascular Excellence
4	14	• Communication, Support, and Service to Primary Care Physicians
3	12	• Outreach/Business Growth
3	12	• Teamwork and Collaboration
3	11	• Successful Cardiac Surgery Program
2	8	• Development of New Programs (electrophysiology, nuclear cardiology)
3	7	• Cardiovascular Administration and Leadership
2	6	• High-Quality Patient Care
2	5	• Timely Response for Consultations and Procedures
2	4	• Seamless Medical Information Systems Between Sites
3	4	• Lean Cost Structure
1	4	• Demonstrated Value to the Organization and Consumers
2	3	• Development and Adherence to Medical Guidelines

Work Activities Summary

Patient Care:

Inpatient
- Consultations
- Rounding
- Call and Call Backup
- Cardiac Care Patient Management and Follow-up
- Patient and Family Counseling/Education

Outpatient/Outreach
- Consultations
- Clinics
- Outreach Hospitals and Clinics
- Pacemaker Follow-up
- Patient and Family Counseling/Education

Noninvasive Cardiology
- Electrocardiography (EKGs/ECGs)
- Echocardiography (Echos)
- Cardioversion

- Treadmill Exercise Tests (TMTs)
- Holter Monitors
- Nuclear Cardiology

Invasive Cardiology

- Cath Lab—Diagnostic
- Cath Lab—Interventional (balloons, atherectomy, stents)
- Pacemaker Implantations (permanent and temporary)
- RV Biopsy
- IABP Placement
- Pericardiocentesis

Administrative/Program Development:

- Program Chairmanships/Directors
  1. Cardiovascular Services
  2. Nuclear Cardiology
  3. RN TMT Clinics and RNs as Clinicians
  4. CCU, PCCU, Cardiac Rehab, Cath Lab, Cardiovascular Research, Cardiology Outreach Directorships
- Committee Memberships
  1. Clinical Quality Committees (QA, CQI)
  2. Critical Care Committee
  3. PreOP Evaluation Committee
  4. Cardiac Arrest Committee
- Guideline Development
  1. Chest Pain Guidelines
  2. Acute MI Guidelines
  3. Emergency Chest Pain Clinical Pathway Development
  4. Lipid Screening Guideline
- Coronary Care Unit Liason
- Cath Lab Liason
- Department/Section Administration

Teaching:

- Interaction with and Supervision of Fellows, Residents, and Students
- Clinical Associate Professorships
- Scheduling and Coordinating Cardiology Fellows and Residents
- Developing Fellowship and Resident Programs
- Perform Entrance and Exit Interviews and Evaluations for Fellows, Residents and Students

- ACLS Lectures
- Other Occasional Lectures
- Reviewer (Journal of the American College of Cardiology, Journal of Catheritization and Cardiovascular Diagnosis)

Research:

- Atherectomy Data Collection
- Pulmonary Artery Wedge Pressure During Angioplasty
- Women's Health Initiative
- Hormone Replacement Study
- CARDIA Study—Echo Support
- CARS Study—Coumadin and Aspirin Reinfarction Study
- VA Digoxin Investigation Group

Source: Sommers, P. A. Internal study. Health Partners/Ramsey Clinic. St. Paul/Minneapolis, MN, 1995-1996.

Benchmarking As a Bridge from Patient to Provider to Payer

During the 1998 Chicago-based MGMA/Northwestern University's J. L. Kellogg Graduate School of Management Conference on Value enhancements in Medical Groups Through Benchmarking Systems, the focus turned back to the development of patient-centered care systems. David Nahrwold, President and CEO, Northwestern Medical Faculty Foundation, stated that health care's fundamental problem is that the system is disconnected—the patient does not pay the physician, does not define quality, and does not measure quality.[12] In other industries, as Nahrwold noted, the consumer pays for the service or product and judges its value. Health care providers must connect patient care, service, and payment to excellence at every level.

Health care providers must be able to proactively link care and service to each patient's defined needs. System functions require alignment—from appointment scheduling to parking; from waiting time to temperature of the exam room and friendliness of staff; from diagnosis to effective treatment; from the billing process to final account resolution; and from answering all the patient's questions to responding to questions from interested family members. Measurement of results related to each function provides benchmarks for both individual patient and medical group system management. Simultaneously, the information can be used to identify practice aspects that can benefit from continuous improvement enhancements.

Once the fear of measurement has been overcome and providers begin to use benchmarking as a continuous improvement tool to help manage the patient care and service process, a shift from trust-based accountability to evidence-based accountability will take place, according to Stephan Shortell, another conference speaker.[12] Measurement is a process to be used by providers for identifying progress (or lack thereof) along the patient care continuum in the direction of healthy outcomes.

FORECASTING/PREDICTING OUTCOMES: THE INFERENTIAL EVALUATION MODEL (IEM)

Survival in the contemporary practice of medicine will depend upon:

1. physicians' ability to adapt to less reimbursement for services provided;
2. consideration of the need to develop an increasingly larger base of patients served;
3. the ability to remain or to become proactively customer-oriented to attract and keep new patients; and
4. the development of strong linkages with sources who refer patients.

Thriving will require all the things necessary for survival and then some. To thrive, physicians will need to:

1. broaden their base of resources, both financial and programmatic;
2. reduce unnecessary expenses incurred by their practice;
3. avoid duplication of services and expenditures; and
4. improve operations.

Managers can provide an essential service by helping the medical staff orchestrate a contemporary practice. Such help will require minimizing the effect of adverse market conditions and maximizing the benefits of trends in reimbursement and in capabilities for delivering services, while adjusting to shifts in the practice's share of the potential market and seeking out opportunities to provide new and/or expanded services to that market.

As resources continue to become even more scarce, managers must be able to conduct the business of medicine more proactively, with an eye on future requirements and probable changes in the market, while simultaneously taking advantage of current and past results associated with the practice. A solution to this complex problem does not exist in a vacuum, nor can it be identified by focusing independently on what are perceived to be the most important elements currently related to a successful medical practice. Instead, what is needed is a technology of evaluation for use by providers of medical services; such technology must appropriately consider the simultaneous effects of important indicators of success in the practice, including financial elements, enabling those providing the services to maximize their abilities to meet their current and future goals and missions.[8,13]

In the practical sense (operations), the role of evaluation in the process of management is a matter of technique. An event occurs, and a record is made of its effects. Careful study and statistical analysis of that record generates quantifiable statements that can serve as inferential indicators which lead to explanations, interpretations, generalizations, predictions, and decisions. Statistical analysis is used to understand and reduce variation for purposes of improving performance.[14] In the theoretical sense (reasoning), evaluation is a matter of using concepts, conceptual systems, constructs, models, and theories. An event can be most accurately studied if those who manage can delineate questions meaningful to the practice as a business, in measurable terms and comprehensive enough to explore all plausible aspects of each problem thoroughly. Such questions require the identification of key concepts or generative ideas that can lead and guide the techniques to be used. Thus, evaluation can be thought of as bringing together conceptual systems (at the theoretical level) and useful techniques (at the level of practical operations).[13]

Many factors may account for the theoretical relationships underlying the practical acts of doing something. To ask or answer questions involving complex relationships and numerous factors, however, necessitates an approach that is suited to considering simultaneously occurring events and activities. If one focuses on a specific relationship, it is apparent that many of the factors theoretically relevant to the concerns of a manager are randomized, when only one or two elements are examined. We may seem to recognize complexities regarding factors that affect the delivery of medical services and operations, but we often fail to conduct analyses that adequately reflect the combined effects of the many elements responsible for the complexities.

Where change in the targeted populations to be provided medical services is rapid and continuous, managers must apply cutting-edge technology to maximize the efficient and effective provision of services.[15,16] As one window of opportunity closes during turbulent times, others will be opening to those leaders in the provision of medical services who are ready to take advantage of the marketplace. The time has come to expand one's thinking about how to address the amalgamation of defined needs and the provision of services proactively. The proactive thought process opens one's mind to the use of multivariate thinking and inferential technology, which can enhance the management of systems for the provision of medical services.[13] Surviving and, more important, thriving as contemporary providers of medical services will require continuous attention to the factors that account for change in the health care delivery systems. It will also require determination of how, when, and to what degree the effects of those changes will hinder and/or enhance their provision of these services.

Why Inferential Management

Since a successful medical practice is based upon the appropriate mix of elements of service and needs for health care in the market to which services are provided, it is necessary to determine both the influence of market conditions on the provision of medical services and the influence upon each other of interactive services and needs.[14] The documented relationships found between and among activity indicators and outcomes are analyzed to determine the degree or inference of the relationship.[17,18,19,20] Some relationships are more important than others in accounting for successful practices. Characteristics to be considered concurrently include, but need not be limited to, the following:

- Operational elements of the practice and services provided, for example:

  1. Shifts in volume (number of patients seen)
  2. Trends in types and timing of clinical activity,
  3. Systems for services providing information to management, medical records, functions of the business office, and communications with patients, to continuously improve quality of outcome
  4. Ratings of consumer satisfaction and other factors

- Changes in the market, for example (to give only three examples among many):

  1. A competitor moves in across the street from your practice and your practice loses 10 percent of its patients seen for primary care.
  2. A business for which your practice has been providing services related to workers' compensation leaves the area and your income from operations decreases 7 percent.
  3. A health care purchasing alliance invites your group to bid on providing capitated health care to the employees of the companies the alliance represents (many of which reside in your area of patient catchment).

- Financial indicators, for example (three of many):

  1. A new 2 percent state tax is assessed against your net revenues.
  2. Your practice is asked by the HMO from which a majority of your patients come to accept bigger discounts (from 20 percent to 30 percent of billed charges).
  3. The resource-based relative value scale (RBRVS) and Medicare reimburse even less than what was in the budget (budget reflected a 13 percent decrease while actual is 18 percent.

- Longitudinal/historical trends and statistically significant changes associated with any important characteristic of your medical practice and/or the hospital(s) where the physicians admit patients
- Demographic shifts within the area of patient catchment that change the composition of the basic population of patients for your primary and referral practice

Multivariate thinking provides managers with an opportunity to consider the role of many factors upon the success—or lack thereof—of the medical practice or of one or more medical services, and also the role of significant elements of the practice, for example:

1. Income from operations
2. Referrals
3. Visits for ambulatory care and admissions to the hospital
4. Overhead expenses
5. Customer satisfaction and other quantifiable factors

Both descriptive and inferential statistics are helpful in illustrating results and relationships that help to understand and reduce variation for purposes of improving performance.[16,17] Descriptive statistics are typically utilized in charts and graphs and include discussion about measures of central tendency (e.g., mean, mode, and median) and about variability (e.g., range, standard deviation, and variance). Inferential statistics yield quantities that are interpreted along the baseline of a distribution of statistical probability. The findings allow for conclusions to be drawn from sampled data and generalized toward defined groups of the population. Inferential statistics are characterized by statistical significance, which illustrates (by a level of probability) a significant departure from what might be expected by chance alone.[18,19]

An individual uses descriptive statistics to talk about the data he or she has. With inferential statistics, an individual can discuss data that he or she does not have, for example, "What do I need to know about today's practice that will enable me to plan for its future success?" Findings are generalizable (inferable) within limits of probability that permit the projection or prediction of results toward other similar populations. For example, a statistically significant finding at a probability level of 0.05 indicates that 95 times out of 100, the same results would predictably occur again (without attribution to chance).[18]

Application to Systems for Delivering Medical Services

Medicine is replete with information—to some degree, more information than is required to conduct an effective business. A process has been needed to enable medical managers to define, monitor, and influence changes in that information, to maximize the impact of the medical products and services they manage. That process is inferential management, used in conjunction with an established strategic plan (business plan). The plan, which represents a preset, agreed-upon direction for the organization, should be based on specific targets or goals in outcome (so you will know where the practice is meant to go) and on strategies with defined objectives, programs, and services that enable you to know how you plan to get there. The objective of inferential thinking is to take systematic advantage, by reasoning, of what is happening or has happened that is reflected in measurable evidence.

Members of the staff who are responsible for each aspect of the business need to develop related, quantifiable goals/objectives to facilitate the measurement of individual outcomes related to overall organizational efforts. Evaluations of performance, considerations of compensation (including incentives), and promotions of personnel should be based upon desired accomplishments of individuals and of the organization. Formation of the annual budget follows development of the strategic business plan, with rank-ordered consideration of financial support and the support of human resources given toward those programs, services, and activities identifiable in the strategic plan as priorities. Routine review of measurable (inferable) performance according to the plan is critical and necessitates at least quarterly assessment, with a comprehensive, in-depth analysis conducted annually.[1,8]

A dynamic business/strategic plan is one that is receptive to changing conditions in the marketplace and is updated at least annually. The plan remains in a "rolling," dynamic, fluid state that evolves proactively and moves in relationship to changing times. If the plan has embraced the organization's mission, it is likely to remain fairly stable, focusing on what your business expects to do over the long-term future. The mission would be supported by a vision statement outlining organizational hopes and dreams and how those who will benefit from the intended health care service will be affected. To write either a statement of mission or of vision, those in management need to agree on values at the core of their understanding of the organization. A statement of core values would reflect expectations concerning the business: how individuals should consider their role, their style of practice or management as it relates within the organization.

As threats to progress and opportunities for development are identified, inferential evaluation is needed to consider the incorporation of such effects, positive and negative. Attentive management with the necessary tools to address change is important to a dynamic plan. It helps minimize the effects of adversity while maximizing proactive contributions (not reactive). The desired outcome is consensus (agreement within the group) on those strategies, defined by reasoning in association with presenting market conditions, which reflect the commitments of the organization aimed at attaining its desired mission and vision.

Strategies may take various forms and shapes. They need specific definition to address issues concerning the medical practice as a business, while emphasizing its reputation for service, its image, and its superior points of difference from the competition that need to be placed in the minds of its customers. Strategies provide direction for clinical and other revenue-producing supporting departments; they should be opportunistically oriented to take advantage of the marketplace. For example, "Here is a specific opportunity; here is how we will use it." Since it is not possible to fund all strategic initiatives sufficiently, each service or program should be rank ordered on the basis of its measured impact and importance on helping the business achieve success in its overall mission and plan. Financial and human resources should be allocated more richly to the top 20 percent of rank-ordered programs that account for a majority of the success of the organization. Multivariate evaluation, specifically multiple linear regression analysis, is well suited to help rank order factors that are the most important predictors of defined success; this analysis helps determine what elements of service or what business activities account for a majority of the variance associated with indicators of business success.

Once the strategic initiatives and measurable objectives have been specified, inferential methodology can be used to facilitate planning and the alignment of resources with those plans. The method infers forecasted outcomes within statistically significant parameters. Probability of a desired outcome is predicted by calculating the cumulative effects of important historical and financial factors and associated trends, with the desired business outcomes, through applied mathematics.

Model for Inferential Management

The model was initially designed, field-tested, copyrighted, and published by the author in 1971 as an inferential evaluative method.[7] Various applications over the years have demonstrated the utility of the inferential approach, as documented by the references for this chapter. The following general structure illustrates how the model operates:

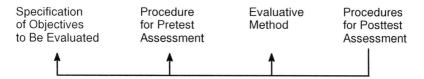

| Specification of Objectives to Be Evaluated | Procedure for Pretest Assessment | Evaluative Method | Procedures for Posttest Assessment |

Specification of Objectives to Be Evaluated

An essential step is the specification of objectives or targets your organization wants to achieve. The process requires a good deal of thought, focusing on those elements which are indicators of business success. Often this is a multiphased process for which it is necessary to understand surveys, studies, and/or financial and historical reviews to specify the objectives or targets of evaluation adequately. Since it is usually impractical and expensive to include in surveys and studies the entire population to be served, techniques for sampling the population and inferential statistics are used to provide results about the population in general. Such techniques are used routinely in political campaigns and election polls; they can accurately forecast ultimate winners from rather small representative samples. If the study or survey identifies a need, managers must establish measurable objectives for exploring the opportunity to serve that need. It is at this point that relatively sophisticated inferential models are most helpful.

When the objectives to be evaluated are identified in quantifiable terms, they serve as benchmarks against which to compare future activity and results. To reduce the risk of a premature evaluation that might assess outcomes before the program has been given a chance to work, or to determine whether there are significant differences before implementing a new service or making changes in an existing program, it is necessary to collect baseline data in advance of introducing elements of change (interventive services or programs). Such information typically includes results of any sampling activity used to gather information about the population in general and historical, financial, and operational data related to the activity or service under study.

Procedures for Pretest Assessment

Prior to instituting a new service or making changes in an existing program, it is important to know as much as possible about the conditions that may influence (or are influencing) success or failure. Steps taken during the pretesting phase include:

1. review of proposed strategies by managers;
2. review of results of existing programs or services, including findings from other institutions that may be appropriate for consideration in current business efforts; and
3. planning of specific procedures, time schedules, and monitoring necessary to implement the strategies.

When a number of strategies are under consideration, multivariate analysis can be applied to illustrate the relative benefits of each, within the limits of probability. This information, in conjunction with data collected during the specification of objectives, is used by managers to select the most parsimonious set of predictors against which to measure the outcomes (achievements) of a program or service.

Information is collected and analyzed to demonstrate relationships between and among elements of the service or program and the objectives evaluated. The pretest findings are used to answer questions such as these:

1. How much of what should be accomplished by the new service, or with changes to an existing service, is already known or desired by the targeted population?
2. Does the population for which the new service or change is intended have the prerequisite behavioral or physical capacity, and/or do they need to benefit from the activity?

Answers to such questions will help managers structure an evaluation that can focus on the service delivered or the change in a program or system and help them understand the effects of preintervention differences in need or readiness between individuals served and groups served. Pretesting attempts to identify bias and other factors that can potentially influence posttest results. Once pretest influences have been identified, it is important to understand the potential problems they might cause and to eliminate those causes or control their impacts on outcomes. Most important, it is essential to identify and control each known biasing factor in advance of the introduction of a new service, program, or system (intervention) to promote a valid evaluative process. This step will keep the focus on the interventions being considered, not the patients or groups of patients.

Managers require accurate information about the state of affairs surrounding the objectives to be evaluated prior to implementing a new or modified service. Following attention to adequate safeguards and the implementation of proposed changes, it is then important to monitor data reflecting the new outcomes. This type of information monitoring is essential as a base for decisions on the maintenance, further modification, or discontinuation of an ongoing program or service.

Evaluative Method

Forecasting procedures can help reflect in statistics the complexities of systems for the provision of medical services that can benefit from data-based evaluation to provide reliable conclusions. A multifaceted question requires a multifaceted methodological approach to achieve an appropriate solution. Multivariate analysis was selected as the basic statistical method of this model of inferential evaluation. It enables managers to delineate, assess, and draw inferences from the conclusions about performance in the program or service from a multifaceted domain.

Multivariate analysis assumes that performance, behavior, or any desired outcome is subject to the influence of more than one variable or condition at a time and that adequate explanation involves more than a single variable or condition. If several variables are proposed as relevant to the outcome, it becomes necessary to measure both the influence of each variable on the targeted outcome or service and their influence upon each other. Multivariate analysis allows administrators to reflect such complexities in the process of management and adds the dimension of predicting future outcomes from past events. The power of forecasting as a tool for management resides in the fact that such benchmarks enable rigorous testing of the adequacy of various trends in the business systems—historical, financial, and operational—affecting the outcome of programs and the results of delivery of services, while predicting the necessary combination of elements accounting for the achievement of predetermined targets (objectives) of the practice as a business.

Procedures for Posttest Assessment

Procedures for posttest assessment (assessment after the evaluative monitoring and predictions) are used to determine if, and to what extent, the specified objectives and targeted outcomes of the medical service have been reached. New business activity, and any service units with an increased allocation of financial and/or human resources, are assessed to determine whether there are any differences between relevant data collected from pretest assessments to posttest assessments. Posttest assessment measures progress toward achievement of defined objectives (the extent of difference within the limits of probability), direction and degree of inference, and predictability of results. Evidence is reviewed to determine whether the business components are performing as expected and what refinements are needed.

It is important to screen the information being collected to detect defects in procedural design and in the process of implementing the service. The purpose of such exchange of information is to monitor the procedures for collecting data and to document the observable effects, not only at the end of the evaluative cycle but throughout the process, to identify potential problems and to correct the operation of systems for delivering the service, as needed. A dynamic, continuously self-improving business system is the desired outcome. The inferential evaluative approach embraces an outcome-based method for continuous enhancement of a medical practice, incorporating improvements when they are called for as a way of doing business. W. Edwards Deming summed it up as follows: the message for management about statistical analysis can be condensed to just a few words—it all has to do with reducing variation.[13]

In summary, the success of an effective business system will ultimately depend on the following:

1. Devising quantitative, operationally defined objectives to be evaluated
2. Before the intervention—new approach—begins, establishing and measuring specific baseline criteria associated with the desired outcomes
3. After the intervention has occurred, comparing subsequent achievement with the predetermined expectations and standards of service
4. Drawing conclusions from the new outcomes that enable the organization to improve, expand, realign resources (financial, human), *or* terminate features of the new service or program, in part or totally

Examples of Applications: How to Apply, Interpret, and Draw Conclusions

The following series of examples illustrates ways and means to apply multivariate and inferential management to the provision of medical services. The four stages of the Inferential Evaluation Model (IEM) have been considered in each example:

1. Objectives to be evaluated have been specified in each case.
2. The status of the environment or targeted population has been

preassessed and defined and quantifiable targeted measures developed.

3. Evaluative method has been selected to measure outcomes and reflect the effects that the service or program has on targeted services, financial results, and/or groups of patients.

4. Desired quantifiable results have been determined for purposes of developing conclusions leading to recommendations for improvement, expansion, and/or other changes.

This section presents examples that illustrate the usefulness of the inferential approach. The various examples illustrate different medical services and managerial settings for which application of the procedures has proven its usefulness.

Points to Keep in Mind As Each Example is Reviewed

What is inferential evaluation? It is a process used to evaluate sources of information and to determine their related values toward the accurate prediction of a defined target. The goal is to identify the predictive indicators for each desired target. Resources are then applied to the key indicators to enhance their impact while eliminating nonproductive/undesirable effects.

Example Definitions

Information	Outcome	Predictor	Resources
• volumes	• new customers	• motif	• human resources
• perceptions	• return customers	• income level	• capital
• attitudes	• net revenue	• age	• operations
• demographics	• staff turnover	• sex	• cash
• financials	• quality product	• distance from service	
• past trends	• highly satisfactory service	• perceptions	
	• exemplary experience	• perceptual expectations	
		• attitudes	
		• feelings	
		• habits	

How is information interpreted and applied? The method infers predictable outcomes within statistically significant parameters. The probability of achieving a desired target outcome is predicted by calculating the cumulative effects of information/factors important to the target.

What are expected results? Desired outcomes will be matched with practice elements required to achieve those outcomes:

1. Increased consumer satisfaction and net revenue, increased market share, increase in new customers, reduction in rate of turnover of customers, and so forth.

2. Elimination of nonproductive/undesirable elements in the practice, with reallocation of expenses toward the creation of priority outcomes.

Example 1

Marshfield Clinic, Marshfield, Wisconsin[21]
Number of Physicians: 400 (1993 MGMA Directory)
Number of employees: 2,730 (1993 MGMA Directory)
Founded: 1916
Type of Group: Multispecialty

Objectives to be evaluated. Determine the level of consumer satisfaction among patients, parents, case coordinators, and sources who refer concerning medical and health care services provided. Also, determine what factors were most important to their current satisfaction and predicted future satisfaction.

Procedures for pretest assessment. Baseline measurement of consumer satisfaction was documented after the first six months of service and thereafter at six-month intervals throughout the cycle studied.

Evaluative method. Multivariate analysis (specifically, multiple linear regression) was used to predict the importance to consumers of various activities of medical service provided them. Analysis of variance (ANOVA) was the inferential method used to describe statistical changes over the course of the study.

Procedures for posttest assessment. Longitudinal assessment was used to determine the stability of consumer satisfaction across multiple elements of service. Five evaluative intervals were measured between July 1, 1975 and February 1, 1978, with the total number of cases (N) being 402. The most important factors related to overall satisfaction as rank ordered by parents included (1) opportunity to ask questions, (2) clarity of medical findings, (3) ease of scheduling appointments, and (4) progress made since medical intervention. The most important factors related to overall satisfaction for case coordinators were how helpful medical findings were in determining specific educational activities for the child and how well medical staff answered questions based upon the child's clinic visit.

Example 2

Gundersen Clinic, LaCrosse, Wisconsin[22]
Number of Physicians: 270 (1993 MGMA Directory)
Number of Employees: 1,200 (1993 MGMA Directory)

Founded: 1919
Type of Group: Multispecialty

Objectives to be evaluated. Validate previous findings (Marshfield study) about consumer satisfaction among patients, parents, case coordinators, and sources who refer, concerning the medical/health care services provided them.

Procedures for pretest assessment. Baseline measurements were provided by the results of the 1980 study.

Evaluative method. Findings from the previous study were validated and expanded. Inferential analyses included multiple linear regression analysis, analysis of variance, and a matched-pair analysis of responses to similar questions on both questionnaires/surveys (to patients and parents, and to case coordinators and sources who refer).

Procedures for posttest assessment. The longitudinal study in Example 1 (Marshfield) was extended from February 1, 1978 to July 31, 1979, adding 152 to the number of cases studied (N = 554). Results from the first analysis (N = 402, from July 1, 1975 to February 1, 1978) were included with the results of the second analysis (N = 152, from February 1, 1978 to July 31, 1979). Statistically significant findings were noted and, as a result of the findings illustrated in the 1980 study, were attributed to changes made in the system for delivering services. Positive gains related to overall satisfaction were noted in all of the case coordinator questions with statistical significance (p = .05) present in eight of ten questions due to focused attention by clinic staff or helping the case coordinators interpret and apply medical information to the child's classroom. A member of clinic staff traveled to the child's school or day care program to complete conversion of medical data into educational program. Parent results centered on two main factors accounting for overall satisfaction: how well medical findings focused on the child's educational needs and having a clinic staff member travel to the child's school to implement medical findings into his or her classroom program in conjunction with teachers.

Example 3

Ramsey Clinic, St. Paul Minnesota[16]
Number of Physicians: 231
Number of Employees: 473
Founded: 1996
Type of Group: Multispecialty

Objectives to be evaluated. Consolidate services given by a group of physicians (Ramsey Clinic) and the hospital receiving a majority of their admissions (St. Paul Ramsey Medical Center) to eliminate duplicated overhead expenses, improve operating efficiencies, and enhance revenues.

Procedures for pretest assessment. Audited financial data, data from the business office, and data on patient volumes prior to consolidation in 1987 were used as baselines, except for measures of outcome (against which to compare performance), which were made from the onset of consolidation (1987). The main focus was on the period of intervention (planned change), measured from 1987 to 1992.

Evaluative method. Basic statistical and inferential longitudinal trend analysis was applied to the data. This included multiple statistical comparisons to analyze the predictability of the results and tests to determine statistically significant trends.

Procedures for posttest assessment. Longitudinal assessment was used to determine the effects of consolidation on the group of physicians over the five-year period. Combined clinic and hospital net revenue was a predetermined success factor. The top predictors of combined net revenue included (1) time (net revenue grew stronger as the clinic-hospital integration proceeded), (2) referrals (new referrals rapidly increased and added significant fee-for-service revenue to both physician group and hospital), (3) physician compensation (the physician turnover rate significantly decreased as compensation increased), and (4) outpatient clinic visits (an increasing outpatient base led to more fee-for-service hospital admissions).

Example 4

Ramsey Clinic, St. Paul, Minnesota[13,17]
Number of Physicians: 231
Number of Employees: 473
Founded: 1966
Type of Group: Multispecialty

Objectives to be evaluated. Physician-hospital organization (PHO) established in 1987 and last measured through 1992 was updated through reevaluation after adding data from 1993 in a continuously refining process of management.

Procedures for pretest assessment. Results from 1993 compared to those from 1992, together with trends of previous six-year period, served as baseline.

Evaluative method. Continuation of previously established longitudinal study. Methods for basic statistical and inferential longitudinal trend analysis were applied to the data.

Procedures for posttest assessment. Methodology for analysis of variance (ANOVA) was used to determine statistical significance of data from 1993 when compared with points of previous data that comprised the longitudinal trend for each defined target in outcome. Best financial outcomes for physician group in its history as a group practice were documented. The hospital also had very good financial performance. The best predictors of combined net revenue included (rank ordered) (1) inpatient days (although average length of stay decreased, the number of patients increased), (2) inpatient referrals (the number of referrals significantly increased [p = .05] leading to more hospital admissions of fee-for-service patients), (3) outpatient clinic visits (number of outpatients increased, expanding overall patient base), (4) physician compensation (compensation increased and physician turnover decreased due to joint clinic-hospital reduction in overhead).

Other Examples

Three additional examples follow, showing how inferential evaluation has been used to benefit management and/or to answer evaluative multidimensional questions.

Example 5:

Public Schools, Mound, Illinois[23]
Number of Children Studied: 52
Type of Service: Special Education District of Southern Illinois

Objectives to be evaluated. Determine whether a test of sensorimotor abilities (the Kinesio-Perceptual Test Battery) could predict racial identity among black and Caucasian students classified as disadvantaged.

Procedures for pretest assessment. Random selection of fifty-two disadvantaged children (twenty-six black, twenty-six white) without severe emotional or neuromuscular problems was made from the population of a rural, public special education district in Southern Illinois to determine whether there were differences, and to what extent, in sensorimotor abilities.

Evaluative method. Following completion of the Kinesio-Perceptual Test Battery by each participant in the study, basic descriptive and inferential statistical procedures were applied to the data. The means, standard deviations, and intercorrelations were obtained. Multiple linear regression analysis was used to predict racial identity.

Procedures for posttest assessment. Scores by black participants were complete to scores by white participants; findings reflected the predictability of race by the test battery in that black participants performed better (p = .001). The information could be further evaluated as an alternative diagnostic and training opportunity to improve the learning capabilities of black children. It should be noted, however, that the regression analysis was not cross-validated in this study; that would be required, before results could be generalized to another population.

Example 6

> Bowen Children's Center, Harrisburg, Illinois; Mound, Illinois, Schools[24]
> Number of Children Studied: 120
> Type of Service: Residence for Mentally Retarded Children; Public Schools

Objectives to be evaluated. Determine whether a test of sensorimotor abilities (the Kinesio-Perceptual Test Battery or KPT) could predict IQ among children in a residence for the mentally retarded.

Procedures for pretest assessment. To determine the usefulness of some commonly measured kinesio-perceptual abilities in predicting IQ, 120 children (67 boys, 53 girls) were randomly selected from a total population of 230 at a state residential center for the mentally retarded in southern Illinois.

Evaluative method. Following completion of the Kinesio-Perceptual Test Battery by each participant in the study, basic descriptive and inferential statistical procedures were applied to the data. Statistical estimates of objectivity, Hoyt's analysis of variance, and test/retest reliability were calculated. Multiple linear regression analysis was used to predict IQ.

Procedures for posttest assessment. Scores made by participants on selected items on the Kinesio-Perceptual Test were related to their IQ. This correlation was found to be statistically significant (p = .001). Unlike other perceptual motor tests reflecting developmental growth patterns, the selected KPT items appear to be indicators of intelligence within this group of retarded children. This information could be used to supplement a diagnostic battery, providing a different type of measure that might offer a direct remedial opportunity to help the retarded to learn. The regression analysis, however, was not cross-validated, which would be necessary before findings could be generalized to another population.

Example 7

> Bowen Children's Center, Harrisburg, Illinois; Mound, Illinois, Schools[25]

Number of Children Studied: 120
Type of Service: Residence for Mentally Retarded Children;
Public Schools

Objectives to be evaluated. Determine whether a test of sensorimotor abilities (the Kinesio-Perceptual Test Battery) can reliably differentiate among those who need remediation and those who do not.

Procedures for pretest assessment. At a state residential center for the mentally retarded in southern Illinois, 120 randomly selected children were given the Kinesio-Perceptual Test Battery. A second random sample of 105 children from a public school was used to cross-validate the findings.

Evaluative method. Descriptive and inferential statistical analyses were applied to the data. Measures of interobserver reliability and estimates of stability were obtained, in addition to predictive validity achieved by application of multiple linear regression analysis.

Procedures for posttest assessment. Cross-validation procedures were applied to the scores of both samples, from the state residential center and from the public school district. None of the cross-validated findings were determined to be significantly greater than zero. Such a result cautions against generalizing the findings beyond the parameters of the population on which the validity studies were conducted. Further application of the Kinesio-Perceptual Test Battery is required before more meaningful interpretations can be made of the data.

ENHANCED DATA SUPPORT METHODOLOGY (EDSM)

EDSM is an integrated point-and-click health care reporting and analysis system developed by Bill Glosemeyer.[26] A menu provides users with hospital, clinic, pharmacy, and enrollment data by specific hospital, clinic, or employer group, or overall. Five levels of drill down are provided. Standardized reports are available through a reporting window. The system integrates EIS drill down and graphic capabilities, quality control, forecasting, and query capabilities. Data are refreshed by a monthly download from mainframe DB2 tables. Data are also imported from other external databases and spreadsheets. The system utilizes various software options, for example, Base, SQL, Access, Graph, AF, SCF, EIS, Quality Control, ETS, GIS, Insight, OR and Query, Neural Networks, and Warehouse Administrator.

The system is used for practitioner profiling, pricing, network coverage evaluation, disease analysis and management, process control evaluation, utilization analysis, and forecasting. The system is utilized by all levels of employees from senior management to nurses. Thirty-six months of claims data currently compose the actual database.

Background

Health care is undergoing a fundamental change. It is becoming, both perceptually and operationally, a business. To succeed in the healthier marketplace, health care providers must adopt contemporary business operating philosophies. Health care has become a commodity with very tight margins. Only those providers who can deliver a product that meets or exceeds the needs/expectations of its customers at cost-effective prices will continue to succeed.

Resource Allocation/Utilization

Strategic Goal:

Improve the health status of patients and members in a cost-effective/ cost-efficient manner while achieving satisfaction with services provided (to individuals, employer/purchasing groups, and other payers).

As with any business, resources are finite. Health care organizations must work smarter by maximizing the use of technology while simultaneously minimizing the need for additional human resources. The fundamental question is how can the healthier system allocate its finite human/ financial resources to optimize the return on its investment? In part, this need can be addressed via the Inferential Evaluation Model (IEM).[1,13,14] The IEM is an outcomes measurement and management tool that is based upon probability theory. Financial, volume, clinical, service, and utilization information is processed through the model, which identifies needed changes and/or new opportunities to achieve desired outcomes. EDSM is one tool to apply to IEM.

The appropriate and effective utilization of outside vendors is another critical component of future success. Situations may exist in which an outside vendor can provide needed data or information services/products in a cost-effective manner. However, the appropriate utilization of outside vendors requires objective analysis of internal resources and systems. EDSM is a tool that will help the health care system minimize its reliance on outside vendors and optimize the use of information in the conduct of business.

Planning for the Future

The health care system will need to demonstrate the effectiveness of clinical decisions and will not only be a supplier of health plans but also a data service bureau supplying its providers, employer groups, and members with direct access to their data. For example, in addition to an employer group receiving a hard copy report, the system must provide the employer group with a database of its summarized claims and financial data, with the attention drawn to the key elements affecting the group from a positive and/or negative perspective. EDSM can serve as the source of data and as the tool for delivery of key information. In addition to providing data, the system can also become a supplier of customized software, providing customers with the necessary capabilities to analyze their data.

Data versus Information

Current buzzwords are data warehouses and data marts/data stores. Basically, these concepts amount to organizing data via subject versus (in AHS/MHP's case) a claims payment system. Information is data organized in a manner that provides the user with the tools to make informed decisions. Health care organizations typically have an abundance of data, but a dearth of information. The transformation of data into information requires information systems (manual or automated). The next level information system must provide management with timely, direct, easy access to information. EDSM is a tool to help build the foundation of physician, hospital, and/or health plan information systems.

EDSM: Beyond the Next Level—What Is It?

EDSM is a level beyond the basic requirement, providing management with immediate access to information, with the patient/member as the primary benefactor. EDSM is a process that integrates business rules with required decisions. Operating information produced from selected data generated by the health care organization is assembled for analysis, interpretation, and reporting purposes. The strategic plan, annual budget assumptions, key indicators, and other essential elements must be built into the EDSM operating structure. Operating information is processed to answer the questions required, apply decision analysis (based on management input), and provide alternative decisions, with the logic for each decision. After a decision is made, EDSM will show the projected impact. A component of each alternative decision will be the financial, human resource, and member satisfaction impact. For example, if reducing provider reimbursement by 4 percent were a component of an alternative decision, this can be directly translated into the financial impact of this decision. If reducing administrative expenses by 0.05 percent were part of an alternative decision, alternative recommendations would be included. This could include reduction in human resources within a specific area or specific reductions from the annual budget in other areas. As surveys are standardized and consistently applied over time, an understanding of the member impact of management decisions can be determined. With this understanding, the implications of specific management decisions upon members can be projected, and subsequently implemented, to maximize the effects.

EDSM will enable the health care organization to implement statistical process control and to determine if specific processes are in or out of control. As a process, upper and lower limits that the average cost per admission should remain within do exist. As the average cost per admission falls outside these limits, the process needs to be reviewed to see if it is out of control. EDSM will permit the health care organization to determine project costs (dollar and human). The cost of a project/work request will be tracked. Then the question can be asked, "If the project sponsor and/or data requester had to pay for the project/request out of his/her department budget, would he/she think it was a worthwhile investment?"—Did the health care organization receive sufficient value to offset the cost of the information?

EDSM consists of fifteen modules: hospital, clinic, pharmacy, enrollment, reporting, databases, product analysis, process control, executive information system, decision analysis, modeling, geographic information system, query window, graphics, and project management. EDSM is parameter driven, requiring the user to select the products, employer groups, and date range for analysis. Figure 6.2 outlines the flow process.

Definitions of EDSM Modules

Clinic: There are three submodules: clinic summary, clinic specific, and trend analysis (graphic format).
Analysis Variables: patient count, cost, visits, per member per month costs, visits/1000, cost/visit, cost/patient
There are five drill downs: major products, subproducts, clinic, physician, and major diagnostic categories.
Databases: This module consists of disease-specific databases that are subsets of the master database. The databases were constructed for user access (e.g., to develop their own queries). For example, six specific databases were constructed to address strategic clinical priorities (colon cancer, breast cancer, pediatric asthma, pregnancy care, cardiovascular disease,

FIGURE 6.2. EDSM Flow Process

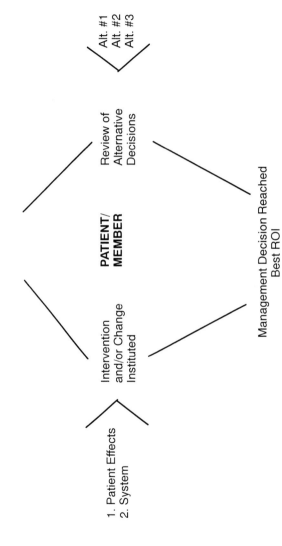

Source: Glosemeyer, B. Enhanced Data Support Methodology (EDSM). Unpublished paper. Burnsville, MN, 1996.

and diabetes). Reporting and analysis of related information for each condition is run against its established database.

Decision Analysis: A module is under development that will be used to show decision makers the impact of their decisions which are based upon experience, data, and intuition. For example, what are the resource implications (human, financial, capital) associated with the most important decisions to be made to achieve each health system strategic target?

Enrollment: There are two submodules: age/sex distribution and monthly enrollment.

Analysis Variables: age, sex, count by month

The analysis consists of an age/sex distribution plot and a monthly enrollment plot over a time period determined by the user.

Executive Information System: The module is utilized by Allina senior management to monitor selected key indicators that reflect the business and operational status of the health system as a whole.

Geographic Information System (GIS): GIS geographically presents the Allina priority databases at the zip code level of analysis across its patient-member catchment area.

Graphics: Graphics interfaces SAS's capabilities for users to develop their own graphic data displays.

Hospital: There are three submodules: hospital summary, hospital specific, and trend analysis (graphic format). The following information is available:

Inpatient Data: patient count, cost, total admissions, number of inpatient days, per member per month costs, cost/day, cost/patient, admissions/1000, days/1000, average length of stay

Outpatient Data: patient count, cost, per member per month costs, visits, visits/1000, cost/visit, cost/patient

There are four drill downs: major products, subproducts, in- or out-patient categories, and major diagnostic categories.

Modeling: This module is utilized to forecast trends on an overall and individual hospital, clinic, and health plan product basis. Forecasts are produced at a summary level and for the major diagnostic categories.

For example, pharmacy information is shown at the summary level and specific therapeutic class. Pharmacy has been the most advanced EDSM application and is in the pilot testing phase with Allina physicians at various clinic locations within the health system.

Pharmacy: There are two submodules: tabular format and graphic format.

Analysis Variables: patient count, prescription count, cost, cost/patient, cost/prescription, average cost/script

There are six drill downs: major products, subproducts, clinic, specialty, physician, and therapeutic class.

Process Control: The purpose of this module is for control chart applications. The analysis identifies random fluctuations or patterns that may indicate that a process is out of control.

Product Analysis: This module combines selected data from the hospital, clinic, pharmacy, and enrollment files and presents the information by product. The drill down consists of product level detail only.

Project Management: This module tracks time and financial expenditures by project. Following the collection of defined data elements, future project time and financial costs are estimated for program planning and budgeting purposes.

Query Window: Users access query windows for ad hoc needs of selected databases represented on the menu.

Reporting: This module consists of reports that are run on a scheduled (monthly, quarterly, semiannual, annual) basis and are parameter driven. The user must specify the date range, employer group numbers, print specifications, and other selection parameters.

EDSM is a closed loop system with interaction and feedback between all parts. No ending point exists since it is a circular flow process. To reach maximum potential, a feedback loop is essential. It will require management feedback. What decision was made and why? How did management reach a specific decision? In addition to EDSM, what other factors were included in the decision-making process? This management decision analysis information will be incorporated into EDSM. Over time, as the management decision analysis database grows, management decision analysis patterns will emerge and be incorporated into future decision analysis. EDSM will learn from management decisions, but only be as good at the data utilized in the process.[22]

MANAGEMENT DECISION PROCESS

Time Frame:	First six months of fiscal year.
Problem:	Medical Trend is running at 5.0 percent. Target is 4.6 percent.
Question:	Is it cost-effective to take corrective actions to lower the medical trend? If so, how can the medical trend be lowered?
Inputs:	
HMO/PPO Databases:	• Utilization is up 5 percent.

- Average cost per procedure is up 3 percent.
- Colon cancer cases are up 10 percent.
- The increase in colon cancer cases will not continue into last six months of fiscal year.

Business Rule:
- Trend cannot exceed target by more than 5 percent.
- Provider reimbursement must remain competitive.

Decision Database:
- Reduce provider fees by 3 percent.
- Reduce administrative expenses by 2 percent.

Strategic Plan:
- Full integration of health care system.
- Optimize distribution of health care providers within specialty across system.

Annual Budget:
- Colon cancer cases will remain consistent with previous year.
- Return on investment target is 1.75 percent.

Surveys:
- Member satisfaction decreases significantly if the health care provider is not included in network.
- Members willing to pay 3 percent more for convenience.

Alternative Decisions:
- Reduce provider fees by 4 percent.
  1. Would save $500,000.
  2. Would make provider fees uncompetitive.
  3. Would result in significant member dissatisfaction.
  ROI Negative
- Reduce administrative expenses by .5 percent.
  1. Would save $100,000.
  2. Would severely hamper ability to meet needs.
  3. Member satisfaction would decrease. Increased delays in clinic/hospital services and/or decrease turnaround in claims payment.

ROI Negative
- Do nothing.
  1. No savings.
  2. Member satisfaction will not be affected.
  3. The number of colon cancer cases are an anomaly. Trend will decrease in last six months.

ROI Neutral

Management Decision: Alternative C
Feedback to decision database
- ROI was neutral.
- Colon cancer cases as a driving factor are an anomaly.
- Appears trend will approach target over remaining six months of fiscal year.
- It is in the best long-term strategic interest of the health system to maintain its current provider network, provider satisfaction level, and member satisfaction level.

PROCESS MAPPING: PHYSICIAN, HOSPITAL, AND HEALTH PLAN BILLING CYCLE REDESIGN

Purpose

To reduce the amount of time between the initial patient encounter and the time the final bill is paid.[27]

Objectives

1. Improve customer service
   - Reduce hassle
   - Increase understanding of cost benefits
2. Enhance information base
3. Reduce administrative costs/overhead
   - Reduce complexity and rework

- Lower accounts receivable
- Reduce processing claims costs

Methods

1. Provide staff and professional support
   - Long-term support required from senior management
   - Staff support for data collection, analysis, logistics, and more
   - Use professionals for coding/transcriptions
2. Increase use of technology
   - E-mail and on-line access
   - Electronic billing, claims, submissions, remits, and payment data
   - ProviderLink
3. Reduce complexity, streamline process
   - Reevaluate billing, contracting, referral processes
   - Eliminate paying ourselves and the associated fees
   - Simplify patient bills

Process mapping was used as a method of initial analysis to determine the current status of billing cycle efficiency for physician's clinics and physician-owned hospitals. The method requires benchmark input with respect to the number of days each component of the billing process should take, from the date of service to the date the bill was settled. Once the desired number of days it should take to resolve a bill has been determined, process mapping analysis compares the days it actually takes.[27]

Figure 6.3 illustrates summarized clinic billing data by each outpatient component involved. In this case, the analysis shows that, from January through October 14, 1996, the actual days numbered forty-eight while the target was thirty-nine days, which yields a nine-day variance. In this case, each day of "accounts receivable" was worth $150,000 or a total of $1,350,000 outstanding. Steps recommended to enhance the collection of the outstanding dollars by billing cycle component is sequentially shown in Figures 6.4 to 6.8. Figures 6.7 and 6.8 show overlap of clinic and hospital billing process.

Hospital experience for the same time interval (January through October 14, 1996) shows a twenty-five-day variance, with each hospital day of accounts receivable worth $500,000 (see Figure 6.9), for a total of $12,500,000 outstanding. Health plan turnaround time from date of service to receipt by claims processing was forty-four days.

FIGURE 6.3. Clinic Billing Process Overview—All Steps

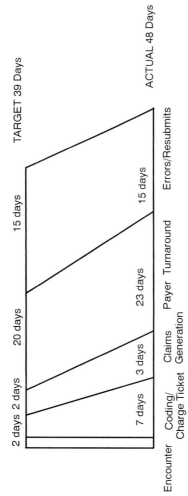

2 days | 2 days | 20 days | 15 days | TARGET 39 Days

7 days | 3 days | 23 days | 15 days | ACTUAL 48 Days

Encounter | Coding/ Charge Ticket | Claims Generation | Payer Turnaround | Errors/Resubmits

Source: Sommers, P. A. and Torgerson, T. Internal study. Allina Health System. Minneapolis, MN, 1997-1998.

FIGURE 6.4. Clinic—Encounter

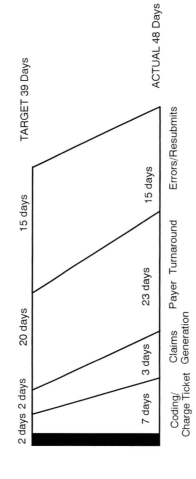

TARGET 39 Days

ACTUAL 48 Days

2 days 2 days   20 days   15 days

7 days   3 days   23 days   15 days

Coding/   Claims   Payer Turnaround   Errors/Resubmits
Charge Ticket   Generation

- Create charge tickets with both the CPT/HCPCS codes and the ICD-9-CM diag-noses codes to allow physician to choose (include top 80 most frequently used codes).
- Collect co-pay prior to providing service.
- Complete charge ticket during and at end of encounter.

Source: Sommers, P. A. and Torgerson, T. Internal study. Allina Health System. Minneapolis, MN, 1997-1998.

FIGURE 6.5. Clinic—Charge Tickets and Health Information

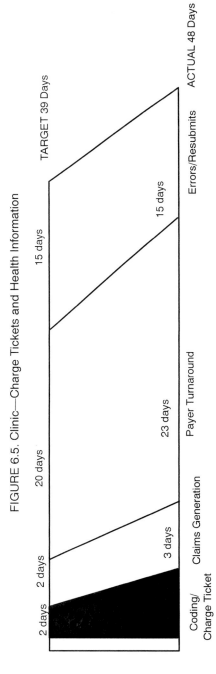

- Providers complete charge ticket at end of encounter; < 24 hour turnaround.
- Create efficient means for physicians to complete record documentation.
- Map how paper flows through your offices. Eliminate the long stay in a physician's office. First priority is to maintain the integrity of the medical record.
- Have a professional coder review and approve your charge tickets annually.
- Have a professional coder provide a quality check on documentation and the resulting charges and codes annually.
- Hire professional staff for coding processing, if possible.
- Process complete and documented billing immediately—no hold period.
- Turnaround transcription with 24 hours—create a variable transcription service—staff up on heavy days; staff down on slow days.
- Consider using transcription staff as other help on staff-down days.
- Prioritize chart completion.

Source: Sommers, P. A. and Torgerson, T. Internal study. Allina Health System. Minneapolis, MN, 1997-1998.

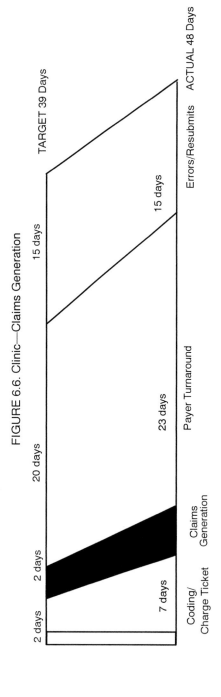

FIGURE 6.6. Clinic—Claims Generation

2 days | 2 days | 20 days | 15 days | TARGET 39 Days

Coding/
Charge Ticket

Claims
Generation

7 days

23 days

15 days

Payer Turnaround

Errors/Resubmits   ACTUAL 48 Days

- Increase number of electronic submissions.
- Track problems with bills requiring correction to focus improvements.
- Reduce bill hold days.
- What percentage of your billing is paper claims? Electronic claims?
- Create communication bridges with key persons in registration and provider staff.

Source: Sommers, P. A. and Torgerson, T. Internal study. Allina Health System. Minneapolis, MN, 1997-1998.

246

FIGURE 6.7. Hospital and Clinic—Payer Turnaround

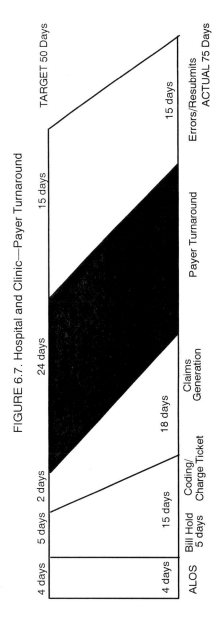

						TARGET 50 Days
4 days	5 days	2 days	18 days	24 days	15 days	15 days
						Errors/Resubmits
4 days	Bill Hold 5 days	Coding/ Charge Ticket	15 days	Claims Generation	Payer Turnaround	ACTUAL 75 Days
ALOS						

- Benchmark process time against Medicare.
- Review claim validation.
  - What are your highest frequency rejects/errors?
  - Which facilities are best/worst? Why?
  - Does ProviderLink have fewer errors? Why or why not?
- Install improved edits to eliminate errors.
- Provide clinics with on-line access to eligibility, benefits, claims status, deductible/co-pay info, on-line certification.
- Assess legal risks.
- Reduce data entry by creating an electronic submission that would not require manual data manipulation, thus increasing accuracy.

Source: Sommers, P. A. and Torgerson, T. Internal study. Allina Health System. Minneapolis, MN, 1997-1998.

247

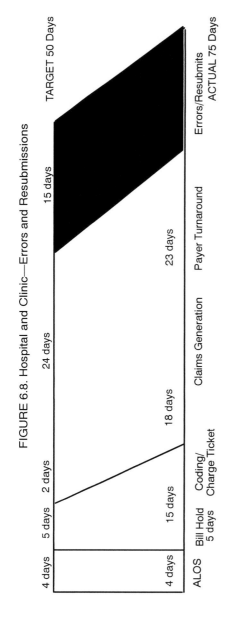

FIGURE 6.8. Hospital and Clinic—Errors and Resubmissions

ALOS: 4 days
Bill Hold: 5 days
Coding/Charge Ticket: 2 days
Claims Generation: 24 days
Payer Turnaround: 15 days
Errors/Resubmits

4 days — 15 days — 18 days — 23 days

TARGET 50 Days
ACTUAL 75 Days

- Breakdown types of bill errors—focus your improvement plans:
  - by facility
  - by payer
  - by cost of error
  - by frequency of error
- Investigate to see if secondary insurance can be submitted immediately.
- Electronic cash posting.
- This is typically a process of 10 to 15 days; benchmark is 10 days.

Source: Sommers, P. A. and Torgerson, T. Internal study. Allina Health System. Minneapolis, MN, 1997-1998.

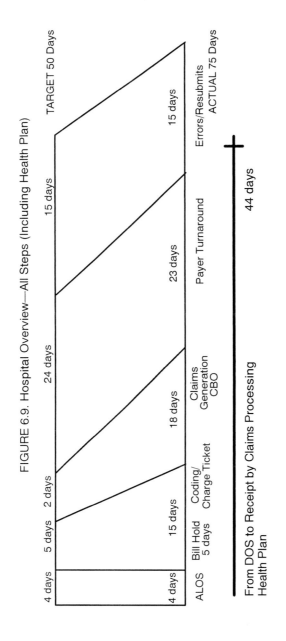

FIGURE 6.9. Hospital Overview—All Steps (Including Health Plan)

Source: Sommers, P. A. and Torgerson, T. Internal study. Allina Health System. Minneapolis, MN, 1997-1998.

Figures 6.10 through 6.12 show recommended steps to be taken to reduce hospital accounts receivable.

Although the health system is not currently prepared to implement the recommendations due to the reorganization of the governance structure, next steps have been planned. The Needs Assessment/Outcomes Management Index in Table 6.12 shows the type of physician/clinic, hospital, and health plan information that will be gathered and centrally monitored on a monthly basis.

INTEGRATION:
PHYSICIAN/HOSPITAL OUTCOMES ANALYSIS

The description that follows focuses on only one part of the 1987 integration between Ramsey Clinic and St. Paul Ramsey Medical Center: the consolidation of two business offices into one.[1,14,17,28,29]

The integration of activities between Ramsey physicians and the hospital where a majority of their patients are admitted was a mutually rewarding, well-planned relationship predicated upon predefined expectations. Since money has the right degree of sensitivity in the process of forming business partnerships, the business office aspect of integration is the focal point of this application.

Each of the subsidiaries (clinic, medical center, foundation) were separate 501(c) 3 organizations, classified as not for profit by the Internal Revenue Service. Ramsey, which bonded legally and spiritually into a unified family through the Ramsey theme, inspires the subsidiaries to examine each opportunity and problem from at least four viewpoints:

1. Impact on the clinic
2. Impact on the medical center
3. Impact on the foundation
4. Overall impact on Ramsey

For example, if a decision is determined to be positive to the Clinic, negative to the medical center, and neutral to the foundation, but overall may be positive to corporate Ramsey, action would be excercised with full knowledge of each potential interaction. Provisions would be made to minimize the negative effects from an organization-wide perspective. Although individual subsidiary situations may change, the goal is to enhance the overall Ramsey perspective.

FIGURE 6.10. Hospital—Average Length of Stay

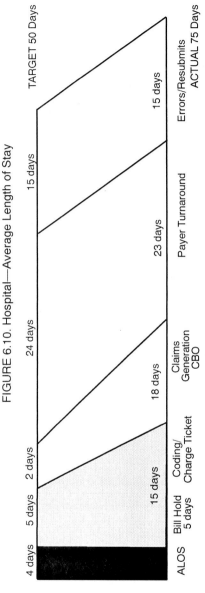

- Examine how this time is used in your facility to collect crucial information and to clarify demographics, insurance information, etc.
- Collection of co-pays for elective admissions.
- Increase preregistration rate.
- Concurrent coding.
- Concurrent signature tagging.
- Concurrent quality and utilization review.
- Combine tasks of quality, utilization, and coding for concurrent review.
- Use patient account reps. who follow patient throughout stay and collect charge tickets and other necessary data.
- Reduce charge ticket lag from ancillary departments, same-day surgery, etc.
- Electronic benefit and eligibility checks.
- Electronic charge ticket capture from caregivers. Eliminate paper.

Source: Sommers, P. A. and Torgerson, T. Internal study. Allina Health System. Minneapolis, MN, 1997-1998.

251

FIGURE 6.11. Hospital—Health Information Processing (Analysis, Coding, and Quality)

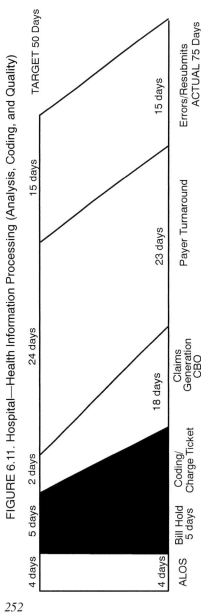

4 days	5 days	2 days	24 days	15 days		TARGET 50 Days
4 days		18 days	23 days	15 days	
ALOS	Bill Hold 5 days	Coding/ Charge Ticket	Claims Generation CBO	Payer Turnaround	Errors/Resubmits ACTUAL 75 Days

- Reduce bill hold days to 5; any longer promotes delay in paperwork completion.
- Reduce number of items analyzed for completion—focus on major items such as discharge summary, history and physical, consultations, operative report, etc. Consult JCAHO recommendations and legal responsibilities.
- Stop nursing deficiency tagging—write responsibility into job description and have them do a quality check every quarter.
- Eliminate hold time for coder—send to coder immediately for follow-up coding if concurrent coder could not flag case for billing.
- Create system outside of suspension to facilitate the provider with chart completion:
  - Have concurrent coders, unit clerk, quality, and utilization staff tag charts on floor for provider signature.
  - Bring discharged charts to floor for provider signature.
  - Bring to office of consulting provider for signature completion.
- Prioritize coding (for example):
  1. Big dollar cases
  2. High number of days out from discharge
  3. Timing of consultant that provides care once a month.
- Stop attestation signatures if you have not already.
- Use qualified coders, ART, RRA, CCS, with quality checks.
- Daily turnover of dictation while patient in-house and improved turnaround for reports dictated after discharge.

Source: Sommers, P. A. and Torgerson, T. Internal study. Allina Health System. Minneapolis, MN, 1997-1998.

FIGURE 6.12. Hospital—Claims Generation

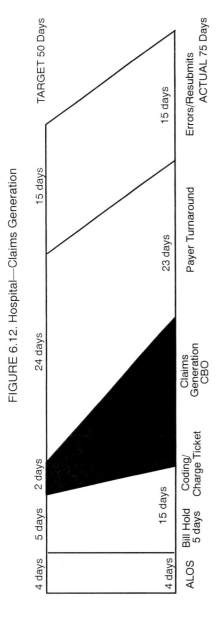

- Reduce bill hold days to 5.
- Create communication bridges with key persons in health information services and admissions.
- Increase the number of electronic submissions your hospital performs.
- Track errors on UB-92 and HCFA 1500 billing and create improvement by working with other departments.
- Look at your payer breakdown.
  - How does this relate to turnaround. Where are your problem products?
  - Medicare = 14 days; BCBS = 14 days; Medicaid = 20 days; Commercial = 30 days; Health Plan = 75 days.

Source: Sommers, P. A. and Torgerson, T. Internal study. Allina Health System. Minneapolis, MN, 1997-1998.

253

TABLE 6.12. Needs Assessment/Outcomes Management Index

Hospital Name: _____

Beds (set up & staffed): ____ Avg. Daily Census: ____ OP Visits: ____

LTC Beds (set up & staffed): ____ Specialty: _____

Clinic Name: ____

Average Daily Encounters: ____ Specialty: _____

	Unit	Description
Average Length of Stay*	Days	Average length of hospitalization of IP discharged
Bill Hold Days	Days	Days after discharge MediPac holds bill before it drops for payer submission. Begins bill delinquency count.
Medical Record Days	Days	Avg. days after discharge to complete coding flag for bill drop.
Uncoded IP Charts*	Charts	Discharged charts that remain completely uncoded after bill hold.
Uncoded OP Days**	Days	Charts that remain completely uncoded after bill hold.
IP Delinquent Charts*	Charts	Discharged charts remaining incomplete after bill hold.
OP Delinquent Charts**	Charts	Charts remaining incomplete after bill hold.
Dictation Needed	Charts	Number requiring dictation.
Transcription Needed	Charts	Number requiring transcription.
Signature Needed	Charts	Number requiring signatures.
Delinquent Bill IP Claims*	Claims	Number of claims not dropped within bill hold days.
Delinquent Bill IP $*	$	Amount of claims not dropped within bill hold days.
Delinquent Bill OP Claims**	Claims	Number of claims not dropped within bill hold days.
Delinquent Bill OP $**	$	Amount of claims not dropped within bill hold days.
Claims Generation Days	Days	Average days to process a bill from coding flag to payer submit.
% Paper claim	%	Percent of claims submitted by manual paper method.
% Electronic claim	%	Percent of claims submitted via electronic method.

Gross Revenue		Total gross revenues accrued during period.
1. Medicare	$	Breakdown of gross revenues by financial class listed (1-10).
2. Medicaid	$	
3. MN Care	$	
4. BC/BS	$	
5. Medica	$	
6. Aetna	$	
7. UBS	$	
8. Select Care	$	
9. Other Commercial	$	
10. Self-Pay	$	
Gross Receivables	$	Total gross receivables accrued during period.
1. Medicare	$	Breakdown of gross receivables by financial class listed (1-10).
2. Medicaid	$	
3. MN Care	$	
4. BC/BS	$	
5. Medica	$	
6. Aetna	$	
7. UBS	$	
8. Select Care	$	
9. Other Commercial	$	
10. Self-Pay	$	

Source: Sommers, P. A. and Torgerson, T. Internal study. Allina Health System. Minneapolis, MN, 1997-1998.

* Hospitals report numbers only.
** Clinics and hospital outpatient report numbers. Hospital outpatient includes SDS.

As a method for dealing with HMOs and Ppos or other agencies requiring the services of more than one Ramsey subsidiary, the Ramsey approach has distinct advantages. Prior to meeting with interested outside agency, clinic, medical center, and/or foundation staff, jointly review administrative and financial perspectives for purposes of most appropriately positioning Ramsey corporate as negotiations proceed.

Increased competition, reduced reimbursements, declining hospital admissions, and rising patient expectations have dramatically altered the way medicine is practiced. Admist these pressures, Ramsey forged a new kind of health care organization—one that combines the strengths of a preeminent medical center, a multispecialty physician group, and a dynamic foundation.

GOALS AND RESULTS OF CLINIC/HOSPITAL INTEGRATION OF BUSINESS OFFICE

Financial Expectations

Expense reduction: Summary comparison of expected and actual financial results based on business office consolidation.

Goals	Results
Increase recovery ratios.	All accounts aged patient receivables (inpatient, outpatient, and combined) and showed continuous improvement between 1987 and 1992.
Decrease the percent of outstanding accounts receivable (AR).	This goal, evaluated with the previous goal (increased recovery ratios), indicated a decrease in the percent of outstanding AR.
Reduce staff by twenty-five FTEs.	Further evaluation is necessary relative to total fees/collection expense and purchased service/utility. A redution in duplicate costs relative to salaries/fringes and medical/other expense occurred. Results of the key informant interviewees stated that the reduction of ten FTEs and combined eighty operations, resulted in savings of approximately $100,000 between the two subsidiaries.

Finance—improved billing and collection performance: Summary comparison of expected and actual financial results based on business office goals and objectives.

Goals	Results
Decrease days for receivables.	Goal not pertinent to hospital. However, the clinic's goal to decrease days receivable from 120 days to 80 days was met and surpassed—decreased to 60 days.
Reduce bad debt.	The percent of bad debts to total operating revenue decreased between 1987 and 1992.
Reduce operating expenses.	The business office consolidation reduced annual operating expenses by $3.5 million for the Ramsey organization overall.
Increase annual interest/ investment income.	Results were inconclusive based on financial evaluation (outside economic factors not taken into consideration). However, key informant interviewees state that, due to improved cash flow, combined operations results in increased annual interest/investment income.
Improve cash flow.	Total operating expense, total operating revenue, and operating fund cash was evaluated along with excess of revenue over expense and indicated positive cash flow results.

Operational Expectations

Operations — coordination of activities: Summary comparison of expected and actual operational results based on business office goals and objectives.

Goals	Results by Key Informant Response
Improve efficiency of operations.	Implemented better systems, eliminated duplicate functions, and cross-trained staff, which led to more efficient and productive day-to-day operations.
Improve equipment utilization.	The major improvement in equipment utilization occurred when the clinic became part of the hospital's automated mainframe computer system.
Reduce duplicate functions.	Integrated billing and collection functions were developed, with duplicate staff functions combined, and clinic and hospital staff cross-trained between the two subsidiaries.

Operations — space reallocation: Summary comparison of expected and actual operational results based on business office goals and objectives.

Goals	Results by Key Informant Response
Improve utilization of space.	The business office (along with other support services) was moved off campus, freeing up vacated space for revenue-producing activities.
Move nonrevenue-producing departments off site into less expensive quarters.	The business office moved into off-campus space. However, the new space had higher rental costs, contributing to an increase in business office expense.
Provide space on campus for revenue producing departments.	The space vacated by the business office was taken over by revenue-generating patient care activities.

Financial Expectations—Expense Reduction

Savings because of lower collection fee/costs. Receivables, uncollectible by in-house collectors, have been routinely turned over to outside collection services each year since 1987. Multiple services have been utilized with different reimbursement arrangements. However, minimal savings were realized from lower collection fees. The most significant financial impact to the physicians' group resulted from the reduction of days in accounts receivable. The forty-five-day reduction in receivables translated to an improvement of more than $3 million in the clinic's cash position.

Increased recovery ratios and decreased percentage of outstanding accounts receivable. Three major factors attributed to increased recovery ratios and decreased percentage of accounts receivable for the hospital and clinic: (1) a reduction in clinic receivable days, (2) automation, and (3) changes instituted in billing and collection.

Hospital receivable days stood at fifty to sixty days from 1987 through 1992, accounting for approximately $400,000 daily in receivables. However, a significant reduction in accounts receivable was realized by the clinic between 1987 and 1992. Prior to consolidation of the business office, the clinic had 120 days or more of revenue tied up in accounts receivable. By 1991, this had been reduced to seventy-five days and, in 1992, subsequently reduced to sixty days.

In 1987, the hospital owned a mainframe computer system (an IBM 4381) through MIS, whereas the clinic leased a computer system (an IBM 38), with one year remaining on its lease. Following expiration of the clinic's lease, all patient billing was assumed by the hospital for both the hospital and clinic.

The hospital has had better receivables management than the clinic, attributable to an automated payer collection system and refined receivables protocols, whereas the clinic employed an outside collection agency. Consolidation efforts incorporated the clinic into the hospital's payer collection system, leading to increased recovery ratios and decreased percentage of accounts receivable.

Staff reductions. Study results indicate that the hospital's business office consolidation goal to reduce staff crossed departmental lines of responsibility. The hospital assumed the billing and collections responsibilities of the clinic, resulting in combined staff functions and cross-training between hospital and clinic personnel. The business office goal to reduce staff had a great financial impact on the clinic, therefore necessitating inclusion of the clinic relative to business office staff reductions.

At the onset of the consolidation in 1987, the business office employed a total of sixty-nine employees: thirty-two hospital FTEs and thirty-seven clinic FTEs. The goal of the merger was to reduce twenty-five FTEs for combined hospital and clinic business office operations; however, it was initially reduced only nineteen FTEs. The goal was not achieved 100 percent because Ramsey changed its way of doing business through eliminating and shifting positions, cross-training, increasing volume of collections, and automating the clinic systems.

Some duplicated positions, in which a hospital employee did the same job as a clinic employee, were eliminated. Some functions were common to both organizations and position shifting occurred. For example, the clinic did not have a credit and collections function prior to the merger. Due to the increased volume of collections between the two entities, the three or four collectors for the hospital were not enough to collect for both. Therefore, current employees performing other functions assumed new positions as collectors and were cross-trained to handle both entities.

After the initial reduction of nineteen FTEs, the business office staff increased by nine FTEs to accommodate line-item posting (due to physician preferences) and added satellite clinics. Seven of the ten business office FTEs who posted cash were employed by the clinic, mainly because physician billing requirements were stricter than hospital billing requirements. Because of less stringent requirements, the hospital was able to post daily charges for submission through an automated computer system. For example, the hospital used diagnosis related groups (DRGs) for its Medicare patients, which did not require posting by line item. The business office submitted a bill and Medicare paid based on diagnosis only. In the past, clinic bills (physician charges) were sent to the insurance company who paid the bottom line total amount. That changed. Because of staff physician demands, the clinic now requires detailed, manually posted billing information, including line-item posting by physician, date, service, CPT code, modifier, cost, diagnosis, and reimbursement received.

As outlined in Table 6.13, at year end 1992, the business office employed twenty-six clinic FTEs, twenty-three hospital FTEs, and ten FTEs who work for both. In 1992, fifty-nine FTEs were doing almost double the volume of work with ten fewer employees, compared to sixty-nine FTEs at the onset of consolidation in 1987. The value of work and demand for staff had increased, but the number of staff had not increased at the same level as volume. The reasons the initial goal to reduce by twenty-five FTEs was not met was due to the combination of increased volume of work and the added detail required for physician billings.

Reduction in duplicate costs. The reduction of ten FTEs in total hospital and clinic combined business office operations resulted in a savings of approximately $100,000.

A major reduction in duplicate costs was reflected when the clinic became part of the hospital's automated mainframe computer system. Annual savings of $288,000 resulted from the clinic's expired IBM System 38 lease and associated maintenance agreement.

TABLE 6.13. Clinic and Hospital Business Office Consolidation (FTE Implications)

	Description	Staff FTEs
Goal:	Projected reduction in FTEs	25
Actual:	Reduction in FTEs ($-19 + 9$)	10
SPRMC BO Staff		32
RC BO Staff		+37
Total Clinic and Hospital Business Office Staff — 1987		69
Less: Reduction in FTEs		-19
Total (Less Staff Reductions)		50
Plus: Increased Clinic Staff to Accommodate Detailed Line-Item Posting and Added Satellite Clinics		+9
Total Clinic-Hospital Business Office Staff Year End 1992		59

Source: Massman, N. Analysis of the Consolidation of Ramsey Clinic and St. Paul Ramsey Medical Center Business Office As a Result of Integration. A theses in partial fulfillment of the master's degree, St. Mary's University Graduate School, Minneapolis, MN, 1996.

Financial Expectations — Improved Billing and Collection Performance

Decreased days for receivables. From 1987 through 1992, the hospital's receivable days remained at fifty-nine to sixty days, due to excellent receivables management. However, the clinic realized a significant reduction in receivable days during this time.

Prior to consolidation of the business office, the clinic stood at 120 receivable days. By 1991, this number had been reduced to seventy-four days, and by year end 1992, receivables had been reduced to an average of between sixty and sixty-two days. Therefore, the clinic goal to decrease days receivable from 120 days to eighty days was met and surpassed.

Factors contributing to the reduction in the number of day's revenue in receivables for the clinic included (1) better systems that provided cleaner claims and (2) increased effort placed on internal collection of RC accounts receivable.

Reduction in bad debt. At the onset of the business office consolidation in 1987, the hospital attributed bad debt to 4.5 percent of its billings. In 1987, the clinic had billings of $55 million, and bad debt was 7.5 percent, or $4.1 million. The clinic's goal was to reduce bad debt from 7.5 percent to 4.5 percent. By 1992, the clinic had reduced its bad debt to the hospital level, which had consistently maintained a 4.5 percent level of bad debt.

Reduction in operating expenses. Overall, business office operating expense increased between 1987 and 1992 due to three major factors: (1) the assignment of space rental expense to the business office following the move off campus; (2) increased collection expense due to increased collection efforts on the clinic's accounts; and (3) normal salary increases due to inflation. No expenses due to unanticipated consequences of the consolidation contributed to the increase in business office expense.

When five clinic departments (OB/GYN, neurology, ENT, anesthesiology, and neurosurgery) decided to use an alternate patient billing system, a minor reduction in business office expenses occurred. This reduction was more than offset, however, by increased expenses in those five departments related to using outside billing services.

In 1987, with the hospital and clinic performing separate billing, data processing, and credit and collection functions, patient billing and data processing operating expenses totaled $5.6 million. With combined hospital and clinic billing, data processing, and credit and collection funds, combined expenses totaled $3.9 million, with a savings of $1.7 million. Organization-wide, the distribution of operating expenses shared on a prorated basis between the hospital and clinic remained the same, with the hospital at 73 percent and the clinic at 27 percent.

Increased annual interest/investment income and improved cash flow. Due to the decreased number of receivable days, and the reduction in bad debt because of enhanced credit and collections follow-up, combined business office operations between the hospital and the clinic resulted in increased annual interest/investment income earned because of improved cash flow.

Operation Expectations—Coordination of Activities

Improved efficiency of operations. Three major factors contributed to improved efficiency of business office operations: (1) coordinated computer systems and improved receivables management led to the implementation of better systems, providing cleaner claims; (2) combined billing and collection functions eliminated duplicate capture of demographic data; and (3) cross-trained staff between the hospital and the clinic provided more efficient and productive day-to-day operations.

Operational Expectations—Space Reallocation

Improved utilization of space. The business office was only one of several support services that have been moved off campus in recent years. As these services have moved, they have been replaced on the main campus by revenue-producing activities that in turn have had a positive financial impact, primarily for the hospital.

Moved nonrevenue producing departments off site into less expensive quarters. In 1988, the business offices located on campus were vacated and moved off campus. However, rental expense associated with the new office space contributed to an increase in business office operation expenses.

Provided space on campus for revenue-producing departments. As previously noted, the business office was only one of several support services that has moved off campus. As these nonrevenue-producing services have moved off campus, the vacated on-campus space has been utilized by revenue-generating patient care activities.

Summary

Ten financial and six operational goals and objectives were studied. Based on financial data and/or key informant interviews, results of three financial goals (savings because of lower collection fees/costs, a reduction in duplicate costs, and an increase in annual interest/investment income) were inconclusive or unmet.

Based on key informant interviews, one operational goal (to remove nonrevenue-producing departments off site into less expensive quarters) was not met. Findings for the remaining twelve goals and objectives previously discussed revealed positive outcomes as a result of the business office integration.

Figures 6.13 and 6.14, and previously shown Figures 2.1 and 2.2 in Chapter 2, pages 34 and 35, illustrate the overall effects of the 1987 integration.

FIGURE 6.13. Total Clinic Visits by Hospital Admissions

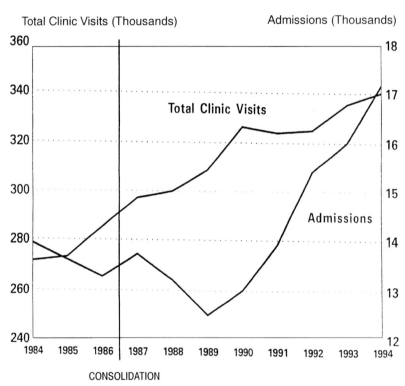

CONSOLIDATION

Source: Sommers, P. A. Internal study. Ramsey Clinic and St. Paul-Ramsey Medical Center, St. Paul, MN, 1995-1996.

KEY INDICATOR DEFINITIONS AND DRILL-DOWN ANALYSIS: PREPARATION FOR ACTION PLAN DEVELOPMENT

Preparations required for accurate action plan development can be enhanced using "drill down." Drill down is defined as the process used to identify the main elements composing a priority or key indicator. Each

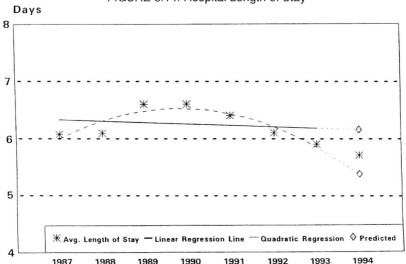

FIGURE 6.14. Hospital Length of Stay

Source: Sommers, P. A. Internal study. Ramsey Clinic and St. Paul-Ramsey Medical Center, St. Paul, MN, 1995-1996.

element may have one or more components leading back to its origin within the health care system.

For example, Sommers reported on this application at the 1997 SAS Institute Annual Health Care Conference using 1996 information.[30,31] The model reflects an organization's set of defined key indicators and illustrates each position on the pathway (see Figure 4.1 in Chapter 4, page 117, showing the pathway with the 1996 key indicator list).

Key Indicator Definitions

Administration Expense: Monitoring it as a percentage of revenue is an internal benchmark that has been set to ensure administrative expenses are in line with revenue growth. Administrative expenses do not include the expenses of workers' compensation and dental departments. Revenue includes both fully insured revenues and an estimate of self-insured premiums, the results being commonly referred to as implicit revenue. The percentages are shown on a calendar year-to-date basis.

Claims Adjustments: The number of claims received in the month per 1000 members that requires a system adjustment in order to generate a correct payment. This may include either a whole or partial, up or down adjustment. Source is the monthly claims status report.

Commercial Members Leaving Health Plans: The percentage of total health plan commercial members that leave the plan each month because their *employer* terminated its relationship. (A transfer between plan products does not represent a termination and thus is not reflected in the percentage.) The measure does exclude those members who leave the plan at open enrollment, provided that the employer stays with the health plan.

Customer Service Average Wait Time: Each individual call received by customer service is directed by an automated voice (interactive voice response—IVR) system. This system prompts callers to enter the first five digits of their member number. After the member number information is entered, the call is routed to the appropriate team to answer the call (Medicaid team, priority team, etc.). Average customer wait time refers to the amount of time the caller remains on hold after this transfer until a "live" representative connects with them.

LAN (Local Area Network) Availability: Actual availability of the information system file servers during normal business hours are compared to target.

Medical Loss Ratio by Product: It is important to monitor the financial performance of each product category. The medical loss ratio (MLR) is the percentage of the premium dollar (net of brokers fees and taxes) that is spent on health care. The percentage is shown on a year-to-year basis. The calculation is done on a "restated basis," meaning that the MLR reflects our most current knowledge of IBNR run-out.

Medicare Members Leaving Plan: The percentage of total Medicare enrollees that leave the plan each month for voluntary reasons. (A transfer between health plan products does not represent a termination and thus is not reflected in the percentage.)

Membership: The number of members reported by each broad classification of products compared to budget.

Operating Income Percentage: The portion of the premium dollar that results in profit in the plan. Thus, it represents net premium revenue less health care costs and administrative expenses. It specifically excludes investment income. Revenue includes an estimate of the premium equivalent for self-insured business (implicit revenue).

Pended Claims: The number of claims over sixty days old from the date received at the plan that are in the process of being adjudicated for a payment status.

Provider Service Average Wait Time: This refers to the average amount of time the provider remains on hold until a "live" representative connects with them. The measure reflects data by coordinators, verification representatives, and dental. The coordinators are responsible for claim and administrative questions, and the verification representatives are responsible for benefit and eligibility questions, and dental is responsible for the dental and provider network.

Provider Service Call Abandonment Rate: Abandonment rate refers to the percentage of provider service calls that disconnect before a "live" representative connects with them.

Trend: A trend factor measures the rate at which health care costs are changing due to such factors as fees paid to providers, changes in frequency and pattern of utilizing various medical services, and the use of new medical technology. Actual year-to-date trend is compared to prior years, current year budget, and the state's required expenditure growth target. The reported percentage is a weighted average across all health plan products.

Application Assumptions

1. Plot trend by month—overall and by product
2. Admissions per 1,000—overall and by product
3. Days per 1,000—overall and by product
4. Physician visits per 1,000—overall and by product
5. Outpatient visits per 1,000—overall and by product
6. Emergency room visits per 1,000—overall and by product
7. Per member per month—overall and by product:
   a. Physician visits
   b. Hospital inpatient
   c. Hospital outpatient
   d. Prescriptions
   e. Mental health/substance abuse
8. Number of catastrophic cases

A 1995 to 1996 performance date was used to identify the position of each indicator as contributed toward the production of operating income.[30,31] Table 4.2 (previously shown on page 118) lists rank order contributions with statistical significance at $p = .05$. Each indicator was individually analyzed with operating income. Table 4.3 (previously shown on page 119) shows the best-fitting combination of indicators, with each indicator competing with the others to show the general proportion of focus (e.g., resource allocation) to consider when establishing "action plan" activities for interventions.

Before action plan development, it is important to "drill down" into the composition of elements responsible for the production of each indicator. A series of figures follow that shows the drill-down process (see Figures 6.15 to 6.18).

Once each indicator's data components have been defined and desired targets set, it becomes possible to predict operational results on a monthly, quarterly, and annual basis. Evaluation will show actual outcomes for comparisons to forecasted targets. As actual results begin to vary from the expected/desired targets, the difference or variance is identified. Depending upon which indicators are off target, one or more action steps are developed and implemented to positively affect the activities responsible for the production of outcomes. Outcomes are monitored throughout the year, with adjustments made as needed. Next year's plans will be developed with knowledge of current year results and the impact of interventions required by the day-to-day changes of the competitive health care marketplace.

Desired Outcome

Determine the most reliable and valid indicators of operating income for the health plans and implement activities to achieve financial targets.

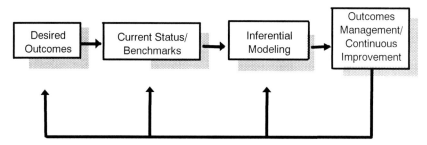

Current status/inferential modeling: four indicators are listed in rank order that account for 93 percent of the variance with the prediction of operating income.

Example

1. Membership (indicator 13)
2. Trend (indicator 8)
3. Customer service average wait time (indicator 7)
4. Administrative expense (indicator 2)

Drill down needs to occur into each component comprising the database for membership, trend, customer service average wait time, and administrative expense. Action plans are required to focus on those indicator elements which are responsible for poor performance.

FIGURE 6.15. Drill Down of Key Indicators

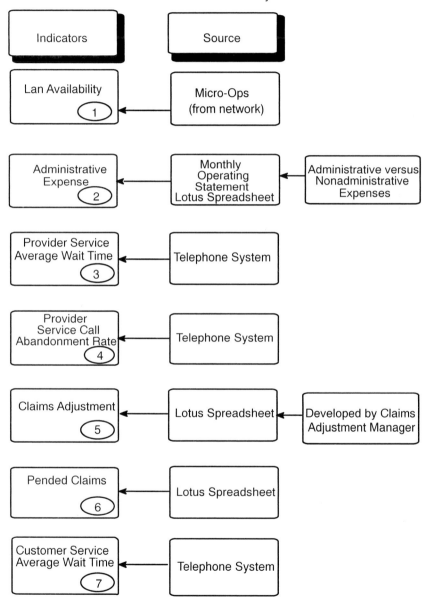

Source: Sommers, P. A. and Glosemeyer, B. Internal study. Allina Health System/Medica Health Plans. Minneapolis, MN, 1997-1998.

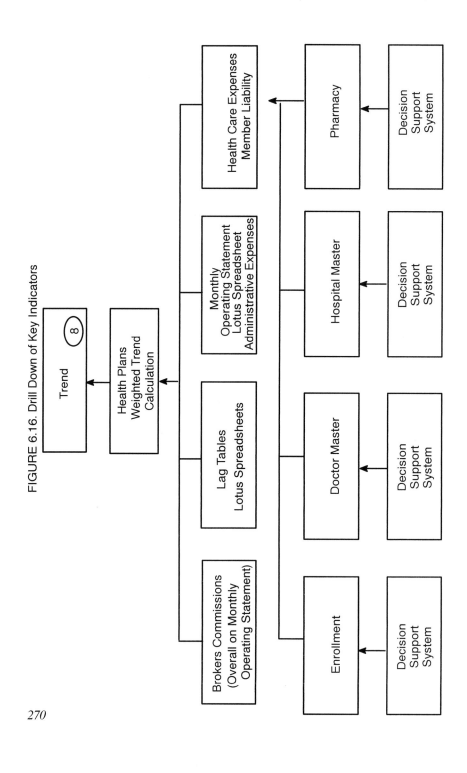

FIGURE 6.16. Drill Down of Key Indicators

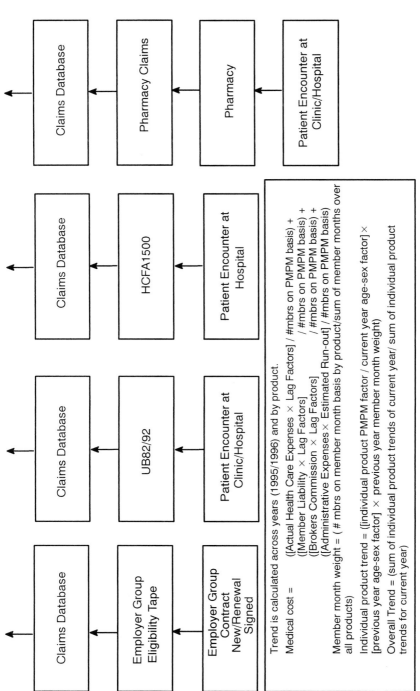

Claims Database ← Pharmacy Claims ← Pharmacy ← Patient Encounter at Clinic/Hospital

Claims Database ← HCFA1500 ← Patient Encounter at Hospital

Claims Database ← UB82/92 ← Patient Encounter at Clinic/Hospital

Claims Database ← Employer Group Eligibility Tape ← Employer Group Contract New/Renewal Signed

Trend is calculated across years (1995/1996) and by product.

Medical cost = ([Actual Health Care Expenses × Lag Factors] / #mbrs on PMPM basis) +
([Member Liability × Lag Factors] / #mbrs on PMPM basis) +
([Brokers Commission × Lag Factors] / #mbrs on PMPM basis) +
([Administrative Expenses × Estimated Run-out] / #mbrs on PMPM basis)

Member month weight = (# mbrs on member month basis by product/sum of member months over all products)

Individual product trend = ([individual product PMPM factor / current year age-sex factor] × [previous year age-sex factor] × previous year member month weight)

Overall Trend = (sum of individual product trends of current year/ sum of individual product trends for current year)

Source: Sommers, P. A. and Glosemeyer, B. Internal study. Allina Health System/Medica Health Plans. Minneapolis, MN, 1997-1998

FIGURE 6.17. Drill Down of Key Indicators

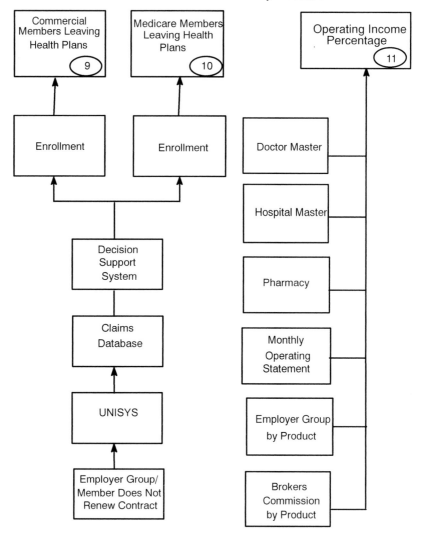

Operating income = (net premium revenue [health care costs + administrative expense])

Source: Sommers, P. A. and Glosemeyer, B. Internal study. Allina Health System/Medica Health Plans. Minneapolis, MN, 1997-1998.

Note: excludes investment income.

FIGURE 6.18. Drill Down of Key Indicators

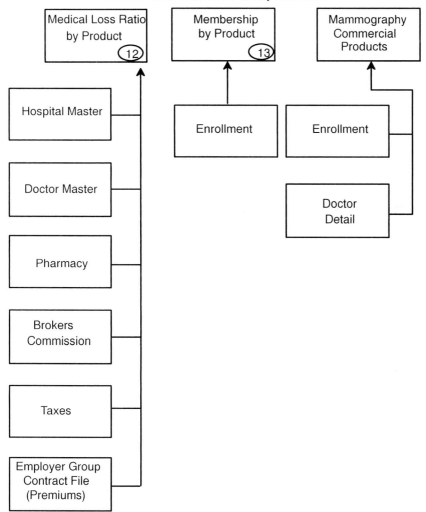

Source: Sommers, P. A. and Glosemeyer, B. Internal study. Allina Health System/Medica Health Plans. Minneapolis, MN, 1997-1998.

Medical loss ratio defined = percentage of premium dollars (net of brokers fees and taxes) that is spent on health care.

Medical loss ratio formula = (sum of amount paid by health plans to doctors, hospitals, and pharmacies [excludes copays/deductibles]/total premiums).

Following the development and implementation of focused action plans, the process is monitored, with outcomes measurements taken on at least a quarterly basis, and comprehensively evaluated at least annually, as additional enhancements are implemented as needed to meet or exceed targets.

REPORT CARDS

Health care organizations use various reports and benchmarks to educate interested groups, individuals, and the public in general about results of their work in the community, throughout the catchment area, and on a larger scale when necessary.[4] One such example, a report card used primarily by health plans, seems to appeal to various audiences interested in this type of information.

The report card can fill an extremely important public information role by establishing in the public's eye an organization's mission, vision, and focus toward improving the health status and lifestyle of those served by the health care system. The report card tells a story from an outcomes perspective, without appearing like a paid advertisement. Health care organizations need to tell their story in a planned, proactive forum versus a reactive manner. For too long, providers have merely reacted to claims of high-cost, poor-quality care, which have come from patient advocate groups, federal and state agencies, and the purchasing community in general.

Table 6.14 illustrates how report-card-type information could be displayed for public awareness and education purposes. State and/or national comparisons used in this case include Healthy People 2000's, a U.S. Department of Health and Human Services' Public Health Science publication outline of national health care goals for the year 2000. The goals established in Healthy People 2000 serve as targets for quality and performance improvement in the delivery of health care services. A second comparison group is the National Committee for Quality Assurance (NCQA) Report Card Pilot Project. The NCQA publishes the results of HEDIS measurements from health plans across the country.[8] HEDIS, developed by NCQA, stands for the Health Plan Employer Data and Information Set and was designed to address two objectives: (1) to educate employers about the value produced by their health care dollars and (2) to provide employers with information about health plan performance while establishing desired levels of accountability. The grand mean/average score for the HEDIS health care indicators of participating health plans serves as a national benchmark of current levels of health care quality, access, and satisfaction.

The third comparative standard in Minnesota is an annual report card of health plan performance published by the Minnesota Department of Health.

Data presented in the following example are organized by four major performance categories:

1. Quality of Care
2. Member Access and Satisfaction
3. Membership and Utilization
4. Finance and Administration

It is the health care organization's responsibility to construct a report card reflective of those elements important to both the organization's internal and external constituencies.

TABLE 6.14. Report Card on Health Care Practices Performance—Grading Criteria: Excellent = 90-100, Strong = 80-89, Average = 70-79, Poor = Below 70

TOPICS	SUBJECTS	SCORING CODE: 1. 1995 Practice Scores 2. 1994 Practice Scores 3. NCQA 1994 Practice Average 4. Healthy People 2000 Goal 5. Other				
		1.	2.	3.	4.	5.
I. Quality of Care	Diabetic Eye Exam Rate*	54%	54%	47%	—	————
	Pap Smear Rate*	77%	78%	77%	85%	————
	Mammography Rate*	76%	68%	—	60%	————
	Pediatric Immunization Rate*	84%	84%	—	—	————
	Prenatal Care Rate*	94%	94%	91%	95%	————
II. Access and Satisfaction	Satisfaction with Care*	97%	96%	—	—	94% 1996 Practice ytd.
	Recommend Provider to Friend*	94%	94%	91%	—	93% 1996 ytd.
	Access (HEDIS) Ages 23-39*	95%	95%	88%	—	————
	Ages 40-64*	96%	96%	91%	—	————
	Thoroughness of Exam*	92%	92%	88%	—	————
	Office Waiting Time*	91%	80%	—	—	————
	Selection of Physicians*	93%	90%	—	—	————
	All Questions Answered by Staff*	86%	85%	—	—	————

III. Stability and Use	Disenrollment Rate for Health Plans, Dropout Rate for Clinics/Hospitals	11.6%	7.9%	23%	—	———————
	ER Use Rate/1000	123	140	—	—	96.3 MN DpHth
	Acute Inpatient Discharge /1000	56	58	—	—	54 MN Dpt Hth
	Acute Inpatient Days/1000	210	230	—	—	205 MN DpHth
	C-Section Rate	18%	17%	—	—	20% MN DpHth
	Pediatric Admission Rate/1000	.9	1.1	1.7	—	———————
IV. Financial and Operations	Administrative Loss Ratio for Health Plans, Administrative Overhead for Clinics and Hospitals	99%	97%	—	—	———————
	Medical Loss Ratio for Health Plans, Net Revenue for Clinics and Hospitals	89%	85%	—	—	———————
	Bills/Claims Turnaround: Physicians	8.7	10.1	—	—	13.8 first qrt., 1996
	Hospital	15.9	16.6	—	—	18.4-1996 ytd.
	Plan Clinics/Medical Review	1.2	1.24	—	—	1.34-1996 ytd.
	Electronic Submission: Physicians*	62%	76%	—	—	59.8% 1996 ytd.
	Pharmacy*	98%	98%	—	—	99% 1996 ytd.
	Hospital*	22%	19%	—	—	31% 1996 ytd.
	Fee/Premium Rate Increase/Decrease	-.4%	2.7%	—	—	———————

Source: Sommers, P. A. Internal study. Allina Health System. Minneapolis, MN, 1997-1998.

* Any rating score less than 90% (Excellent) is not acceptable for those categories graded on 0-100% scale.

PHYSICIAN/PRACTITIONER INFORMATION SYSTEMS

One key to effective and efficient provider-directed quality patient care is founded on the principle of using practice information for self-directed education and continuous improvement.[32,33,34,35] The goal is to define each aspect of the provider's practice in terms of required operations and desired outcomes. Each aspect that is deemed important must be quantified for measurement and then monitored toward desired targets important to the type of practice (e.g., primary care, specialty, other). Physicians' data must be useful to their practice, timely, accurate, case-mix adjusted for severity, and statistically significant. It has been documented that successful physician change programs have the following characteristics in common: individualized, specific feedback; peer comparison; face-to-face communication; continuous education and feedback; knowledge of cost information; and financial arrangements whereby physician income is placed at risk and based on performance.[36,37]

Once a profile of the provider's practice has been established, the information becomes a bridge toward success, as illustrated by the various patterns established. Patterns of practice can be reflected as a patient treatment episode (PTE), which is defined as all hospital inpatient and ambulatory care services— including prescription drugs—incurred in treating an individual's medical condition within a specific period.[34]

In the process of establishing a PTE, traditional managed care readiness measures are monitored by many health care systems. Per member per month (PMPM) expense indicators, previously discussed in Chapter 6, are computed for each managed care plan served by the health system. Since the physician is responsible for providing or directing the use of health care resources, it is important to monitor, and subsequently manage, the impact of resource use to achieve an effective patient outcome, while optimizing the return on investment. Typical areas requiring resource management include resource use by volume, by medical condition, and by service category.

Inpatient Facility (Excluding Alcohol/Drug Abuse and Pysch)

For benchmarking purposes, actuarial firms provide comparative data from across the United States.[4,8] With benchmarking information, an organization can determine the broad characteristics of its group's practice patterns in comparison to others. For purposes of comparing physician practices, profiles, and resource use, the practice conditions and type of patients served must be carefully managed to ensure accurate and meaningful analysis. Episode Treatment Groups (ETGs) are applied to the information to group individual patients by the same unit of analysis. Ambulatory Care Groups (ACGs) are based on the premise that a measure of a population's illness burden can help explain variation in health care resource consumption. ACGs represent a simple method for classifying individuals based on age, sex, and diagnosis, as assigned by their providers during care delivery. Once less-than-acceptable patterns have been identified in one or more areas, such as lab or pharmacy, for example, it is possible to drill down to the provider- and/or clinic-specific level. Examples of reports shown in Figures 6.19 and 6.20 and Tables 6.15 and 6.16. They reflect pharmacy use, first at a physician-specific level and then at the clinic level.[26]

DEVELOPING TRUST BETWEEN PROVIDERS AND A HEALTH PLAN

Without providers, health plans will go out of business. Without payers, providers and hospitals will go out of business. Without excellent care and service, consumers will go elsewhere—a lose, lose, lose situation that offers significant opportunity for correction.[37,38]

The purpose of health care must be redesigned around customer needs. Physicians' groups, hospitals, and health plans must understand that excellence in care and service is based on sensitive consumer perceptions. Without health care staff at every level voluntarily committing to work collaboratively on the patient's behalf, the probability of failing to achieve excellence, and therefore satisfaction, is most certainly assured.[39,40,41]

Health plans and their providers lack trust and confidence in each other. It is believed that consumer satisfaction improvements can be a bridge between providers and health plans, since satisfied consumers benefit both groups and promote customer loyalty. A "Pilot Project" is being used as a vehicle to develop a joint partnership between Wellness Health Plans and All Physicians Clinic to improve plan member and clinic employee satisfaction, increase customer loyalty, and simultaneously improve the clinic's bottom line as it pertains to plan members.[36]

The research objective of the pilot project is to improve health plan member and employee satisfaction while developing trust with the care and service providers. Research implications include the following:

1. The lack of trust and confidence between health plans and their providers supports continuing failures.
2. Health plans must develop trust with providers and hospitals by establishing joint partnerships.
3. Satisfaction improvement toward excellence must be a focused priority among providers, hospitals, and the health plan on behalf of the patients/members.
4. Satisfaction improvement will be the result of a connection between customer and employee satisfaction, measured by increased customer loyalty.

FIGURE 6.19. Physician-Specific Pharmacy Profile

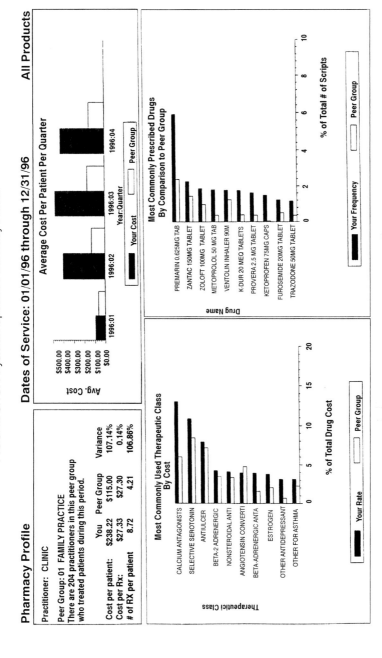

Source: Sommers, P. A. and Glosemeyer, B. Internal study. Allina Health System, Minneapolis, MN, 1997-1998.

279

FIGURE 6.20. Pharmacy Profile Clinicwide

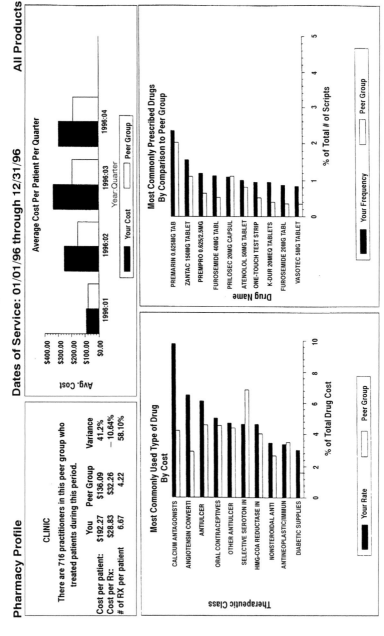

Source: Sommers, P.A. and Glosemeyer B. Internal study. Allina Health System. Minneapolis, MN, 1997-1998.

TABLE 6.15. Physician-Specific Pharmacy Profile

Practitioner: CLINIC — Peer Group: 01 FAMILY PRACTICE

Quarterly	Total # Rx	Total # Patients	Total Ingred. Cost	Avg # Rx/ PPPQ*	Avg Rx Cost	Avg Cost PPPQ*	% Generic	% Formulary Compliance
1996 01	1,360	397	$37,636	3.48	$27.27	$94.81	36.33	
1996 02	1,475	99	$39,606	14.9	$26.85	400.06	37.49	
1996 03	1,603	93	$44,179	17.2	$27.56	475.04	38.68	
1996 04	1,582	104	$43,663	15.2	$27.60	419.84	39.32	
Peer Gr	396,639	94,140	$10,826,326	4.21	$27.30	115.00	42.31	

*PPPQ= Per UTILIZING Patient Per Quarter

Top Therapeutic Classes by Total Cost

Practitioner: Rank		% Total	Avg Cost/Rx	Peer Group: 01 FAMILY PRACTICE Rank		% Total
1	OTHER ANTIULCER	2.2	93.64	1	OTHER ANTIULCER	4.0
2	OTHER ANTIPARKI	2.1	79.54	2	OTHER ANTIPARKI	0.4
3	ANTIULCER	7.9	71.77	3	ANTIULCER	7.2
4	SELECTIVE SEROT	10.9	66.10	4	SELECTIVE SEROT	8.4
5	ORAL CONTRACEPT	2.0	55.63	5	ORAL CONTRACEPT	4.7
6	HMG-COA REDUCTA	1.8	48.80	6	HMG-COA REDUCTA	5.4
7	CALCIUM ANTAGON	13.0	44.91	7	CALCIUM ANTAGON	6.0
8	TO PREVENT AND	1.4	44.30	8	TO PREVENT AND	3.0
9	ANALGESICS	1.5	41.50	9	ANALGESICS	0.4
10	OTHER FOR ASTHM	3.1	40.05	10	OTHER FOR ASTHM	2.2
11	OTHER ANTIHYPER	2.2	36.99	11	OTHER ANTIHYPER	0.5
12	DIABETIC SUPPLI	3.1	34.02	12	DIABETIC SUPPLI	2.1
13	BETA-2 ADRENERG	4.2	31.44	13	BETA-2 ADRENERG	3.5
14	OTHER ANTIDEPRE	3.1	30.05	14	OTHER ANTIDEPRE	0.7
15	NONSTEROIDAL	4.1	29.98	15	NONSTEROIDAL	3.4
16	ANGIOTENSIN CON	4.0	29.96	16	ANGIOTENSIN CON	4.7
17	ORAL HYPOGLYCEM	2.7	23.77	17	ORAL HYPOGLYCEM	2.1
18	SECONDARY AMINE	1.8	16.89	18	SECONDARY AMINE	0.3
19	BETA-ADRENERGIC	3.9	15.53	19	BETA-ADRENERGIC	1.5
20	ESTROGEN	3.8	13.26	20	ESTROGEN	2.0
		78.9				62.6

Top Drugs by Number of Scripts

Practitioner: Rank		% Total	Avg Cost/Rx	Peer Group: 01 FAMILY PRACTICE Rank		% Total
1	PROZAC 20MG CAP	1.1	82.14	1	PROZAC 20MG CAP	1.4
2	ZANTAC 150MG TA	2.2	79.06	2	ZANTAC 150MG TA	1.4
3	ZOLOFT 100MG TA	1.9	67.87	3	ZOLOFT 100MG TA	1.0
4	PAXIL 20MG TABL	1.0	53.05	4	PAXIL 20MG TABL	0.7
5	ULTRAM 50MG TAB	1.0	42.81	5	ULTRAM 50MG TAB	0.4
6	GLYBURIDE 5MG T	1.0	36.23	6	GLYBURIDE 5MG T	0.4
7	PROCARDIA XL 30	1.1	35.25	7	PROCARDIA XL 30	0.4
8	KETOPROFEN 75MG	1.5	34.67	8	KETOPROFEN 75MG	0.0
9	VENTOLIN INHALE	1.8	28.06	9	VENTOLIN INHALE	1.2
10	NORTRIPTYLINE 5	0.9	24.94	10	NORTRIPTYLINE 5	0.1
11	TOPROL XL 50MG	0.9	23.64	11	TOPROL XL 50MG	0.1
12	PREMPRO 0.625/2	1.0	16.15	12	PREMPRO 0.625/2	0.7
13	K-DUR 20MEQ TAB	1.7	14.01	13	K-DUR 20MEQ TAB	0.4
14	PREMARIN 0.625M	5.9	12.42	14	PREMARIN 0.625M	2.4
15	METOPROLOL 100M	0.9	10.19	15	METOPROLOL 100M	0.2
16	PROVERA 2.5MG T	1.6	10.08	16	PROVERA 2.5MG T	0.4
17	METOPROLOL 50MG	1.8	9.12	17	METOPROLOL 50MG	0.4
18	ATENOLOL 50MG T	1.1	4.15	18	ATENOLOL 50MG T	1.1
19	TRAZODONE 50MG	1.2	3.09	19	TRAZODONE 50MG	0.4
20	FUROSEMIDE 20MG	1.2	1.26	20	FUROSEMIDE 20MG	0.5
		30.6				13.6

Source: Sommers, P. A. and Glosemeyer, B. Internal study. Allina Health System. Minneapolis, MN, 1997-1998.

TABLE 6.16. Pharmacy Profile Clinicwide

CLINIC

Peer Group: All Clinics

Quarterly	Total # Rx	Total # Patients	Total Ingred. Cost	Avg # Rx/ PPPQ*	Avg Rx Cost	Avg Cost PPPQ*	% Generic	% Formulary Compliance
1996.01	18,871	5,875	$532,628	3.21	$28.22	$90.66	62.01	
1996.02	19,301	2,187	$552,347	8.83	$28.62	$252.56	61.81	
1996.03	20,171	1,760	$589,517	11.5	$29.23	$334.95	62.12	
1996.04	21,165	2,100	$617,693	10.1	$29.18	$294.14	60.82	
All Clinics	1,367,842	324,444	$44,136,314	4.22	$32.27	136.04	59.80	

*PPPQ = Per UTILIZING Patient Per Quarter

Top Therapeutic Classes by Total Cost

Peer Group: All Clinics

Rank		% Total	Avg Cost/Rx
1	ANTINEOPLASTIC/	3.4	104.21
2	OTHER ANTIULCER	4.7	86.21
3	HMG-COA REDUCTA	4.6	73.51
4	ANTIULCER	6.1	71.86
5	SELECTIVE SEROT	4.6	60.82
6	QUINOLONES	1.4	57.00
7	ORAL CONTRACEPT	5.0	54.43
8	ANTIHISTAMINES	1.7	48.08
9	TO PREVENT AND	1.4	46.19
10	CALCIUM ANTAGON	9.8	43.35
11	OTHER FOR ASTHM	2.9	40.43
12	CEPHALOSPORINS	1.5	38.26
13	ANGIOTENSIN CON	6.5	31.27
14	DIABETIC SUPPLI	3.0	31.00
15	BETA-2 ADRENERG	2.8	30.69
16	NONSTEROIDAL	3.5	28.36
17	ORAL HYPOGLYCEM	2.7	26.89
18	ORAL ANTICOAGUL	1.6	25.49
19	ESTROGEN	2.2	15.14
20	BETA-ADRENERGIC	2.3	13.78
		71.6	

Top Drugs by Number of Scripts

Peer Group: All Clinics

Rank		% Total	Avg Cost/Rx	% Total
1	PRILOSEC 20MG C	1.1	98.37	1.1
2	PROZAC 20MG CAP	0.7	78.90	1.2
3	ZANTAC 150MG TA	1.6	76.28	1.1
4	PRAVACHOL 20MG	0.7	64.85	0.5
5	CLARITIN 10MG T	0.8	53.38	1.3
6	ONE TOUCH TEST	1.0	45.89	0.5
7	VASOTEC 5MG TAB	0.8	40.03	0.3
8	NORVASC 5MG TAB	0.8	39.15	0.4
9	ATROVENT INHALE	0.7	27.87	0.3
10	VENTOLIN INHALE	0.7	27.26	1.0
11	PRINIVIL 10MG T	0.7	25.32	0.5
12	COUMADIN 5MG TA	0.7	23.04	0.4
13	K-DUR 20MEQ TAB	0.9	18.41	0.4
14	PREMPRO 0.625/2	1.2	16.35	0.6
15	PREMARIN 0.625M	2.4	13.65	2.0
16	LANOXIN 0.25MG	0.7	5.82	0.3
17	ATENOLOL 50MG T	1.0	3.30	0.8
18	ACETAMINOPHENC	0.7	1.96	1.1
19	FUROSEMIDE 40MG	1.1	1.58	0.5
20	FUROSEMIDE 20MG	0.9	0.99	0.4
		19.3		14.9

Source: Sommers, P. A. and Glosemeyer, B. Internal study. Allina Health System. Minneapolis, MN, 1997-1998.

282

Project support is being provided through the department of Health Measurement, Analysis, and Research (a pseudonym), Anytown, USA. Wellness Health Plan (a pseudonym) is the managed care/insurance plan component of the Wellness Health System.

History

All Physicians Clinic staff indicated that their efforts toward the improvement of consumer satisfaction began in 1994 and asked that the information collected during 1994 and 1995 be considered in development of the pilot project. A summary of 1994 and 1995 activities and results follows:

1994 Activities

1. Quality improvement activities for service issues:
   - Survey conducted to assess access, wait times, and satisfaction.
   - Internal time study of the phone and scheduling systems was completed.
   - Program to acknowledge physicians with high satisfaction was implemented.
   - Results: unknown.
2. Quality improvement activities from patient feedback forms:
   - Through these forms, the area of hold times was identified as an area for improvement.
   - Results: hold times were reduced through a major enhancement to the telephone system.
   - Measurable Improvements:

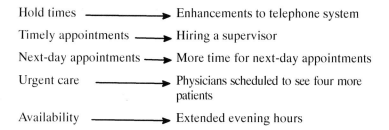

Hold times ⟶ Enhancements to telephone system

Timely appointments ⟶ Hiring a supervisor

Next-day appointments ⟶ More time for next-day appointments

Urgent care ⟶ Physicians scheduled to see four more patients

Availability ⟶ Extended evening hours

1995 Activities

1. Clinic-focused survey for All Physicians Clinic done by Wellness Health Plans Method.

2. 226 capitated members with visits from July through December 1995 sent survey in March-April 1996.
3. 238 premium option members with visits from July through December 1995 sent survey in June-July 1996.
   • Results: areas for improvement identified:
     a. Access to clinic for advice or help with problems
     b. Amount of time it takes to get an appointment for routine care
     c. Amount of time it takes to get an appointment when the condition requires prompt attention
     d. Amount of time patients wait between scheduled appointment time and when seen by a provider
   • Survey comments identified specific problems:
     a. Amount of time it takes to get an appointment
     b. Amount of time patients wait between scheduled appointment time and when seen by a provider
     c. Phone waiting time
     d. Member not seeing regular doctor but other doctor

Customer Service Steering Committee Formed to Address Issues

Background. All Physicians Clinic identified the following elements as being important to patients:
1. Attentive providers and high quality medical care
2. Helpful and courteous staff
3. Easy and timely access to appropriate medical care
4. Minimal wait time in the office
5. Timely follow-up on test results
6. Information/education in written form

Goals: All Physicians Clinic focused their attention on the following service areas:

1. Improve customer service, measured by:
   a. improved HMO satisfaction survey scores,
   b. reduction in trends from feedback forms, and
   c. improved internal customer satisfaction survey scores.
2. Decrease wait time in the office, measured by:
   a. improved HMO satisfaction survey scores,
   b. wait time less than twenty minutes, and
   c. reduction in trends from feedback forms.

3. Improve job satisfaction, measured by:
   a. climate survey scores improvement, identifying barriers to providing good patient care/service and improved communication of staff, and
   b. employee turnover decrease.

Improvements: All Physicians Clinic designated the following areas for improvement:

1. Attention to what patient has to say: improvement plans were implemented for specific physicians, and physicians were sent to communication courses.
2. Access to medical care: steering committee formed to address the most common areas identified as "most important" by customers in each survey in 1995. Addressed first was wait time in the office and customer service.

1995 PHYSICIAN-FOCUSED WELLNESS MEMBER SATISFACTION SURVEY DONE BY WELLNESS HEALTH PLAN

This survey assessed twelve physicians at All Physicians Clinic in the areas of access, clinical aspects, interaction with physicians, and facility assessment.

- Premium Option and Capitated members responded to the survey for visits from January through December 1995.
- One physician scored well below other physicians in their specialty.
- Eight physicians had low satisfaction related to their access of care.
- Five physicians had low satisfaction related to clinical aspects of the visit.
- Seven physicians had low satisfaction related to their interaction with patient.
- Three physicians had low satisfaction related to facility.

Survey questions correlated (r) the highest with physician satisfaction were:
1. Ability to get response from doctor or the "on call" staff after hours (.5)
2. Length of time waiting in the waiting room to see doctor (.46)
3. Doctor paying attention to concerns (.63)
4. Doctor reassurance and support (.60)
5. Doctor spending enough time with patient during visit (.56)

1996 INTERNAL ALL PHYSICIANS CLINIC SURVEY

As a follow-up to the 1996 Physician-Focused Wellness Member Satisfaction Survey done by Wellness Health Plan, All Physicians Clinic did their own internal survey, with more specific questions to compare their physicians with their peers. Results: unknown.

Method

Annually, Wellness Health Plan conducts a survey of member ratings and comments about their satisfaction with the care and services they received from system providers. From the 1996 analysis, one medical group (All Physicians Clinic, a pseudonym for an active health plan medical provider group) was offered and accepted the opportunity to participate in the pilot study due to the nature of their satisfaction scores. The intent was to collaborate with the medical group practice staff for purposes of specifically identifying the reasons for poor performance; developing strategies to correct deficiencies; implementing action plans; and remeasuring the effects toward excellence. Due to sensitive trust issues between the health plan and medical providers, an outside business improvement group, Success, Inc. (a pseudonym), was retained by the Department of Health Measurement, Analysis, and Research (a pseudonym) to provide direct consultation while developing and implementing improvement action plans in conjunction with the medical providers, clinic management, and rank-and-file employees of All Physicians Clinic. An introduction to the member/patient satisfaction survey and research methods used follows.

The survey's main goal was to collect Wellness members' satisfaction ratings regarding their physicians and to incorporate the results into the physician evaluation program. A secondary goal was to use the survey results to give clinics in the Medica network a baseline performance evaluation to be used for educational purposes. Other uses of the survey included:

- identifying commonalties across specialties;
- providing physicians in each specialty the ability to compare themselves with their peers;
- providing clinics in the Wellness network the ability to compare themselves with other clinics;
- supporting Wellness strategic goals; and
- identifying areas where physicians and clinics are doing well and areas that need improvement.

The 1996 Physician-Focused Wellness Member Satisfaction Survey was a mail survey that measured Wellness Premium Option and Wellness Capitated members' satisfaction ratings with physicians in seven specialties: dermatology, family practice, internal medicine, obstetrics/gynecology, ophthalmology, orthopedics, and pediatrics. The survey was coordinated by the Department of Health Measurement, Analysis, and Research at Wellness Health Plans and administered by National Information Systems or NIS (a pseudonym).

Survey Design

The survey's design was built around five dimensions of care that were selected to measure physician and clinic performance in relationship to member satisfaction:

- Access to care (for clinic performance only)
- Clinical aspects of visit
- Clinic staff (for clinic performance only)
- Interaction with doctor
- Overall satisfaction with physician

Survey questions contributing to each dimension were developed utilizing the following resources:

- 1995 Physician Evaluation Survey and results;
- Evaluation surveys previously conducted by United Health Care plans;
- Externally coordinated Wellness Satisfaction Surveys.

National Information Systems created a scan-ready graphical design for the survey. The survey was a two-page booklet, with the cover letter and member's mailing address on the first page, and the survey questions on the remaining pages. Cronbach's alpha was used to measure the reliability of the survey. This statistic measures the internal consistency of the survey questions.

The value of Cronbach's alpha was large (.97 out of 1.0), indicating that the survey instrument is reliable. Reliability of the survey questions in each dimension ranged from .88 to .97.

Population and Sampling Design

A sample of members who received services between January 1996 and November 1996 from dermatologists, family practitioners, general intern-

ists, obstetricians, gynecologists, ophthalmologists, orthopedists, and pediatricians were selected for the survey. These members were enrolled
during this time period in the Wellness Premium Option and/or Wellness
Capitated Products. Adults, ages eighteen to sixty-five, and guardians/
parents of children ages zero to twelve were selected to complete the
survey. The types of services used to select members were generated using
CPT4 codes denoting ambulatory, face-to-face encounters. Excluded from
the survey were members in the following groups: members between the
ages of thirteen and seventeen years, Wellness Health System employees,
NIS employees, members in unions, and Medicaid members. These members were excluded from the survey due to confidentiality issues, member
bias, contractual issues, and survey design.

The physicians included in the sample had provided services to 150 or
more unique members from July 1995 through June 1996. The clinics
included in the sample were those where members received services from
the selected physicians.

Data Collection Methods

National Information Systems (NIS) conducted the mail survey. The
Department of Health Measurement, Analysis, and Research at Wellness
provided NIS with member names in October and December of 1996.
During these same months, NIS mailed the surveys to members. Seven
days after the survey was mailed, the member received a follow-up post-
card. Each week NIS scanned the surveys and sent Wellness any comments attached to the surveys. Comments that warranted follow-up were
given to the Quality Improvement Integration Department. A member was
picked only once in the sample; however, a member could be sent more
than one survey if his or her child/children were also selected in the
sample. Therefore, 22.5 percent of the households received more than one
survey.

Response Rates

NIS sent out 118,131 surveys to members, representing 1,285 physicians and 316 clinics. Nine hundred and twenty surveys were nondeliverable. Taking into consideration the nondeliverable surveys, 39,539 surveys
were completed for an overall response rate of 34 percent.

Table 6.17 shows the number of physician types and clinics included in
the final analyzed data, the original sample, and in the Wellness Premium
Option and Capitated Network. The final analyzed data consisted of only

physicians and clinics with more than twenty-seven completed surveys. The original sample data was derived by the physicians providing services to 150 or more unique members from July 1995 through 1996. Thus, 23 percent of the physicians and 33 percent of the clinics in the network were included in the reporting.

TABLE 6.17. 1996 Physician Performance Evaluation of Physicians and Clinics

Physician Type	Final Analyzed Data *	Sample Data *	Wellness Premium Option/Capitated Network *
	# Percent of Network Total	# Percent of Network Total	Total
Dermatology	38 30	41 42	127
Family Practice	514 27	643 40	1,887
Internal Medicine	116 15	141 24	778
OB/GYN	138 24	145 30	574
Ophthalmologist	82 30	83 38	277
Orthopedist	45 13	60 23	361
Pediatrician	157 33	172 40	476
Total Physicians	1,090 23	1,285 33	4,697
Total Clinics	284 36	316 36	868

Source: Sommers, P. A. and Deml, L. Internal study. Allina Health System. Minneapolis, MN, 1997-1998.

* Includes only physicians with valid Social Security numbers, provider numbers, and group practice identification numbers

Error Rates

Table 6.18 below shows the completed surveys per physician and clinic. The survey sample size for the physicians who received a scored profile provides an accuracy rating of ± 9 percent to ± 11 percent when generalized to each physician. The survey sample size for the clinics included in the overall clinic score provides an accuracy rating of ± 3 percent to ±11 percent when generalized to each clinic. The confidence interval for the samples is 95 percent.

TABLE 6.18. 1996 Physician Performance Evaluation—Margin of Error

Physician Type	Number of Completed Surveys	Margin of Error Actual or Average 95% Confidence Interval
Per Physician	27 to 47	± 9% to ± 11%
Per Clinic	27 to 841	± 3% to ± 11%

Data Analysis

NIS scanned the surveys and sent frequencies and the survey data to Wellness in a text file format. SPSS (Statistical Package for the Social Sciences) was used to analyze the data and to produce the graphics in the aggregate report. The survey dimensions were equally weighted to produce the overall scores for each physician, specialty, clinic, and all clinics.

Overall specialty scores and overall clinic scores were calculated by using only physicians and clinics with more than twenty-seven completed surveys. The physician evaluation profiles for physicians and clinics and the aggregate report denoted survey scores in two ways:

• The percentage of member responses
• The mean of member responses on a five-point rating scale of Poor (1), Fair (2), Good (3), Very Good (4), and Excellent (5).

Limitations of Methodology

Limitations of the sampling design included difficulty in finding a large number of members in a four-month time period and physicians not seeing enough members to achieve twenty-seven completed surveys in lieu of the estimated response rates. As such, eighteen physicians had five to nine surveys completed, sixty-two physicians had ten to fourteen surveys completed, twenty-one physicians had fifteen to nineteen surveys completed, and ninety-four physicians had ten to twenty-six surveys completed.

Completed Surveys

Physician and clinic profiles were sent out in March of 1997. To receive scored survey results, the physician needed a minimum of twenty-seven unique members to complete the survey. Physicians who did not receive twenty-seven complete surveys were given a profile for educational purposes (1,095 physicians received scored profiles, and 195 physicians received profiles for educational purposes). In addition, all clinics were given a profile for educational purposes.

Table 6.19 shows the number of completed surveys and the number of physicians and clinics who received more than twenty-seven completed surveys.

TABLE 6.19. 1996 Physician Performance Evaluation—Number of Physicians and Completed Surveys.

Physician Type	Number of Physicians/Clinics	Number of Completed Surveys
Dermatology	38	1,254
Family Practice	514	16,723
Internal Medicine	116	3,781
Obstetrics/Gynecology	138	4,667
Ophthalmology	82	2,709
Orthopedist	45	1,411
Pediatrician	157	5,162
All Physicians	1,285	35,707
All Clinics	284	38,629

As one of many medical groups participating in the survey, All Physicians Clinic was selected as an "initial pilot" because of their request for help and the interest expressed in working toward excellence. The remainder of this chapter will focus on All Physicians Clinic and the specific consumer satisfaction elements most important to that group, as reflected by the Wellness members whom the group served during the study period.

Results

In September 1997, All Physicians Clinic staff met with Wellness Health Measurement, Analysis, and Research staff and Success, Inc., the outside business improvement group that would be working directly with All Physicians Clinic. Results from the 1996 Wellness Physician-Focused Member Satisfaction Survey was presented to serve as a baseline for the pilot.

1996 Baseline Results

- Eighteen physicians from All Physicians Clinic received satisfaction evaluations from at least twenty-seven different health plan members who received services during the study period.
- Premier Option and Capitated members responded to the survey for visits from January through December 1996.
- Scores related to the five dimensions of care previously discussed revealed the following:
  1. Four physicians scored well below other physicians in their specialties.
  2. Six physicians had low satisfaction with the clinical aspects of visit scores.
  3. Five physicians had low satisfaction with the interaction with doctor scores.
- Clinic areas for improvement were identified by standard deviations away from overall clinics' mean scores and correlation (r) with physician satisfaction:
  1. Ability to phone doctor or staff for advice during regular hours: − 1.9 (.52)
  2. The wait to get a routine care appointment: − 1.6 (.38)
  3. Ability to contact doctor or on call staff after hours: − 1.5 (.52)
  4. Ease of getting through to make an appointment: − 1.4 (.36)
  5. Education on prevention of illness and good health care habits: − 1.3 (.68)
  6. Clarity of information and advice received by phone during office hours: − 1.3 (.47)
- Physician areas for improvement were identified by standard deviations away from overall clinics' mean scores and correlation (r) with physician satisfaction:
  1. Instructions for prescribed medication and treatments: − 1.3 (.70)
  2. Education on prevention of illness and health care habits: − 1.3 (.68)
  3. Reminders and encouragement to seek preventive care: − 1.2 (.66)
  4. Doctor respecting your privacy: − 1.1 (.69)
  5. Timeliness of the follow-up reports on lab tests and procedures: − 1.0 (.68)

Pilot Project Results

An improvement team process at All Physicians Clinic was chartered by the Medical Group's Board of Directors in November 1997. Membership includes physicians, administrative staff, rank-and-file employees who "do the work" at the appropriate level to understand and provide real-world recommendations, which, when implemented, will solve each identified problem. Success, Inc., staff are coordinating activities and serve as a resource for the improvement team.

Between November 1997 and February 1998, a problem solving model has been implemented that includes the following elements, which the board has asked the improvement team to address:

- Identify project parameters based on current data (including the assessment of employee attitudes).
- Prioritize key areas.
- Scope down key areas for improvement, identify opportunities and barriers along with the required resources to achieve desired results.
- Set measures of success and tie to bottom line results.
- Recommend improvement projects for All Physicians Clinic board approval.
- Implement and manage project activities.
- Measure effect of implementing improvement team recommendations, as well as determining the impact (both financial and programmatically) if the recommendations are not implemented.
- Report results back to the board on a regular basis.

Summary of Results

A perception of systemic problems:

- Repetition of low scores has occurred over the years.
- Improvements made do not appear to have a direct, positive, measurable impact.
- Responsibility for tasks and actions is unclear.
- It is difficult to determine if the problems are process, behavior, or system related.
- The gap between patient/member and employee perceptions of what is important needs to be eliminated.

Recommendations Based on Results

The following three improvement project goals and measurable objectives were assembled following a three-day focused in-service that reviewed past and current information.

Response Time to Patient Messages

1. Problem: amount of time between when the message is taken and a response is received is not acceptable.
2. Goal: reduce patient complaints regarding length of time it takes to respond to messages.
   a. Establish a policy on message response time.
   b. Place a higher rating on the patient satisfaction survey regarding responses to messages.
   c. Encourage better physician and patient rapport.
   d. Reduce worker frustration in the communication center.

Overall Time Spent in the Waiting Room from Scheduled Appointment to When the Patient Is Brought into the Exam Room

1. Problem: patients are waiting too long.
2. Goal: shorten the actual and patient perception of wait time:
   a. Increase patient registration.
   b. Improve patient satisfaction with wait time.
   c. Improve co-worker satisfaction with wait time.
   d. Increase patient retention.

Timeliness of Response to Patients Regarding Test Results

1. Problem: patients are not being notified of test results in a timely fashion.
2. Goal: develop and implement a new policy on the timely delivery of test results to patients.
   a. Decrease risk management issues in this area.
   b. Shorten the actual and patient perception of time it takes.
   c. Improve patient satisfaction with response time.
   d. Improve co-worker satisfaction with test response time.

The third improvement project listed is recommended and approved by the board for initial implementation.

Summary

A pilot project was implemented in November 1997 between Wellness Health System/Wellness Health Plans and All Physicians Clinic for purposes of cooperatively developing and implementing the following plans:

1. Improve health plan member satisfaction with services received at All Physicians Clinic.
2. Improve clinic employee satisfaction at All Physicians Clinic.
3. Increase plan member loyalty to both Wellness Health Plans and All Physicians Clinic based upon the excellent care and services provided.
4. Improve the bottom line of All Physicians Clinic as it pertains to Wellness Health Plans members, based upon increased enrollment and membership retention.

Survey results and previous improvement activities from 1994, 1995, and 1996 were used as part of the needs assessment information base. A current organizational assessment survey was conducted in November 1997 and provided feedback from patient/members and employees at All Physicians Clinic to serve as a snapshot in time that can be compared from one year to the next. Specific pilot goals and objectives were developed by the improvement team following analysis of the needs assessment data. Three improvement projects were outlined by the improvement team (as illustrated in the results section). The one selected for initial development and implementation beginning in January 1998 was "Timeliness of Response to Patients Regarding Test Results."

By the end of February 1998, an improvement plan will be complete and implemented, which includes an operational redesign of how All Physicians Clinic conducts each test procedure, the involvement of participating outside vendors, and the process mapping of each test from the time the patient/member received the test to when and how the results were communicated back to the patient/member.

Significance

The significance of a successful pilot at All Physicians Clinic will be reflected on multiple levels:

1. The ability of Wellness Health Plans to begin to regain the trust and confidence of its practicing physicians through cooperative activities

is paramount to Wellness Health System's current and future success.

2. When health plan member satisfaction improves at All Physician Clinic the following effects will be measurable:
   - Employee satisfaction will increase.
   - Plan member loyalty to both Wellness and All Physicians Clinic, based upon excellent care and service, will increase and be demonstrated through increased enrollment and membership retention.
   - The All Physicians Clinic's bottom line will improve as it pertains to Wellness Health Plans members.
   - Wellness Health Plans' bottom line will improve in relationship to the members served at All Physicians Clinic.

Next Steps

1. The successful pilot will be expanded to address the remaining two improvement projects previously identified at All Physicians Clinic:
   - Overall time spent in the waiting room from scheduled appointment time to when the patient is brought into the exam room
   - Response time to patient messages
2. In 1998, the hospital(s) where All Physicians Clinic admits its patients will be included in the pilot. Wellness is interested in determining how many of the health plan members cared for by Wellness physicians are receiving hospital services from Wellness hospitals. Second, does consumer satisfaction with services at All Physicians Clinic affect where the Wellness Health Plan members are sent to receive hospital services?

It is believed that excellent care and service will be delivered at the clinic level and will "pull through" Wellness members to a health system hospital. In total, excellent care and service will account for increased enrollment and membership retention.

SUMMARY

- Briefly describe each application and indicate one or more situations in which the health care organization would benefit from its implementation. Begin with the end in mind.
- Are there other applications that can be added to the outcomes management process? If yes, include them.

- Using an outcomes management system approach (see Table 4.4 on p. 123) list each activity that is an organization priority and complete the information requested in each category of the grid.
- Return on investment for each outcome achieved will add value to the decision-making process. Work effort and resources must be focused on the most important indicators of each target to have optimum effectiveness. What are two of the top five indicators for each of the health care organization's top priorities?
- What is current level of alignment within the health care organization as a whole? Does each functional unit and department directly contribute to customer-focused care and the other priorities? How will you use what has been learned about alignment of organizational priorities and resources?

Resources

Information about health plans, hospitals, and physicians is available through each organization's association office. Primary contact can be made for various information sources (e.g., costs, compensation, best of practice, benchmarks, and other related databases) and for contact information about other organizations that may be helpful.

HEALTH PLANS

American Association of Health Plans (AAHP)
1129 20th Street NW, Suite 600
Washington, DC 20036

National Committee for Quality Assurance (NCQA)
1350 New York Avenue, Suite 700
Washington, DC 20005

HOSPITALS

American Hospital Association
737 North Michigan Avenue
Chicago, IL 60611-2615

Joint Commission on Accreditation of Healthcare Organizations (JCAHO)
1 Renaissance Boulevard
Oakbrook Terrace, IL 60181

PHYSICIANS

American Medical Association (AMA)
515 North State Street
Chicago, IL 60610

American Medical Group Association (AMGA)
1422 Duke Street
Alexandria, VA 22314-3430

Medical Group Management Association (MGMA)
104 Inverness Terrace East
Englewood, CO 80112-5306

Notes

Chapter 1

1. Sommers, P. A. *Medical Group Management in Turbulent Times: How Physician Leadership Can Optimize Health Plan, Hospital, and Medical Group Performance.* Binghamton, NY: The Haworth Press, 1998.
2. Dunevitz, B. Physician Compensation Stays Flat for a Second Straight Year. *Medical Group Management Update,* 37(19): 1, 9, 1998.
3. American Hospital Association. *Recent Trends in Employer Health Insurance Coverage and Benefits.* Insurance editorial. Chicago, IL: American Hospital Association News, September 3, 1996.
4. Editorial. Industry Guide Indicates HMO Performance Slipping. *Capitation Rates and Data,* 2(5): 49-60, National Health Information, LLC, Marietta, GA, May 1997.
5. Ellwood, P. and Kaiser, L. *The Medical Organization of the Future.* Alexandria, VA: American Group Practice Association, 1985.
6. Halvorson, G. C. *Strong Medicine.* New York: Random House, 1993.
7. Allina Health System. *INSIDE: Market and Network Services,* November 1996; *Healthy Living Is Our Choice,* June 1997; *Winning Health,* Summer 1997. Information is available by contacting ALLINA, 5601 Smetana Drive, P. O. Box 9310, Minneapolis, MN 55440-9310.
8. Stodghill, R. II. Gordon Sprenger Interview: What's a Ton of Prevention Worth? Allina Health System Is Trying to Heal the Sick by Healing Society. *Business Week,* 8: 162-163, October 28, 1996.
9. HealthPartners. *Health Plan Members Materials Related to Prevention of Disease and Healthy Lifestyle Development.* Minneapolis, MN: HealthPartners Today, Fall 1997.
10. Wetzell, S. and Hamacher, F. Buyers Health Care Action Group (BHCAG). Request for proposal for 1997. Bloomington, MN: BHCAG, distributed in 1995.
11. Howatt, G. HealthPartners to Emphasize Wellness in Goal-Setting Prevention Program. *Minneapolis Star Tribune,* Tuesday, February 22, 1994, D1.
12. Majeski, T. Largest HMO Bringing Bid for Wellness to Home Office. *St. Paul Pioneer Press,* Tuesday, February 22, 1994, 1.
13. Editorial. An HMO Tries Talking Members into Healthy Habits. *The Wall Street Journal,* Wednesday, April 6, 1994.
14. Ornish, D. *Dr. Dean Ornish's Program for Reversing Heart Disease.* New York: HarperCollins, 1992.

15. Allina Health System. 1997-1998 Clinical Priorities. Allina-Wide Clinical Action Group (CAG) Focus, *Allina Today,* March/April: 5, 1998.

16. Ehlen, J. K. and Sprenger G. M. On the Road Toward Integration: Allina's Journey Continues. *The Medical Journal of Allina,* 6(2):2-4, Spring 1997.

17. Kleinman, J. H. Allina's Efforts to Provide an Excellent Healthcare Experience. *The Medical Journal of Allina,* 6(2):5-6, Spring 1997.

18. Lewin, L. S. A Paler Shade of Gray: Or, Returning the Physician to the Center of Health Care. *Medical Group Management Journal,* 45(5): 60-64, September/October 1998.

19. Schneider, P. Stone Soup: When Providers and Vendors Throw Their Ideas into the Pot, the Informational Technology Infrastructure That Results Can Satisfy Them Both. *Healthcare Informatics,* 9(3):58-60, September 1998.

20. National Committee for Quality Assurance. *The State of Managed Care Quality* (1997). Washington, DC: NCQA, 1997.

21. Health Resouces Publishing. Directions: Looking Ahead in Healthcare. *Executive Briefing,* 1(1), 1998.

22. The University of Michigan. *Health Risk Appraisal.* Ann Arbor, MI: Fitness Research Center, 1998.

23. Barnhardt, D. L. and Dunevitz, B. Patients Disconnected from Health Care System: That's Why Benchmarking Is So Important. *Medical Group Management UPDATE,* 37(14):1-2, July 15, 1998.

Chapter 2

1. Sommers, P. A. Using Technology for Competitive Advantage in the Management of Integrated Health Care Services. *Executive Solutions—SAS Institute Magazine for Business Decision Makers,* First Quarter 1997 (2): Keynote address at SAS Institute World Headquarters Annual Health Care Conference, Cary, North Carolina, January 15-16, 1997.

2. Sommers, P. A. and Torgerson, T. Billing Cycle Redesign Analysis for Health Plan/Care Delivery Organization (HP/CDO). Internal study. Allina Health System 1996-1997. Presented at Allina Leadership Forum on October 25, 1996.

3. Sommers, P. A. Managing Medical Services Outcomes by Predicting and Achieving Success: An Inferential Approach. *American Medical Group Association,* 44:3, 24, 26-28, 30, May/June 1995.

4. Sommers, P. A. Longitudinal Analysis of a Physician-Hospital Collaboration That Works: The Ramsey Model (1987-1991). *American Medical Group Association,* 43:3, 14, 16-18, 20, 22-23, 26, 66, 1994.

5. Sommers, P. A. Multivariate Analysis Applied to the Delivery of Medical Services: A Focus on Evaluation and Replication. *International Journal of Applied Psychology,* 34(2):203-224, 1985.

6. Eccles, R. G. The Performance Measurement Manifesto. *Harvard Business Review/Reprint Collection on Measuring Corporate Performance,* Product #49516, Reprint #91103, January/February: 55-62, 1991.

7. Kaplan, R. S. and Norton, D. P. Using the Balanced Scorecard as a Strategic Management System, *Harvard Business Review/Reprint Collection Measur-*

ing Corporate Performance, Product #49516, Reprint #96107, January/February: 1-13, 1996.

8. Drucker, P. F. The Information Executives Truly Need. *Harvard Business Review/Reprint Collection Measuring Corporate Performance,* Product #49516, Reprint #95104, January/February:36-44, 1995.

9. Sommers, P. A. Maximizing Group Practice Medicine: Unifying Ramsey Clinic and Hospital Services. *American Medical Group Association,* 41(3): 51-58, May/June 1992.

10. Sommers, P. A. A Consolidated Approach to Physician/Hospital Bonding—Ramsey Clinic Style. *American Medical Group Association,* 39(6):24-33, November/December 1990.

11. Sommers, P. A. A Natural Partnership—Physician and Hospital: The Ramsey Clinic Model. *American Medical Group Association* 38(2):34-53, March/April 1989.

12. Sommers, P. A. Preparing for 2000 and Beyond through Physician Group, Hospital and Health Plan Integration. *American Medical Group Association,* 43(6):38-43, November/December 1994.

13. Kelly, F. J., Beggs, D. L., and McNeil, K. *Multiple Regression Approach.* Carbondale, IL: Southern Illinois University Press, 1969.

14. Rust, R., Zahorik, A. and Zeiningham, T. *Return on Quality.* Chicago and Cambridge: Probus Publishing Company, 1994.

15. Popham, W. J. *Educational Statistics.* New York: Harper and Row, 1967.

16. Center for Research in Ambulatory Health Care Administration. *CRAHCA Physician Services Practice Analysis Comparison (PSPA): 1993 Medians.* Englewood, CO: MGMA, 1994.

17. *Managed Care Digest, 1997: Medical Group Practice Edition, Hoechst Marion Roussel Managed Care Digest, Medical Group Practice Digest,* Kansas City, MO, 1997. Data supplied by Medical Group Management Association (MGMA), Englewood, CO, and American Medical Group Association (AMGA), Alexandria, VA.

18. National Committee for Quality Assurance (NCQA). *The State of Managed Care Quality* (1997). Washington, DC: NCQA, 1997.

Chapter 3

1. Sommers, P. A. *Medical Group Management in Turbulent Times: How Physician Leadership Can Optimize Health Plan, Hospital, and Medical Group Performance.* Binghamton, NY: The Haworth Press, 1998.

2. Sommers, P. A. Preparing for 2000 and Beyond Through Physician Group, Hospital and Health Plan Integration. *American Medical Group Association,* 43(6):38-43, November/December 1994.

3. Sommers, P. A. Using Technology for Competitive Advantage in the Management of Integrated Health Care Services. *Executive Solutions—SAS Institute Magazine for Business Decision Makers,* First Quarter 1997, 2: 22. Keynote address at SAS Institute World Headquarters Annual Health Care Conference, Cary, North Carolina, January 15-16, 1997.

4. The following information is reprinted with permission from the National Committee for Quality Assurance (NCQA). *The State of Managed Care Quality (1997).* Washington, DC: NCQA, 1997. Copyright ©1997 by NCQA.

Chapter 4

1. Sommers, P. A. The Inferential Evaluation Model. *Journal of Educational Technology,* 2(3):31-32, May 1973.

2. Sommers, P. A. Managing Medical Services Outcomes by Predicting and Achieving Success: An Inferential Approach. *American Medical Group Association,* 42(3): May-June 1995.

3. Sommers, P. A. and Deml, L. Medica Health Plans Key Indicator Analysis. Internal study of 1995 and 1996 information. Minneapolis, MN: Allina Health System, 1997.

4. Sommers, P. A. Using Technology for Competitive Advantage in the Management of Integrated Health Care Services. *Executive Solutions—SAS Institute, Magazine for Business Decision Makers,* First Quarter 1997 (2):22. Keynote address at SAS Institute World Headquarters Annual Health Care Conference, Cary, North Carolina, January 15-16, 1997.

5. Glosemeyer, W. J. Enhanced Data Support Methodology (EDSM). Unpublished paper. Burnsville, MN, 1996.

Chapter 5

1. Sommers, P. A., Luxenberg, M. G., and Sommers, E.P. Continuous Quality-Improvement (CQI) Longitudinally Applied to Integrated Service Outcomes: An Inferential Evaluation Model (IEM) Approach. *Medical Group Management Association (MGMA),* 42(2):50-54, 56-58, 80-82, 1995.

2. Allina Health System/Medica Health Plans. 1997 Environmental Assessment Internal Allina study. Minneapolis, MN: Allina Health System, 1997.

3. Sommers, P. A., Bartelma, R., and Whelan, M. Market Medicine the Old-Fashioned Way: Consumer Satisfaction. *strategic Health Care Marketing,* 8(7): 10-12, 1991.

4. Sommers, P. A. Malpractice Risk and Patient Relations. *Grand Rounds on Medical Malpractice.* American Medical Association/Harvard Medical Institutions, Inc.: Article 1.1:20-22, 1990 (originally published in *Journal of Family Practice,* 20(3):299-301, 1985).

5. Sommers, P. A. Minimizing Malpractice Risk: A Patient Approach. *American Medical Group Association,* 36(5): 86-90, 1987.

6. Albrecht, K. and Zemke, R. *Service America: Doing Business in the New Economy.* Homewood, IL: Dow Jones-Irwin, 1985, pp. 1-18.

7. Sommers, P. A. Getting the Most Out of Your Visit to the Doctor. *Executive Health Report,* 26(1):1,4-5, 1989.

8. Sommers, P. A. What Physicians Should Know About Consumer Satisfaction. *The American Journal of Medical Sciences,* 295(5):415-417, 1988.

9. Sommers, P. A. *Medical Group Management in Turbulent Times: How physician leadership can optimize health plan, hospital, and medical group performance.* Binghamton, NY: The Haworth Press, 1998.

10. Joint Commission on Accreditation of Healthcare Organizations. *Accreditation Manual.* Oakbrook Terrace, IL: JCAHO, 1997.

11. Kongstvedt, P. R. The Managed Health Care Handbook, Third Edition. Gaithersburg, MD: Aspen Publishers, Inc., 1996.

12. National Committee for Quality Assurance (NCQA). *NCQA Accreditation Process Manual.* Washington, DC: NCQA, 1997.

13. Dacso, S. T. and Dacso, C. C. Managed Care Answer Book, Second Edition. Gaithersburg, MD: Aspen Publishers, Inc., 1997.

14. Sommers, P. A. and Thompson, M. A. The Best Malpractice Insurance of Them All: Consumer Satisfaction. *Health Marketing Quarterly,* 1(1):83-92, 1983; and in Winston, W. (Ed.), *Marketing the Group Practice: Practical Methods for the Health Care Practitioner.* Binghamton, NY: The Haworth Press Inc., 1983, pp. 83-92.

15. Sommers, P. A. Active Consumer Participation in the Health Delivery System: An Evaluation of Patient Satisfaction. (In English) *Bulletin of the Pan American Health Organization,* 16(4):367-383, 1982. (In Spanish) *Boletin de la Oficina Sanitaria Panamericana,* 94(1): Emero, 1983.

16. Sommers, P. A. and Fuchs, C. Pediatric Care for Exceptional Children: An Inferential Procedure Utilizing Consumer Satisfaction Information. *Medical Care,* 18(6):657-667, 1980.

17. Sommers, P. A. Consumer Satisfaction with Medical Care. *American Medical Group Association,* 29(7):5-8, 20, 1980.

18. Sommers, P. A. *Consumer Satisfaction in Medical Practice.* Binghamton, NY: The Haworth Press, Inc., in press.

19. Sommers, P. A. *Medical Group Management in Turbulent Times:* How Physician Leadership Can Optimize Health Plan, Hospital, and Medical Group Performance. Binghamton, NY: The Haworth Press, Inc., 1998.

20. Sommers, P .A. and Nycz, G. A. Procedure to Study the Efficiency of Clinical Services Provided to Children with Exceptional Health and Educational Needs: A Question of Consumer Satisfaction. *American Journal of Public Health,* 68(9):903-905, 1978.

21. Sommers, P. A. Multivariate Analysis Applied to the Delivery of Medical Services: A Focus on Evaluation and Replication. *International Journal of Applied Psychology,* 34:203-224, 1985.

22. Nelson, A. A Consumer Satisfaction Evaluation Study of Ramsey Clinic Services. Internal study. Minneapolis/St. Paul, MN: Nelson Research Services, Inc., 1987.

23. Kilmann, R. H. *Management of Corporate Culture.* New York: John Wiley and Sons, 1988.

24. Silversin, J. and Kornacki, M.U. Employee Values and Commitment to Service. *Medical Group Management Association,* October 1989.

25. Hoxie, L. *Department of Ambulatory Healthcare—Accreditation Services Study.* Chicago, IL: Joint Commission on Accreditation of Healthcare Organizations, January/February 1991.

26. *Accreditation Manual for Hospitals* (AMH). Chicago, IL: Joint Commission on Accreditation of Healthcare Organizations, August 1993.

27. Kaplan, R. S. and Norton, D. P. Using the Balanced Scorecard as a Strategic Management System. *Harvard Business Review/Reprint Collection Measuring Corporate Performance,* Product #49516, Reprint #96107, January/February:1-13, 1996.

Chapter 6

1. Sommers, P. A., Luxenberg, M. G., and Sommers, E. P. Continuous Quality Improvement (CQI) Longitudinally Applied to Integrated Service Outcomes: An Inferential Evaluation Model (IEM) Approach. *Medical Group Management Association (MGMA),* 42(2):50-58, March/April 1995.

2. Anderson D. Documented Clinical Priorities from Current and Previous Work As a Quality Improvement Analyst. Minneapolis, MN: Allina Health System, 1996.

3. Premier, Inc. *Best Practices in Healthcare: A Series of Reports Describing Successful Benchmarking Efforts and Research.* Charlotte, NC: Premier, Inc., 1996.

4. Spendolini, J. F. *The Benchmarking Book.* New York: AMACOM, a division of American Management Association, 1992.

5. Editor. *Capitation Rates and Data,* Volume II. Marietta, GA: National Health Information LLC, 1997 and 1998.

6. Editorial. Industry Guide Indicators HMO Performance Slipping, *Capitation Rates and Data,* 2(5):49-60. National Health Information LLC, Marietta, GA, May 1997.

7. American Healthcare Consultants: Beat Insurers at Their Own Game—MD Groups Launch Direct Contracting. *Physicians Managed Care Report* 3(9):97-98, 100, 1996.

8. National Committee for Quality Assurance (NCQA). *NCQA Accreditation Process Manual.* Washington, DC: NCQA, 1995.

9. Minnesota Department of Health (MDH). *1995 HEIS Measures Acrosss Health Plan Comparisons.* St. Paul, MN: MDH, 1996.

10. Center for Research in Ambulatory Health Care Administration. *CRAHCA Physician Services Practice Analysis Comparison (PSPA): 1993 Medians.* Englewood, CO: MGMA, 1994.

11. *Managed Care Digest, 1997: Medical Group Practice Edition, Hoechst Marion Roussel Managed Care Digest, Medical Group Practice Digest,* Kansas City, MO, 1997. Data supplied by Medical Group Management Association (MGMA), Englewood, CO, and American Medical Group Association (AMGA), Alexandria, VA.

12. Barnhardt, D. L. and Dunevitz, B. Patients Disconnected from Health Care System: That's Why Benchmarking Is So Important. *Medical Group Management UPDATE*, 37(14):1, July 15, 1998.

13. Sommers, P. A. An Inferential Model: Systematic Analysis to Hasten a Technology of Evaluation in the Behavioral Sciences. PhD dissertation. Carbondale, IL: Southern Illinois University. Copyright 1971.

14. Sommers P. A. Managing Medical Services Outcomes by Predicting and Achieving Success: An Inferential Approach. *American Medical Group Association*, 41(3): 24, 26-28, 30, 1995.

15. Balestracci, D. Statistical Tools to Help Manage Utilization and Costs. American Group Practice Association, 45th Annual Conference on "Quality-Change Management—Managed Care," January 18-21, New Orleans, LA, 1995.

16. Sommers, P. A. and Luxenberg, M. J. Physician-Hospital Integration, Ramsey Style. *Minnesota Medicine,* 77:22-25, 1994.

17. Sommers, P. A. Longitudinal Analysis of a Physician-Hospital Collaboration That Works: The Ramsey Model (1987-1991). *American Medical Group Association*, 43(3): 3, 14, 16-18, 20, 22-23, 26, 66, 1994.

18. Kelly, F. J., Beggs, D. L., and McNeil, K. *Multiple Regression Approach.* Carbondale, IL: Southern Illinois University Press, 1969.

19. Popham, W. J. *Educational Statistics.* New York: Harper and Row, 1967.

20. Sommers, P. A. The Inferential Evaluation Model. *Journal of Educational Technology,* 2:33-34, May 1970.

21. Sommers, P. A. and Fuchs, C. Pediatric Care for Exceptional Children: An Inferential Procedure Utilizing Consumer Satisfaction Information. *Medical Care,* 18(6):657-667, 1980.

22. Sommers, P. A. Multivariate Analysis Applied to the Delivery of Medical Services: A Focus on Evaluation and Replication. *International Review of Applied Psychology,* 34(2):203-224, 1985.

23. Sommers, P. A., Holt, L. E., Joiner, L. M., Gross, J. C., William, M. A., and Mainord, J. C. Kinesio-Perceptual Abilities as Predictors of Race: A Study of the Disadvantaged. *The Negro Educational Review,* 114-123, 1970.

24. Sommers, P. A., Joiner, L. M., Holt, L. E., and Gross, J. C. Reaction Time, Agility, Equilibrium and Kinesio-Perceptual Matching as Predictors of Intelligence. *Journal of Perceptual and Motor Skills,* 31:460-462, 1970.

25. Gross, J. C., Joiner, L. M., Holt, L. E., and Sommers, P. A. A Kinesio-Perceptual Test's Reliability and Validity with Retarded Subjects. *The Journal of Special Education,* 6(2):223-231, 1970.

26. Glosemeyer, B. Enhanced Data Support Methodology (EDSM). Unpublished paper. Burnsville, MN, 1996.

27. Sommers, P. A. and Torgerson, T. Health Plan/Care Delivery Organization Billing Cycle Redesign. An Internal Allina Health System study. Results presented to the Allina Leadership Council in October, 1966, and at a National Conference on Integrated Health Care Organizations, Albuquerque, NM, 1997.

28. Sommers, P. A. A Consolidated Approach to Physician/Hospital Bonding: Ramsey Clinic Style. *American Medical Group Association*, 39(6):24-33, November/December 1990.

29. Massman, N. Analysis of the Consolidation of Ramsey Clinic and St. Paul Ramsey Medical Center Business Office As a Result of Integration. A thesis in partial fulfillment of the master's degree, St. Mary's University Graduate School, Minneapolis, MN, 1996.

30. Sommers, P. A. Using Technology for Competitive Advantage in the Management of Integrated Health Care Services, *Executive Solutions—SAS Institute Magazine for Business Decisions Makers,* First Quarter 1997 (2):22. Keynote address at SAS Institute World Headquarters Annual Health Care Conference, Cary, North Carolina, January 15-16, 1997.

31. Sommers, P. A. and Deml, L. Medica Health Plans Key Indicator Analysis. Internal Allina Health System study of information 1995/1996, 1997.

32. Cave, D. G. The Marketbasket Approach to Cost Control in Capitated Plans. *Managed Health Care,* 6(5):46-60, May 1996.

33. Cave, D. G. and Geehr, E. C. Analyzing Patterns-of-Treatment Data to Provide Feedback to Physicians. *Medical Interface:* 117-128, July 1994.

34. Goldfield, N. and Boland, P. *Physician Profiling and Risk Adjustment.* Gaithersburg, MD: Aspen Publishers, Inc., 1996.

35. Equifax Healthcare Analytical Services. Peer-A-Med Physician Practice Profiling Analysis. An internal service/report provided for ConnectiCare, Inc., Baltimore, MD, February 1996.

36. Sommers, P. A. and Deml, L. Implementing Consumer Satisfaction Improvement While Developing Trust with Providers for Medica Health Plan Members. 1998 Minnesota Health Services Research Conference, Minneapolis, MN, February 24, 1998.

37. Sommers, P. A. *Medical Group Management in Turbulent Times: How Physician Leadership Can Optimize Health Plan, Hospital, and Medical Group Performance.* Binghamton, NY: The Haworth Press, Inc., 1998.

38. Sommers, P. A. *Consumer Satisfaction in Medical Practice.* Binghamton, NY: The Haworth Press, 1999.

39. Silversin, J. and Kornacki, M. J. Employee Values and Commitment to Service. *Medical Group Management Association,* 34(3):27-30, September/October 1989.

40. Kilmann, R. H. *Management of Corporate Culture.* New York: John Wiley and Sons, 1988.

41. Caldwell, C. *Mentoring Strategic Change in Health Care.* Milwaukee, WI: ASCQ Quality Press, 1995.

Glossary

accountability: Responsibility with the authority of a person or team to take action or achieve goals.

administration expense (as a health plan key indicator): Managing costs as a percent of revenue to ensure administrative expenses are in line with revenue growth.

analysis: Separating a process or function into parts to determine relationships between and among each component.

bar graph: An illustration composed of parallel and vertical bars showing dimensions to reflect specified quantities in a set of data.

benchmarking: Comparing standards of practice or operations to other similar organizations on a national and regional level.

brainstorming: A technique used to stimulate as many ideas as possible in a short time period; a way of obtaining group members' participation toward specific issues and/or required actions.

cause-effect diagram: A visual display (e.g., fishbone diagram) that illustrates the relationship between a problem and its contributing causes.

commercial members leaving health plans (as a health plan key indicator): The percent of total health plan commercial members that leave the plan each month because their employer terminated the relationship. The measure excludes those members who leave the plan at open enrollment, provided that the employer stays with the health plan.

consumer: An individual or group who receives a service or the production of goods (e.g., patient, physician, employee, regulator, payer, supplier, community).

control chart: A chart that graphically displays statistical data over time to monitor activity and events related to the completion of specific events or project activities. It serves to identify variations from expected or desired standards that reflect the need for corrections to keep activity on target.

cost-benefit analysis: An analysis used to calculate the costs and benefits associated with the proposed solutions of a problem.

Author's note: A number of the definitions were adapted from Quality Principles, and Tools and the Medica Health Plans Key Indicator Report, both internal work projects of Allina Health System, Minneapolis, MN, 1996 and 1997.

customer expectation: The need to perceive/receive a desired level of satisfaction.

customer focus: Services and goods are designed and delivered to meet specifically defined customer needs.

customer requirement: The results of successfully meeting defined customer needs, which leads to satisfaction.

customer service average wait time (as a health plan key indicator): Each individual call received by customer service is directed by an automated voice (interactive voice response—IVR) system that routes the call to the appropriate team to handle the customer request. The average customer wait time refers to the amount of time the caller remains on hold after this transfer until a live representative connects with them.

data: Information collected and recorded about the activities and events comprising the totality of what it takes to operate a health care organization.

decision matrix: A grid used to rate possible options/recommendations against prioritized and/or weighted criteria.

deliverable: A product or service that is produced by the system and provided to customers.

descriptive statistics: Math calculations that describe the key characteristics of a set of data that is known (e.g., mean, median, mode, and standard deviation), or graphical representations (e.g., histograms and line graphs).

discrepancy: The difference between actual and desired results if the two measures are not identical.

effectiveness: Achievement of the appropriate results.

efficiency: The manner in which the appropriate result is achieved.

enhanced data support methodology (EDSM): EDSM is an integral point-and-click health care reporting and analysis system. Through a menu system, users can view hospital, clinic, pharmacy, and enrollment data by specific hospital, clinic, or employer groups, or overall. Up to five levels of "drill down" are provided. Standardized reports are available through the reporting window. The system integrates EIS "drill down" and graphic capabilities, quality control, forecasting and query capabilities. Data are refreshed by a monthly download from mainframe DB2 tables. Data are also imported from other external databases and spreadsheets. The system utilizes Base, SQL, Access, Graph, AF, SCF, EIS, Quality Control, ETS, GIS, Insight, OR, and Query. The system is used for provider profiling, pricing, network coverage evaluation, disease analysis and management, process evaluation, utilization analysis, and forecasting. The system is utilized by all levels of employees, from senior management to nurses.

flowchart: An illustration showing the sequential steps or processes involved in a project or activity from beginning to end.

Health Plan Employer Data and Information Set (HEDIS): Developed by the National Committee for Quality Assurance (NCQA), HEDIS was designed to address two objectives: (1) educate employers about the value produced by their health care dollars, and (2) provide employers with information about health plan performance while establishing desired levels of accountability.

histogram: A bar chart graph that illustrates the frequency distribution of data. Observation frequencies are presented as bars on the chart.

inferential evaluation model (IEM): The IEM is an outcomes measurement and management tool that is based upon probability theory. Information processed through the model can point to needed changes and/or new opportunities. As new or changing patterns are identified, "drill down" to each of the data source's origin is applied to determine the nature and need of adjustment. It serves as a forecasting and validation instrument that determines by percent of variance the relationship between a criterion variable (e.g., operating income) and one or more key indicator variables (e.g., plan members, hospital admissions, outpatient visits, medical loss ratio, etc.). The IEM is used to predict desired outcomes (e.g., strategic targets associated with activities and functions of the health care system).

inferential statistics: Inferential statistics yield quantities that are interpreted along the baseline of a distribution of statistical probability. The findings allow for conclusions to be drawn from sampled data and generalized toward defined groups of the population. Inferential statistics are characterized by statistical significance, which illustrates (by a level of probability) a significant departure from what might be expected by chance alone.

LAN (local area network) availability (as a health plan key indicator): Actual availability of the file servers during normal business hours is compared to target.

line graph: A series of lines connecting data points showing the functional relationship between two or more variables.

Malcom Baldrige National Quality Award: A national award that recognizes service and manufacturing businesses that demonstrate exemplary quality in their practices, products, and services. The establishment of a comprehensive set of criteria to evaluate applicants has provided business leaders with a consistent set of standards by which they can evaluate their organizations.

medical loss ratio by product (as a health plan key indicator): The medical loss ratio is the percentage of the premium dollar (net of brokers' fees and taxes) that is spent on health care.

Medicare members leaving plan (as a health plan key indicator): The percent of total Medicare enrollees that leave the plan each month for voluntary reasons.

membership: The number of members reported by each insurance product compared to budget.

mission: Defines the broad purpose for which an organization exists. It addresses the fundamental question of why an organization exists, or why it is in business.

mission statement: A description of the activities needed to be carried out to achieve an end result.

operating income percentage (as a health plan key indicator): The portion of the premium dollar that results in profit to the health plan.

Pareto principle: The circumstances in which a relative few factors account for the majority of an effect. Also known as the 80/20 rule, where 80 percent of the desired result can be achieved by focusing on 20 percent of the desired result key indicators.

payer: Those (insurance company, employer) who reimburse the health care provider for services rendered.

pended claims: Claims over sixty days old from the date received that are being prepared for payment.

process mapping: A process that is used to describe and graphically display each project or activity component to be sequentially completed.

process performance: Measurement associated with the ways a project or activity was completed.

provider service average wait time (as a health plan key indicator): Provider service average wait time refers to the average amount of time the provider remains on hold until a live health plan representative connects with them. The measure reflects data by coordinators, verification representatives, and dental. The coordinators are responsible for claims and administrative questions, and the verification representatives are responsible for benefits and eligibility questions, and dental is responsible for the dental and provider network.

provider service call abandonment rate: The percentage of provider service calls that disconnect before a live representative connects with them.

quality: Achieving excellence related to customer requirements for care, service, and value.

quality improvement: The process of achieving excellence related to care, service, and value by increasing effectiveness and efficiency of activities and processes through continuous improvement.

redesign: Reorganizing existing elements into a more efficient and effective activity pattern.

stakeholder (or key stakeholder): A person or constituency who has a vested interest in a project, activity, or function.

team charter: A written statement used by a team that defines its purpose, and measurements or indicators that are used to evaluate its effectiveness.

threshold: The standard of performance below which improvement is needed.

trend (as a health plan key indicator): A trend factor measures the rate at which health care costs are changing due to such factors as fees paid to providers, changes in frequency and pattern of utilizing various medical services, and the use of new medical technology. Year-to-date trend is compared to prior years, current year budget, and the state's required expenditure growth target.

Bibliography

Albrecht, K. and Zemke, R. *Service America: Doing Business in the New Economy.* Dow Jones-Irwin, Homewood, IL, 1985, pp. 1-18.

Allina Health System. *Inside: Market and Network Services,* November 1996: Healthy Living Is Our Choice, June 1997; Winning Health, Summer 1997. Allina Health System, Minneapolis, MN, 1996 and 1997.

Allina Health System. Clinical Strategies: Allina-Wide Clinical Action Group (CAG) Focus. *Allina Today,* March/April:5, 1998.

Allina Health System/Medica Health Plans. Environmental Assessment. Internal Allina study. Allina Health System, Minneapolis, MN, 1997.

American Healthcare Consultants. Beat Insurers at Their Own Game—MD Groups Launch Direct Contracting. *Physicians Managed Care Report* 3(9):97-98, 100, 1996.

American Hospital Association, Insurance Editor. *Recent Trends in Employer Health Insurance Coverage and Benefits.* American Hospital Association, Chicago, IL, September 3, 1996.

Anderson, D. Documented Clinical Priorities from Current and Previous Work As a Quality Improvement Analyst. Internal study. Allina Health System, Minneapolis, MN, 1996.

Balestracci, D. Statistical Tools to Help Manage Utilization and Costs. AGPA 45th Annual Conference on "Quality-Change Management—Managed Care," January 18-21, New Orleans, LA, 1995.

Barnhardt, D. L. and Dunevitz, B. Patients Disconnected from Health Care System: That's Why Benchmarking Is So Important. *Medical Group Management UPDATE,* 37(14):1-2, July 15, 1998.

Caldwell C. *Mentoring Strategic Change in Health Care.* ASQC Quality Press, Milwaukee, WI, 1995.

Cave, D. G. The Marketbasket Approach to Cost Control in Capitated Plans, *Managed Health Care,* 6(5):46-60, May 1996.

Cave, D. G. and Geehr, E. C. Analyzing Patterns-of-Treatment Data to Provide Feedback to Physicians, *Medical Interface,* July:117-128, 1994.

Center for Research in Ambulatory Health Care Administration. *CRAHCA Physician Services Practice Analysis Comparison (PSPA): 1993 Medians.* Medical Group Management Association, Englewood, CO, 1994.

Dasco, S. T. and Dasco, C. C. *Managed Care Answer Book,* Second Edition. Aspen Publishers, Inc., Gaithersburg, MD, 1997.

Drucker, P. F. The Information Executives Truly Need. *Harvard Business Review/ Reprint Collection Measuring Corporate Performance,* Product #49516, Reprint #95104, January/February:36-44, 1991.

Dunevitz, B. Physician Compensation Stays Flat for a Second Straight Year. *Medical Group Management UPDATE,* 37(19):1, 9, 1998.

Eccles, R. G. The Performance Measurement Manifesto. *Harvard Business Review/Reprint Collection Measuring Corporate Performance,* Product #49516, Reprint #91103, January/February:55-62, 1991.

Editorial. An HMO Tries Talking Members into Healthy Habits. *The Wall Street Journal,* Wednesday, April 6, 1994.

Editorial. Industry Guide Indicates HMO Performance Slipping. *Capitation Rates and Data,* 2(5), National Health Information, LLC, Marietta, GA, May 1997.

Ehlen, J. K. and Sprenger, G. M. On the Road Toward Integration: Allina's Journey Continues. *The Medical Journal of Allina,* 6(2):2-4, Spring 1997.

Ellwood, P. and Kaiser, L. *The Medical Organization of the Future.* American Group Practice Association, Alexandria, VA, 1985.

Equifax Healthcare Analytical Services. Peer-a-Med Physician Practice Profiling Analysis. An internal service/report provided for ConnectiCare, Inc., Baltimore, MD, February, 1996.

Glosemeyer, B. Enhanced Data Support Methodology (EDSM). Unpublished paper. Burnsville, MN, 1996.

Goldfield, N. and Boland, P. *Physician Profiling and Risk Adjustment.* Aspen Publishers, Inc., Gaithersburg, MD, 1996.

Gross, J. C., Joiner, L. M., Holt, L. E., and Sommers, P. A. A Kinesio-Perceptual Test's Reliability and Validity with Retarded Subjects. *The Journal of Special Education,* 6(2):223-231, 1970.

Halvorson, G. C. *Strong Medicine.* Random House, New York, 1993.

HCIA, Inc. *The Guide to the Managed Care Industry,* 1997 Edition. HCIA, Inc., Baltimore, MD, 1997.

HealthPartners. *Health Plan Member Materials Related to Prevention of Disease and Healthy Lifestyle Development.* HealthPartners Today, Minneapolis, MN, 1997.

Health Resources Publishing Editor. Directions: Looking Ahead in Healthcare. *Executive Briefing,* 1(1), 1998.

Howatt, G. HealthPartners to Emphasize Wellness in Goal-Setting Prevention Program. *Minneapolis Star Tribune,* Tuesday, February 22, 1994, p. D1.

Hoxie, L. *Department of Ambulatory Healthcare—Accreditation Study.* Joint Commission on Accreditation of Healthcare Organizations, Chicago, IL, January/February, 1991.

Joint Commission on Accreditation of Healthcare Organizations (JCAHO). *Accreditation Manual for Hospitals (AMH).* JCAHO, OakBrook Terrace, IL, August 1993.

Joint Commission on Accreditation of Healthcare Organizations (JCAHO). *Accrediation Manual.* JCAHO, OakBrook Terrace, IL, 1997.

Kaplan, R. S. and Norton, D. P. Using the Balanced Scorecard As a Strategic Management System. *Harvard Business Review/Reprint Collection Measuring Corporate Performance,* Product #49516, Reprint #96107, January/February:1-13, 1996.

Kelly, F. J., Beggs, D. L., McNeil, K., Eichelberger, T., and Lyon, J. *Multiple Regression Approach.* Southern Illinois University Press, Carbondale, IL, 1969.

Kilmann, R. H. *Management of Corporate Culture.* John Wiley and Sons, New York, 1988.

Kleinman, J. H. Allina's Efforts to Provide an Excellent Healthcare Experience. *The Medical Journal of Allina,* 6(2):5-6, Spring 1997.

Kongstvedt, P. R. *The Managed Health Care Handbook,* Third Edition. Aspen Publishers, Inc., Gaithersburg, MD, 1996.

Lewin, L. S. A Paler Shade of Gray: Or, Returning the Physician to the Center of Health Care. *Medical Group Management Journal,* 45(5):60-64, September/October 1998.

Majesky, T. Largest HMO Bringing Bid for Wellness to Home Office. *St. Paul Pioneer Press,* Tuesday, February 22, 1994, p. 3.

Managed Care Digest, 1997: Medical Group Practice Edition, Hoechst Marion Roussel Managed Care Digest, Medical Group Practice Digest. Kansas City, MO, 1997. Data supplied by Medical Group Management Association (MGMA), Englewood, CO, and American Medical Group Association (AMGA), Alexandria, VA.

Massman, N. Analysis of the Consolidation of Ramsey Clinic and St. Paul-Ramsey Medical Center Business Office As a Result of Integration. A thesis in partial fulfillment of the master's degree, St. Mary's University Graduate School, Minneapolis, MN, 1996.

Medica Health Plans Key Indicator Report. An internal work document of Allina Health System, Minneapolis, MN, 1996-1997.

Medical Group Management Association (MGMA). *The Academic Practice Management Survey: 1994 Report Based on 1993 Data.* MGMA, Englewood, CO, 1994.

Minnesota Department of Health (MDH). *1995 HEDIS Measures Across Plan Comparisons.* MDH, St. Paul, MN, 1996.

National Committee for Quality Assurance (NCQA). *NCQA Accreditation Process Manual and Quality Compass.* NCQA, Washington, DC, 1995 and 1996.

National Committee for Quality Assurance (NCQA). *The State of Managed Care Quality (1997).* NCQA, Washington, DC, 1997.

National Health Information, LLC. *Capitation Rates and Data,* Volume II. National Health Information, LLC, Marietta, GA, 1997.

Nelson, A. Consumer Satisfaction Evaluation Study of Ramsey Clinic Services. Internal study conducted by Nelson Research Services, Inc., Minneapolis/St. Paul, MN, 1987.

Ornish, D. *Dr. Dean Ornish's Program for Reversing Heart Disease.* HarperCollins, New York, 1992.

Popham, W. J. *Education Statistics.* Harper and Row, New York, 1967.

Premier, Inc. *Best Practices in Healthcare: A Series of Reports Describing Successful Benchmarking Efforts and Research.* Premier, Inc., and related companies, Charlotte, NC, 1996.

Quality Principles and Tools. An internal work document of Allina Health System, Minneapolis, MN, 1996.

Rust, R., Zahorik, A., and Zeiningham, T. *Return on Quality.* Probus Publishing Company, Chicago and Cambridge, 1994.

Schneider, P. Stone Soup: When Providers and Vendors Throw Their Ideas into the Pot, the Informational Technology Infrastructure That Results Can Satisfy Them Both. *Healthcare Informatics,* 9(3):58-60, September 1998.

Schuller, R. H. Five Universal Principles for Today and Tomorrow. *Hour of Power,* weekly television program. Crystal Cathedral Ministries, Garden Grove, CA, November 1, 1998.

Silversin, J. and Kornacki, M. J. Employee Values and Commitment to Service. *Medical Group Management Association,* 34(3):27-30, September/October 1989.

Siren, P. B. and Laffel, G. L. Quality Management in Managed Care. In Kongstvedt, P. R., *The Managed Health Care Handbook,* Third Edition. Aspen Publishers, Inc., Gaithersburg, MD, 1996, pp. 402-422.

Sommers, P. A. The Inferential Evaluation Model. *Journal of Educational Technology,* 2(3):31-32, May 1973.

Sommers, P. A. Consumer Satisfaction with Medical Care. *American Medical Group Association,* 29(7):5-8, 20, 1980.

Sommers, P. A. Get the Most Out of Your Visit to the Doctor. A booklet published by the National Research Bureau, Inc., Employee Communications Division, Burlington, IA, June 1982.

Sommers, P. A. Active Consumer Participation in the Health Delivery System: An Evaluation of Patient Satisfaction. (In English) *Bulletin of the Pan American Health Organization,* 16(4):367-383, 1982; (In Spanish) *Boletin de la Oficina Sanitaria Panamericana,* 94(1): Emero, 1983.

Sommers, P. A. Managing Multispecialty Medical Services: A Focus on Special Children and the Elderly. *Medical Group Management Association,* 31(2):50-55, 62, 1984.

Sommers, P. A. Multivariate Analysis Applied to the Delivery of Medical Services: A Focus on Evaluation and Replication. *International Journal of Applied Psychology,* 34:203-224, 1985.

Sommers, P. A. Minimizing Malpractice Risk: A Patient Approach. *American Medical Group Association,* 36(95):86-90, 1987.

Sommers, P. A. What Physicians Should Know About Consumer Satisfaction. *The American Journal of Medical Sciences,* 295(5):415-417, 1988.

Sommers, P. A. A Natural Partnership—Physician and Hospital: The Ramsey Clinic Model. *American Medical Group Association,* 38(2):34-53, March/April 1989.

Sommers, P. A. Getting the Most Out of Your Visit to the Doctor. *Executive Health Report,* 26(1):4-5, 1989.

Sommers, P. A. A Consolidated Approach to Physician/Hospital Bonding—Ramsey Clinic Style. *American Medical Group Association,* 39(6):24-33, November/December 1990.

Sommers, P. A. Malpractice Risk and Patient Relations. *Grand Rounds on Medical Malpractice.* The American Medical Association/Harvard Medical Institutions, Inc., Article 1.1, pp. 20-22, 1990. (Originally published in *Journal of Family Practice,* 20(3):299-301, 1985.)

Sommers, P. A. Maximizing Group Practice Medicine: Unifying Ramsey Clinic and Hospital Services. *American Medical Group Association,* 41(3):51-58, May/June 1992.

Sommers, P. A. Longitudinal Analysis of a Physician-Hospital Integration, Ramsey Style. *Minnesota Medicine,* 43(3):3, 14, 16–18, 20, 22-23, 26, 55, 1994.

Sommers, P. A. Preparing for 2000 and Beyond Through Physician Group, Hospital, and Health Plan Integration. *American Medical Group Association,* 43(6):38-43, 1994.

Sommers, P. A. Internal study. Ramsey Clinic, St. Paul, MN, 1994-1995.

Sommers, P. A. Managing Medical Services Outcomes by Predicting and Achieving Success: An Inferential Approach. *American Medical Group Association* 44(3):24, 26-28, 30, 1995.

Sommers, P. A. Internal study. Ramsey Clinic/St. Paul-Ramsey Medical Center, St. Paul, MN, 1995.

Sommers, P. A. Internal study. Allina Health System, Minneapolis, MN, 1995-1996.

Sommers, P. A. Using Technology for Competitive Advantage in the Management of Integrated Health Care Services. *Executive Solutions—SAS Institute Magazine for Business Decision Makers,* (2):22, First Quarter 1997. Keynote address at SAS Institute World Headquarters Annual Healthcare Conference, Cary, NC, January 15-16, 1997.

Sommers, P. A. Internal study. Allina Health System, Minneapolis, MN, 1997-1998.

Sommers, P. A. *Medical Group Management in Turbulent Times: How Physician Leadership Can Optimize Health Plan, Hospital, and Medical Group Performance.* The Haworth Press, Inc., Binghamton, NY, 1998.

Sommers, P. A. *Consumer Satisfaction in Medical Practice.* The Haworth Press, Inc., Binghamton, NY, 1999.

Sommers, P. A., Bartelma, R., and Whelan, M. Market Medicine the Old-Fashioned Way: Consumer Satisfaction. *Strategic Health Care Marketing,* 8(7):10-12, 1991.

Sommers, P. A. and Deml, L. Medica Health Plans Key Indicator Analysis. Internal Allina Health System study (1995/1996), 1997.

Sommers, P. A. and Deml, L. Implementing Consumer Satisfaction Improvement While Developing Trust with Providers for Medica Health Plan Members. Minnesota Health Services Research Conference, Minneapolis, MN, February 24, 1998.

Sommers, P. A. and Fuchs, C. Pediatric Care for Exceptional Children: An Inferential Procedure Utilizing Consumer Satisfaction Information. *Medical Care,* 18(6):657-667, 1980.

Sommers, P. A., Holt, L. E., Joiner, L. M., Gross, J. C., Willis, M. A., and Mainord, J. C. Kinesio-Perceptual Abilities As Predictors of Race: A Study of the Disadvantaged. *The Negro Educational Review,* 114-123, 1970.

Sommers, P. A., Joiner, L. M., Holt, L. E., Gross, J. C. Reaction Time, Agility, Equilibrium, and Kinesio-Perceptual Matching As Predictors of Intelligence. *Journal of Perceptual and Motor Skills,* 31:460-462, 1970.

Sommers, P. A. and Luxenberg, M. J. Physician-Hospital Integration, Ramsey Style. *Minnesota Medicine,* 77:22-25, 1994.

Sommers, P. A., Luxenberg, M. G., and Sommers, E. P. Continuous Quality Improvement (CQI) Longitudinally Applied to Integrated Service Outcomes: An Inferential Evaluation Model (IEM) Approach. *Medical Group Management Association,* 42(2):50-54, 56-58, 80-82, 1995.

Sommers, P. A. and Nycz, G. A Procedure to Study the Efficiency of Clinical Services Provided to Children with Exceptional Health and Educational Needs: A Question of Consumer Satisfaction. *American Journal of Public Health,* 68(9):903-905, 1978.

Sommers, P. A. and Thompson, M. A. The Best Malpractice Insurance of Them All: Consumer Satisfaction. *Health Marketing Quarterly,* 1(1):83-92, 1983; and in Winston W. (Ed.), *Marketing the Group Practice—Practical Methods for the Health Care Practitioner.* The Haworth Press, Inc., Binghamton, NY, 1983, pp. 83-92.

Sommers, P. A. and Torgerson, T. Health Plan/Care Delivery Organization Billing Cycle Redesign. Internal Allina Health System study. Results presented to the Allina Leadership Council in October 1996 and at a National Conference on Integrated Health Care Organizations, Albuquerque, NM, 1997.

Sommers, P. A. and Torgerson, T. Internal study. Allina Health System, Minneapolis, MN, 1997-1998.

Spendolini, M. J. *The Benchmarking Book.* AMACOM, a division or American Management Association, New York, 1992.

Stodghill, R. II. Gordan Sprenger Interview: "What's a Ton of Prevention Worth? Alliance Health System Is Trying to Heal the Sick—By Healing Society." *Business Week,* October 28, 1996, pp. 162-163.

The University of Michigan. *Health Risk Appraisal.* Fitness Research Center, Ann Arbor, MI, 1998.

Wetzell, S. and Hamacher, F. Buyers Health Care Action Group (BHCAG). Request for proposal for 1997. Distributed in Bloomington, MN, 1995.

Index

Page numbers followed by the letter "f" indicate figures; those followed by the letter "t" indicate tables.

Order Your Own Copy of
This Important Book for Your Personal Library!

ALIGNMENT
A Provider's Guide to Managing the Practice of Health Care

_____ in hardbound at $39.95 (ISBN: 0-7890-0635-9)

COST OF BOOKS _____

OUTSIDE USA/CANADA/
MEXICO: ADD 20% _____

POSTAGE & HANDLING _____
(US: $3.00 for first book & $1.25
for each additional book)
Outside US: $4.75 for first book
& $1.75 for each additional book)

SUBTOTAL _____

IN CANADA: ADD 7% GST _____

STATE TAX _____
(NY, OH & MN residents, please
add appropriate local sales tax)

FINAL TOTAL _____
(If paying in Canadian funds,
convert using the current
exchange rate. UNESCO
coupons welcome.)

☐ **BILL ME LATER:** ($5 service charge will be added)
(Bill-me option is good on US/Canada/Mexico orders only;
not good to jobbers, wholesalers, or subscription agencies.)

☐ Check here if billing address is different from
shipping address and attach purchase order and
billing address information.

Signature _____

☐ **PAYMENT ENCLOSED: $** _____

☐ **PLEASE CHARGE TO MY CREDIT CARD.**

☐ Visa   ☐ MasterCard   ☐ AmEx   ☐ Discover
☐ Diners Club
Account # _____

Exp. Date _____

Signature _____

Prices in US dollars and subject to change without notice.

NAME _____

INSTITUTION _____

ADDRESS _____

CITY _____

STATE/ZIP _____

COUNTRY _____ COUNTY (NY residents only) _____

TEL _____ FAX _____

E-MAIL_____
May we use your e-mail address for confirmations and other types of information? ☐ Yes   ☐ No

Order From Your Local Bookstore or Directly From
The Haworth Press, Inc.
10 Alice Street, Binghamton, New York 13904-1580 • USA
TELEPHONE: 1-800-HAWORTH (1-800-429-6784) / Outside US/Canada: (607) 722-5857
FAX: 1-800-895-0582 / Outside US/Canada: (607) 772-6362
E-mail: getinfo@haworthpressinc.com
PLEASE PHOTOCOPY THIS FORM FOR YOUR PERSONAL USE.